D1452956

Predatory Value Extraction

Predatory Value Extraction

*How the Looting of the Business Corporation
Became the U.S. Norm and
How Sustainable Prosperity Can Be Restored*

WILLIAM LAZONICK AND JANG-SUP SHIN

OXFORD
UNIVERSITY PRESS

OXFORD
UNIVERSITY PRESS

Great Clarendon Street, Oxford, OX2 6DP,
United Kingdom

Oxford University Press is a department of the University of Oxford.
It furthers the University's objective of excellence in research, scholarship,
and education by publishing worldwide. Oxford is a registered trade mark of
Oxford University Press in the UK and in certain other countries

First Edition published in 2020
Impression: 1

Published in the United States of America by Oxford University Press
198 Madison Avenue, New York, NY 10016, United States of America

British Library Cataloguing in Publication Data
Data available

Library of Congress Control Number: 2019941476

ISBN 978-0-19-884677-2

DOI: 10.1093/oso/9780198846772.001.0001

Printed and bound in Great Britain by
Clays Ltd, Elcograf S.p.A.

Preface

Our collaboration for this book began in earnest in 2015 when the U.S. activist hedge fund Elliott Associates attacked Samsung Group, Korea's most successful business group. By then, Lazonick, whose *Harvard Business Review* article, "Profits Without Prosperity," had exposed the use of stock buybacks to loot the U.S. business corporation, was engaged in a study of the role of hedge funds in this value-extraction process. Shin wrote several articles about the battle between Samsung and Elliott, including "The Reality of 'Actions' by Activist Hedge Funds and Public Policies on *Chaebols*" published in *KERI insight*, and wanted to undertake in-depth research on hedge-fund activism. In August 2015, at a workshop in Kyoto on "Financial Institutions for Innovation and Development," funded by the Ford Foundation, we decided to work together on a project that would explain the rise of hedge-fund activism, its institutional support in the United States, and its consequences for economic growth and income distribution.

The result of our collaboration since then is this book on "predatory value extraction": the process by which powerful financial interests extract value from business corporations that is far in excess of their contributions to the value-creation process. Critical to understanding value extraction is a coherent analysis of the process of value creation as it occurs in business corporations. For this analysis, we employ Lazonick's "theory of innovative enterprise," with its focus on three social conditions: "strategic control," "organizational integration," and "financial commitment." In this book, we show how the powerful combination of corporate executives as value-extracting insiders, institutional investors as value-extracting enablers, and hedge-fund activists as value-extracting outsiders has resulted in strategic control of corporate resource allocation that amounts to nothing less than the legalized looting of the U.S. business corporation.

In the course of writing this book, Lazonick travelled to Singapore twice and Shin travelled to the United States twice, and we also met in Korea once, while communicating frequently by email. It has been a stimulating intellectual collaboration for both of us. We give our special thanks to researchers at the Academic-Industry Research Network (theAIRnet), a non-profit organization of which Lazonick is co-founder and president: Matt Hopkins for his assiduous research on hedge funds; Ken Jacobson, who integrated his knowledge of the book's subject matter with his extraordinary copy-editing capability to transform complexity into clarity; Mustafa Erdem Sakınç for contributing his data expertise; and Emre Gömeç for valuable research assistance. We also are grateful to Tom Ferguson, research director of the Institute for New Economic Thinking (INET), for his recognition of the importance of an analysis of the financialization of the U.S. business corporation for understanding instability and inequity in the U.S. economy as a whole. We were greatly helped by Shin's research assistants at the National University of Singapore: Divya Sampath, Louis Lim Bei Long, Suzie Shin, and Shawn Wong Jun Kit.

Lazonick received financial support from INET through theAIRnet; European Union Horizon 2020 Research and Innovation Programme under grant agreement No. 649186 (Innovation-Fuelled Sustainable and Inclusive Growth) through the University of Ljubljana; Korea Economic Research Institute; and Ford Foundation project on Financial Institutions for Innovation and Development through UMass Lowell. Shin is grateful to the National University of Singapore (C-122-000-031-001) and the Laboratory Program for Korean Studies (AKS-2018-LAB-1250001) for their financial support.

Lazonick dedicates this book to the amazing team of researchers at theAIRnet. Shin dedicates this book to his wife Kate Lim who wholeheartedly supported this long journey and endured him using their home as his office.

Contents

List of Figures

List of Tables

1

The Growing Imbalance between Value Creation and Value Extraction

This book explains how, in the United States, an ideology of corporate resource allocation known as "maximizing shareholder value" (MSV), which emerged in the 1980s and came to dominate strategic thinking in business schools and corporate boardrooms, undermined the social foundations of sustainable prosperity, resulting in employment instability, income inequity, and slow productivity growth. In explaining what happened to sustainable prosperity in the United States, we focus on the growing imbalance between *value creation* and *value extraction* in the U.S. economy. At the center of this imbalance are the corporate-governance institutions that determine the relation between value creation and value extraction in the nation's major business corporations. The imbalance has become so extreme in the United States that *predatory value extraction* has become a central economic activity, to the point at which the U.S. economy as a whole can be aptly described as a *value-extracting economy.*

Value creation is a process that generates the high-quality, low-cost goods and services that are the essence of productivity growth. *Value extraction* is the process of appropriating portions of the value that has been created. Balancing the contributions of economic actors to value creation with their power to extract value provides the foundation for stable and equitable economic growth. An imbalance occurs when certain economic actors are able to assert their power to extract far more value than they contribute to the value-creation process. This book is about how that imbalance has become extreme, with dire economic, political, and social consequences.

1.1 From Retain-and-Reinvest to Downsize-and-Distribute

Since the late 1970s, the richest American households have increased their power to extract value that the American working class is helping to create. This change in the value-extracting power of the richest Americans has manifested itself in an ever-increasing gap between the rate of growth of labor productivity and the rate of growth of real wages, with wage growth falling further and further behind productivity growth, as shown in Figure 1.1. Major reasons why the rate of growth of wages tracked the rate of growth of productivity in the post-World War II

Predatory Value Extraction: How the Looting of the Business Corporation Became the U.S. Norm and How Sustainable Prosperity Can Be Restored. William Lazonick and Jang-Sup Shin, Oxford University Press (2020). © William Lazonick and Jang-Sup Shin.
DOI: 10.1093/oso/9780198846772.001.0001

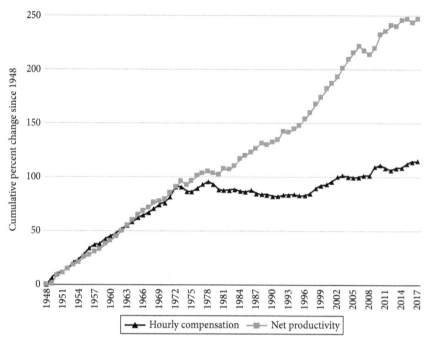

Fig. 1.1. The growing imbalance between productivity and compensation in the United States, 1948–2017

Source: Economic Policy Institute, at https://www.epi.org/productivity-pay-gap/

decades were the "retain-and-reinvest" resource-allocation regime and the "career-with-one-company" (CWOC) employment practice of the business corporations that then dominated the U.S. economy. By the same token, the prime cause of the growing gap between productivity growth and wage growth from the late 1970s was the abandonment of the "retain-and-reinvest" regime, in which CWOC was rooted, and the transition to the "downsize-and-distribute" resource-allocation regime, characterized by contingent employment relations.[1]

Under the retain-and-reinvest regime, senior executives made corporate resource-allocation decisions that, by retaining people and profits within the company, permitted reinvestment in productive capabilities that could generate competitive (high-quality, low-cost) products.[2] The social foundation of retain-and-reinvest was employment relations that offered decades-long job security, in-house promotion opportunities, rising real earnings, and health-insurance coverage, with a defined-benefit pension at the end of a long career. The retain-and-reinvest regime, combined with the CWOC norm, enabled both white-collar

---

[1] Lazonick and O'Sullivan (2000b); Lazonick (2009a); see also Lazonick (1994a).
[2] Lazonick (2015c).

and blue-collar workers to join a growing middle class. In sharp contrast, under downsize-and-distribute, a company is prone to downsize its labor force and to distribute to shareholders, in the form of cash dividends and stock buybacks, corporate cash that it might previously have retained.

The vast majority of these buybacks have been done as open-market share repurchases with the purpose of giving manipulative boosts to the company's stock price. Buybacks are massive. Over the decade 2008–2017, corporations in the S&P 500 Index repurchased $4.0 trillion, equal to 53 percent of net income. That was in addition to 41 percent of net income paid as dividends, the traditional way of providing shareholders with a yield for, as the name says, *holding* the company's stock. In contrast, the gains from stock buybacks go to those share-*sellers* who are best positioned to time their stock sales to take advantage of buyback activity done as open-market repurchases. These privileged sharesellers include not only senior executives on the inside, especially through the timing of stock-option exercises and the vesting of stock awards, but also hedge-fund managers and investment bankers on the outside who are in the business of making money by influencing stock prices and timing the purchase and sale of corporate stock.

Buybacks come at a great cost to working people. The corporate cash spent on buybacks could have been used to provide increased job stability and higher earnings to the broad base of employees who helped to generate the company's profits. Instead, by raising the gains of those sharesellers with the most informa-tion and influence, buybacks contribute to the widening gap between increases in wages and increases in productivity in ways that concentrate income at the very top of the U.S. income distribution. Figure 1.2 displays data for 1916 to 2011 on the income shares of the top 0.1 percent of U.S. households. As can be seen, the largest component of the incomes of the richest households from the mid-1980s has been "salaries," supplemented by spikes in capital gains at the peaks of the stock-market booms in 2000 and 2007. The salaries data, which also display spikes representing stock-market booms, include substantial stock-based pay taxed at ordinary rates, pay that is not distinguished as stock based in the data that scholars have collected from personal income-tax returns. Corporate ex-ecutives, hedge-fund managers, and investment bankers are well represented among the top 0.1 percent.

In the post-World War II decades, as now, large corporations have dominated U.S. economic activity. In 2012 (the most recent complete data available), 1,906 business enterprises with 5,000 or more employees in the United States averaged 20,366 employees and accounted for 34 percent of all business employees, 38 percent of all business payrolls, and 44 percent of all business revenues.[3] The quantity and

---

[3] United States Census Bureau (2016).

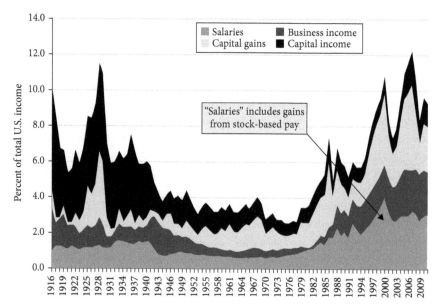

Fig. 1.2. Top 0.1% income share and its components in the United States, 1916–2011

Notes: Data from the U.S. databases published by this project are only available with these categorizations of the components to 2011.

The category "salaries" includes compensation from the realized gains on exercising stock options and the vesting of stock awards.

Source: The World Wealth and Income Database: https://wid.world/country/usa: United States, top 0.1% income composition.

quality of employment opportunities that the U.S. economy offers, both within these large companies and in millions of smaller firms with which the large companies or their employees do business, depend heavily on the investment strategies, organizational structures, and financial behaviors of this relatively small number of larger firms. U.S. institutions of corporate governance vest power over major resource-allocation decisions in the hands of senior executives, supported by their corporate boards. Given the enormous size of the major business corporations and their centrality to economic activity, the resource-allocation decisions made by senior executives of major U.S. corporations profoundly influence the operation and performance of the economy as a whole—including the availability, or not, of secure and well-paid employment opportunities.

In the decades after World War II, these employment opportunities reflected a CWOC norm that provided stable employment and rising real incomes as employees of major U.S. companies shared in corporate productivity gains. For blue-collar workers, the CWOC norm was rooted in union representation and its seniority principle of "first hired, last fired." In the aftermath of World War II, mass-production unions enabled blue-collar workers with high-school educations—and, in many cases, not even that—to secure the realistic promise of career employment with one company, with wages and benefits that could support a middle-class standard of living over decades of work and retirement. Although those occupying such positions were overwhelmingly white males in the 1950s, African Americans made progress in gaining access to these middle-class jobs in industries such as automobiles, electrical equipment, and steel.[4]

In white-collar professional, technical, and administrative positions, the dominance of white males, who were increasingly college-educated, was even more complete. These white-collar employees also had the expectation of a career with one company even in the absence of union representation, which was virtually non-existent among these "managerial" personnel. When a company had invested money in training a white-collar male employee who exhibited dedication to the organization, it then sought to retain him through the prospect of promotion and the promise of a defined-benefit pension after, typically, thirty years of service. In his 1956 best-seller, *Fortune* magazine editor William H. Whyte called this species of white-male American "the organization man."[5]

Our basic thesis in this book is that there is an integral relation in the U.S. economy between the explosion of the incomes of the richest households and the erosion of middle-class employment opportunities that has occurred over the past four decades. Since the early 1980s, employment relations in U.S. industrial corporations have undergone three major structural changes, summarized as "rationalization," "marketization," and "globalization," that have eliminated existing middle-class jobs.[6] From the early 1980s, *rationalization*, characterized by plant closings, terminated the jobs of high-school educated blue-collar workers, most of them well-paid union members. From the early 1990s, *marketization*, characterized by the end of the career with one company as an employment norm, placed the job security of middle-aged white-collar workers, many of them college educated, in jeopardy. From the early 2000s, *globalization*, characterized by the offshoring of employment to lower-wage nations, has left all U.S. workers vulnerable to displacement, whatever their educational credentials and employment experience. Exacerbating the rate of job loss and limiting business investment in new career-employment opportunities has been the financialization of the business corporation, manifested by massive stock buybacks in addition to expanding dividend payments.[7] In the process, we argue, the relation between value creation and value extraction within major business corporations has become unbalanced, and, given the importance of big business to the U.S. economy, this imbalance has affected the entire U.S. economy.

---

[4] See Lazonick et al. (2019).   [5] Whyte (1956).   [6] Lazonick (2015c).
[7] Our analysis focuses on the looting of the publicly traded company. For the role of private equity in the looting of the business enterprise, see Appelbaum and Batt (2014).

The decline of the American middle class, with all its economic, social, and political ramifications, cannot be remedied simply by "creating jobs." To lead a middle-class existence, a person needs to earn a decent income over thirty to forty years of his or her working life, with enough left over to support a dignified standard of living for some twenty years, on average, in retirement. And these incomes must also support family investment in the next generation of the labor force: future workers will require more and better education to remain productive in an increasingly knowledge-based economy with intense global competition. Especially in a high-wage economy such as that of the United States, middle-class standards of living must be supported by decades-long involvement in occupations through which, as the result of collective and cumulative learning, commensurately high levels of productivity can be generated. With technology, market, and competitive conditions constantly changing, the new middle class must be engaged in employment that offers lifelong-learning experiences that become embodied in the higher-quality, lower-cost goods and services that make the business enterprise for which they work competitive on product markets. At a national level, the emergence and sustainability of a broad middle class requires that a substantial proportion of the labor force—perhaps 100 million people in the United States—be employed by what can be called an "innovative enterprise": a business organization with the capability of generating the higher-quality, lower-cost products that can support the middle-class incomes of its labor force.

1.2 Innovative Enterprise and Shareholder Value

Unfortunately, the vast majority of economists, including those who seek to shape economic policy to achieve stable and equitable growth, have little conception of how innovation occurs in business enterprises and how it affects growth and distribution in the economy. Most PhD economists learn, and then teach, that the ideal economy is characterized by very small firms that compete with each other without seeking to transform the technological and market conditions that they face. They glorify an economy in which large numbers of very small firms compete in an industry by selling undifferentiated products—that is, commodities—with product prices to consumers falling to levels that eliminate profit margins. They give this state of economic affairs the label "perfect competition," with the expressed implication that, even if not the reality, an economy in which perfect competition were to prevail would be the ideal of economic efficiency.

The problem is that these firms in "perfect competition" are so numerous and small because they are so unproductive.[8] If this so-called ideal of economic

---

[8] For systematic critiques of this neoclassical view of the world from the innovative-enterprise perspective, see Lazonick (2015b, 2017b).

efficiency actually prevailed, we would all be living in poverty. Productivity growth is driven by companies that differentiate themselves from others in their industry by investing in collective and cumulative learning processes that can, if successful, enable these companies to develop *higher-quality products* than their rivals. These higher-quality products enable innovative firms to attain a large share of the market, which spreads the high fixed costs of developing the higher-quality product over large volumes of sold output, resulting in economies of scale that *drive down the unit costs* of producing and selling these higher-quality products. We call a firm that can differentiate itself from its industry rivals by generating higher-quality products at lower unit costs an *innovative enterprise*. These innovative enterprises generate productivity growth in the economy. They are highly profitable because of the investments in their workforces that enable collective and cumulative learning, and these enterprises can use their high profits to reward employees with stable and equitable employment opportunities. While contradicting the neoclassical textbook nonsense of "perfect competition" as the ideal of economic efficiency, these innovative enterprises create the foundation on which an economy can achieve stable and equitable economic growth—or what we call "sustainable prosperity."

The Theory of Innovative Enterprise, which we will explain in detail in Chapter 2, is fundamental to understanding the micro-foundations that an economy must have if it is to be able to achieve stable and equitable economic growth. This theory is also fundamental to understanding how those micro-foundations can be undermined. The Theory of Innovative Enterprise explains how, in the United States during the twentieth century, a "retain-and-reinvest" allocation regime enabled a relatively small number of business enterprises in a wide range of industries to grow to employ tens of thousands, and in some cases hundreds of thousands, of people per firm and to attain dominant product-market shares. Companies retained corporate profits and reinvested them in productive capabilities, including first and foremost collective and cumulative learning. Into the 1980s, companies integrated personnel into learning processes through CWOC employment. Under retain-and-reinvest, companies shared the gains of innovation with employees in the forms of more employment security, higher incomes, and greater benefits. A steady stream of dividend income and higher stock prices based on innovative products gave public shareholders an interest in retain-and-reinvest.

Based on the nonsensical theory of the "unproductive firm" as the ideal of economic efficiency that underpins conventional economic analysis, the economic ideology that arose in the 1970s and 1980s to justify the transition from retain-and-reinvest to downsize-and-distribute holds that, for the sake of superior economic performance, a company should be run to "maximize shareholder value" (MSV). Lacking a theory of innovative enterprise, MSV ideology views the business corporation as a "market imperfection" that, by engaging in what we call "retain-and-reinvest," is hoarding labor and finance that need to be "disgorged" from the firm so that these resources can be re-allocated to the most efficient uses. Hence the logic of downsize-and-distribute: downsize a company's labor force and distribute a company's cash to shareholders, and the markets for labor and finance will allocate these resources to achieve greater efficiency. The problem is that the economists who espouse MSV ideology *lack a theory of how those more efficient uses come into being.* That is, with their view of the operation and performance of the economy rooted in a theory that, quite absurdly, posits the highly unproductive firm as ideal, they give up on constructing a theory of innovative enterprise. As a result, as we will show in this book, while the proponents of MSV purport to be articulating a theory of value creation, they are actually promulgating a theory of value extraction.

1.3 The Value-Extracting Insiders, Enablers, and Outsiders: The Organization of this Book

In this book, we will show how, whether wittingly or not, *corporate executives as insiders, institutional investors as enablers,* and *hedge-fund activists as outsiders* have embraced MSV as an ideology that legitimates their extracting value at a level that is unmatched by their contributions to its creation. Across the United States economy, centered on cash distributions to shareholders in the form of dividends and buybacks, unbalanced value-extracting activity has been carried out through what amounts to the generalized looting of the industrial corporation, with devastating impacts on employment stability, income equity, and productivity growth. We explain the historical evolution of this imbalance between value creation and value extraction. Once the sources of the imbalance are understood, we can develop a viable perspective on how to initiate the economic, political, and social processes that the rebalancing of value creation and value extraction requires.

Chapter 2 presents a theoretical perspective—the Theory of Innovative Enterprise—that enables us to understand the evolving relation between value creation and value extraction. The Theory of Innovative Enterprise posits that business enterprises are central to the achievement of stable and equitable economic growth and offers an analytical framework for understanding the processes of value creation and value extraction as prime micro-level determinants of macroeconomic outcomes. Specifically, the Theory of Innovative Enterprise analyzes the dynamic interaction of three social conditions of innovative enterprise—strategic control, organizational integration, and financial commitment—in determining both the value-creating capability of a business enterprise—its ability to generate higher-quality products at lower unit costs—and the distribution of value created by the enterprise among participants in the value-creation process. The Theory of Innovative Enterprise provides a rigorous and relevant alternative to the prevailing market-based theories of the firm that lack an analysis of the process of value creation and that view value extraction as a process that operates through demand and supply on labor, finance, and product markets rather than through social relations within business organizations.

Foremost among the prevailing market-based theories of the firm is agency theory, which views the operation of the business enterprise as the potential source of an "agency problem" because shareholders as the firm's so-called principals have to delegate the management of the firm to corporate executives, who act as their agents. The agency problem is that these executives, who wield power over corporate resource-allocation decisions, may utilize this power for their own personal benefit rather than for the benefit of shareholders, the principals who purportedly employ them. The resolution of the agency problem, in the view of the agency theorist, is to create an incentive system for corporate executives to align their interests with those of shareholders by providing them with stock-based remuneration.

Our exposition of the Theory of Innovative Enterprise in Chapter 2 sets the stage for a fundamental critique of MSV in Chapter 3, where we argue that public shareholders, for whose benefit agency theorists claim the firm should be run, are generally value extractors who are unwilling and unable to participate in the value-creation process. We will show that MSV is an ideology of value extraction that, implemented by agency theory, lacks a theory of value creation. As such, MSV has done great damage to the achievement of sustainable prosperity. MSV has now been the dominant ideology of corporate governance for three decades. By justifying the agency theory mantra that, for the sake of economic efficiency, corporations should, to use Michael Jensen's ideologically-laden terms, "disgorge" the "free" cash flow,[9] MSV has contributed to unstable employment, inequitable income, and slowing productivity.

In Chapter 4, "The Value-Extracting Insiders," we focus on the general transformation of senior corporate executives in the United States from industrialist leaders dedicated to value creation into financial engineers intent on value extraction. Incentivized by stock-based pay and legitimized by MSV ideology, in the 1980s senior executives of major American corporations began to turn their backs on long-standard practices of resource allocation: Ceasing to retain profits and reinvest them for the future, many executives placed the emphasis on cost-cutting and passed out profits to shareholders in the form of not only dividends, but also stock buybacks. Under "retain-and-reinvest," a business corporation looks to improve and enlarge its productive capabilities, a process that includes training and retaining corporate employees and sharing profits with them in the form of

---

[9] Jensen (1986).

stable employment and higher incomes. Under a downsize-and-distribute regime, in contrast, the corporation reduces the size, pay, and competence of its labor force while distributing its profits in cash to shareholders as dividends and stock buybacks. Downsizing can be achieved by cutting employees' wages and benefits or simply dismissing them; selling off assets; bidding out work previously done in house to contractors (outsourcing); and moving production and other basic functions overseas (offshoring). Some companies' distributions to shareholders—financed by eating into corporate cash reserves, taking on debt, disposing of assets, and laying off longstanding employees—have exceeded 100 percent of net income for years, even decades, on end. In addition, for the sake of higher after-tax profits out of which distributions to shareholders can be increased, corporate executives may have the companies that they control engage in tax avoidance, price gouging, squeezing suppliers and franchisees, and defrauding buyers—all in the name of MSV.

Chapter 5, "The Value-Extracting Enablers," focuses on government agencies and economic actors that have made significant contributions to the largely legal looting of the U.S. business corporation that the regime of downsize-and-distribute represents. These enablers have included the U.S. Securities and Exchange Commission, notably with the adoption of Rule 10b-18 in 1982, and with proxy-rule changes in 1992 that allowed shareholders "free communication and engagement" among themselves as well as with corporate management. Another important enabler was Robert Monks, a businessperson who, in 1984, took the post of administrator of the U.S. Department of Labor (DOL) Office of Pension and Welfare Benefit Programs. Upon leaving the DOL after one year, Monks set up Institutional Shareholder Services (ISS) to offer proxy advice to institutional investors. A fervent advocate of activist public shareholders, in the late 1980s Monks pioneered elevating proxy voting to the status of a fiduciary duty for pension funds. Public-sector pension funds, most notably the California Public Employees' Retirement System (CalPERS) and the California State Teachers' Retirement System (CalSTRS), also entered the vanguard of shareholder activism by setting up the Council of Institutional Investors (CII) in 1985 and lobbying to increase the collective power of institutional investors through changes in rules concerning proxy voting, board elections, and institutional-investor engagement with management.

These efforts at shareholder activism had a fatal flaw: They accepted the ideology that companies should be run to maximize shareholder value. The institutional investors criticized high executive pay but not the tying of executive pay to a company's stock-price performance. They railed against the evils of incumbent management but did not offer a theory of the value-creation process that could guide good managerial practice. They objected to greenmail—the buying back of the shares of corporate raiders at premium prices—but they allied with corporate raiders in looting industrial corporations rather than setting up governance mechanisms for sustainable value creation and balanced value extraction. And they not only failed to question massive open-market re-purchases, they even instigated them. Moreover, institutional investors have evolved toward being less interested in and less capable of proxy voting and engagement as index funds—whose low fee structure is based on tracking indexes without paying attention to individual companies—have increasingly become dominant. Institutional investors have conflicts of interest even more serious than those of the corporate executives whom they presume to "correct" by relying on their ever-growing voting power. Despite their incapacity for and conflicts of interest in proxy voting, hedge-fund activists and proxy-advisory firms have exerted inordinate influence over the ways in which corporations allocate resources.

Chapter 6, "The Value-Extracting Outsiders" exposes a particularly aggressive species of activist shareholder ready to take advantage of changes in proxy-voting and engagement rules to enhance their value-extracting power and to build private "war chests" that serve to enhance their value-extracting power even more. In the 1980s and 1990s this ultra-active shareholder was known as a "corporate raider," a predatory actor epitomized by Carl C. Icahn. In the 2000s and 2010s this predatory breed, now known as the "hedge-fund activist," was again epitomized by Icahn. In the interim, with the help of financial regulatory changes in the 1980s and the 1990s, he and other shareholder activists—promi-nent names being William Ackman, David Einhorn, Daniel Loeb, Nelson Peltz, and Paul Singer—built their financial power by accumulating war chests through value extraction. We examine the evolution and the current state of hedge-fund activism. After explaining this phenomenon's origin and expansion, we investi-gate in particular Carl Icahn's transition from the most representative corporate raider to one of the most "successful" hedge-fund activists.

Over the decades during which MSV has been doing its damage as an ideology that justifies predatory value extraction, the leading academic proponents of MSV changed as well. In the 1980s and 1990s, the chief academic cheerleader for MSV was Michael C. Jensen, a Chicago School economist by way of the ultraconserv-ative University of Rochester business school who was recruited to Harvard Business School in 1985.[10] We critique Jensen's views in Chapter 3. In the 2000s and 2010s, the role of leading academic agent of activist aggression has been played by Lucian Bebchuk, a professor at Harvard Law School with Harvard doctorates in both law and economics. In Chapter 7, we use innovation theory to provide both a general theoretical critique and a selective empirical critique of the use of agency theory to rationalize the looting of the U.S. business corporation as enhancing economic efficiency. First, focusing on Bebchuk and Fried, *Pay Without Performance* (2004), we argue that the authors fail in their objective to

---

[10] See McDonald (2017b: 42–9).

demonstrate that U.S.-style stock-based pay undermines "shareholder value," while we contend that, from the perspective of innovation theory, shareholder value is an illegitimate measure of corporate performance. We then zero in on Bebchuk, Brav, and Jiang, "The Long-Term Effects of Hedge-Fund Activism" (2015), which purports to demonstrate empirically that the exercise of shareholder power improves corporate operating performance, return on assets, and stock returns over periods as long as five years. Our analysis casts serious doubt on their findings. Half of the companies in their dataset "disappeared" within five years, with no explanation for their demise. For those companies that remain, the supposed improvements in corporate performance could very well have resulted from cost-cutting that increased profits at the expense of the labor force rather than from productivity gains from the generation of higher-quality products at lower unit costs—gains of innovative enterprise that are typically shared with the firm's employees. Finally, we turn to a step-by-step critique of Fried and Wang, "Short-Termism and Capital Flows" (2017). This paper takes issue with the central argument in Lazonick's article "Profits Without Prosperity" (2014d) that massive distributions to shareholders in the forms of dividends and buybacks have come at the expense of investment in innovation and higher wages. Fried and Wang (2017) claim that a number of other sources of funds (debt issues, stock issues) and uses of funds (remuneration, R&D, acquisitions, venture capital) result in innovation and good wages. We demonstrate that Fried and Wang make a series of assertions about the economic impacts of financial flows—which they incorrectly call "capital flows"—that lack substance. We conclude Chapter 7 by arguing that, for analyzing the operation and performance of the economy, innovation theory should replace agency theory. Agency theorists do not address, let alone explain, why, since the 1980s, the United States has experienced an extreme concentration of income among the richest households and the erosion of middle-class employment opportunities.

More generally, we contend that MSV ideology as promulgated by agency theorists has contributed to inferior corporate and economic performance. The critical issue for understanding the role of corporate governance in supporting or undermining economic performance is the relation between value creation and value extraction for those "stakeholders" engaged in the development and utilization of the company's productive capabilities. Innovative enterprise solves the agency problem. By incentivizing and rewarding the real value creators, the innovative enterprise can mobilize the skill, effort, and finance that, by generating high-quality, low-cost products, can improve the performance of the economy—defined in terms of stable and equitable economic growth.

In the final chapter, Chapter 8, we suggest changes to the United States' corporate-governance regime that can get the U.S. economy back on the path to sustainable prosperity. This concluding chapter lays out a basic agenda for combatting predatory value extraction and restoring sustainable prosperity.

There are five broad planks in the scaffolding on which a value-creating economy can build:

- Rescind SEC Rule 10b-18 and ban open-market stock repurchases.
- Redesign executive pay to incentivize and reward value creation, not value extraction.
- Reconstitute corporate boards of directors to include representatives of households as workers, as taxpayers, and as savers as well as households as founders—and exclude the predatory value extractors.
- Reform the corporate tax system so that it returns profits to taxpaying households and funds government spending on infrastructure and knowledge for the next generation of innovative products.
- Redeploy corporate profits and productive capabilities to support collective and cumulative careers, and thus enable widespread upward socioeconomic mobility.

2

The Business Enterprise as a Value-Creating Organization

Given the importance of major business enterprises to the growth of the economy as a whole, the balance between value creation and value extraction within those enterprises has a major impact on the balance between production and distribution in the macroeconomy. In the process of sharing the gains of innovation with those who contribute to the process, the innovative enterprise tends to strike a balance between value creation and value extraction, and hence the innovative enterprise provides a foundation for sustainable prosperity. In this chapter, we explain the main concepts of the Theory of Innovative Enterprise to show why and how it can underpin stable and equitable economic growth. Next, drawing on the history of the United States, we show how government investments in physical infrastructure and the human knowledge base can support innovation. Then, having shown how the interaction of business strategy and government policy—that is, the interaction between the innovative enterprise and the developmental state—can structure a balance between value creation and value extraction, we will be in a position to consider how predatory value extractors can subvert the social conditions of innovative enterprise to capture for themselves the gains from innovation that others have created and from which customers also have previously benefited.

2.1 The Schumpeterian Challenge

In 1911, at the age of 28, Joseph Schumpeter published *The Theory of Economic Development*, in which he argued that capitalism must be conceptualized as an economic system in which innovation constantly disrupts the general equilibrium of market exchange. Indeed, Schumpeter argued that innovation is "the fundamental phenomenon of economic development," and some three decades later, in *Capitalism, Socialism, and Democracy*, he recognized that the business enterprise that grows to be large is "the most powerful engine of progress":

> What we have got to accept is that [the large-scale enterprise] has come to be the most powerful engine of [economic] progress and in particular of the long-run expansion of total output not only in spite of, but to a considerable extent

Predatory Value Extraction: How the Looting of the Business Corporation Became the U.S. Norm and How Sustainable Prosperity Can Be Restored. William Lazonick and Jang-Sup Shin, Oxford University Press (2020).
© William Lazonick and Jang-Sup Shin.
DOI: 10.1093/oso/9780198846772.001.0001

through, the strategy that looks so restrictive when viewed in the individual case and from the individual point in time. In this respect, perfect competition is not only impossible but inferior, and has no title to being set up as a model of ideal efficiency.[1]

The research now available on the growth of industrial corporations is vastly richer than that which Schumpeter could consult when he wrote those words in 1942. In the forefront of the research effort have been business historians stimulated by the work of Alfred D. Chandler, Jr. (1918–2007), who synthesized huge bodies of research in his three monumental books: *Strategy and Structure* (1962), *The Visible Hand* (1977), and *Scale and Scope* (1990).[2] Business-history research on the evolution of the large corporation leaves little doubt that the capability of producing massively greater quantities of output at lower costs, which could be sold at lower prices, enabled the most productive enterprises to achieve large market shares in the industries where they competed.

One of Schumpeter's great strengths as an economist was his recognition of the need to integrate history and theory so that empirical research on, in this case, the rise and dominance of the large corporation would not be simply a catalogue of facts.[3] Rather, in doing this research, economists can gain what Schumpeter called the "historical experience" of constructing a theory of the growth of the firm that can comprehend the rise to dominance of the large corporation. The pioneering work in this regard is Edith Penrose's *The Theory of the Growth of the Firm*, published in 1959.[4] In this book, Penrose depicts the large industrial corporation as one that grows by investing in organizational learning while paying constant attention to diversifying into new businesses by redeploying capabilities—especially its human assets—that have been developed in existing businesses. As Chandler (1962) shows in *Strategy and Structure*, published three years after Penrose's book, from the 1920s through the 1950s U.S. industrial firms implemented the multidivisional organization to enable the growth of the firm, in line with Penrose's theoretical argument.

Yet, despite Schumpeter's warning that "perfect competition is not only impossible but inferior, and has no title to being set up as a model of ideal efficiency," and notwithstanding the subsequent intellectual breakthroughs of Penrose and Chandler and their influence on many economists and historians (we would claim to be both), the neoclassical conception of perfect competition as an ideal state of industrial organization still pervades the textbooks and mindsets of conventional economists. Every year, tens of thousands of PhD economists teach millions of economics students that "perfect competition" is the ideal of economic efficiency.

---

[1] Schumpeter (1942).
[2] Chandler (1962, 1977, 1990). On Chandler's work, see Lazonick (2012).
[3] Schumpeter (1954); Lazonick (1994b, 2002).   [4] Penrose (1959).

Conventional neoclassical economists have thus been unable to comprehend the rise of the large corporation and its potential for and actual importance to the superior operation and performance of the modern economy.

2.2 The Illogical Neoclassical Theory of the Optimizing Firm

The neoclassical theory of the firm idolizes perfect competition in the market and trivializes strategy, organization, and finance in the firm.[5] The ideal company is one that optimizes, subject to technological and market constraints, to equate marginal costs with marginal revenues to maximize profits. It is assumed that "entrepreneurs" do *not* devise strategies to overcome those constraints. Instead, they are supposed to react to the appearance of profit opportunities in a particular industry as a result of exogenous changes in technology and markets, and to allocate resources to produce in that industry. Having invested in an industry, the management of the firm reduces to a mere exercise in "substitution at the margin" in the choice of its profit-maximizing output; that is, what economists call "constrained optimization." It is indeed, as we shall see, a *loss of control* over the internal organization of production that is essential for achieving this "optimal" neoclassical outcome. Financing the transformation of productive resources into revenue-generating products is non-problematic because the theory assumes that at each and every point in time the firm can borrow finance at the prevailing market rate and can sell all of its output, covering the cost of finance.

There are three major assumptions contained in the neoclassical theory of the firm that limit its ability to understand innovative enterprise. These assumptions result in the well-known U-shaped cost curve, in which average cost decreases as the firm expands its output but then, at a certain point, changes direction and increases. First, the neoclassical theory assumes that *the entrepreneur plays no role in creating the disequilibrium condition* that triggers the reallocation of resources from one industry to another. In effect, it posits the entrepreneur as an arbitrageur who exploits disequilibrium conditions, rather than as someone whose actions *create* disequilibrium conditions. The neoclassical entrepreneur only chooses the industry in which he wants to engage by allocating resources to it because the exogenous appearance of a disequilibrium condition creates supernormal profits to be made. The disequilibrium condition disappears as entrepreneurs reallocate resources to this particular industry, and, as long as equilibrium conditions persist across all industries, there will be no incentive for the entrepreneur to shift resources from one industry to another.

---

[5] For elaborations on the illogical neoclassical theory of the optimizing firm, see Lazonick (2015b, 2019).

Second, the neoclassical theory assumes that *the entrepreneur requires no special expertise to compete in one industry rather than another.* All that is required of the entrepreneur is that he follow the principle of profit maximization in the choice of industry in which to compete. A critical supposition here is the distinction between "fixed costs" and "variable costs." Fixed costs are exogenously determined by existing technology and prevailing factor prices, and *the entrepreneur does not choose the firm's level of fixed costs and the particular productive capabilities embodied in them as part of his firm's investment strategy.* Given the firm's fixed costs, the entrepreneur determines only the quantity of complementary variable inputs at prevailing factor prices in accordance with given technological and market requirements of achieving the amount of output at which profits are maximized. Thus, variable costs per unit of output are added to the fixed costs per unit of output to yield total unit costs, with the average cost curve mapping these total unit costs for different levels of output. If variable costs were to remain constant as output expanded, the average cost curve would slope downwards continuously (although at a declining rate) as fixed costs are spread over more units of output.

Third, the neoclassical theory at this point makes a critical assumption that causes the average cost curve to change direction and slope upwards, thus yielding the U-shaped cost curve found in every introductory economics textbook. The assumption is that the addition of variable factors of production to the firm's fixed factors of production results in declining average productivity of these combined factors. In deriving the U-shaped cost curve, neoclassical theorists have put forward two theses as to why productivity should decline as output expands, both of which treat labor as the key variable factor. One thesis holds that as more variable factors are added to the fixed factors, increasingly crowded factory conditions reduce the productivity of each variable factor as, for example, workers continuously bump into one other. According to the other thesis, as more workers are added to the production process, the entrepreneur, as the fixed factor whose role is to organize productive activities, experiences "control loss" because of the increasing number of workers that he has to supervise and monitor. If and when the increase in average variable cost outweighs the decrease in average fixed cost, the line that maps average total cost (the sum of fixed and variable costs) turns upward, yielding the U-shaped cost curve. Under these assumptions, the optimal production for a firm becomes the point where the marginal cost (MC) curve intersects the marginal revenue (MR) curve, which represents demand for the firm's product (Figure 2.1). Under conditions of "perfect competition"—the neoclassical ideal of economic efficiency—the firm is so small relative to the size of the industry in which it competes that it can sell all of its profit-maximizing output without affecting the product price, and hence average revenue (AR) equals marginal revenue (MR). Moreover, free entry into the industry by identical small firms bids down product price to the lowest point of the average cost curve,

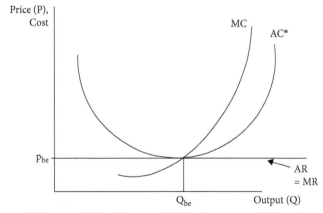

* AC is average total cost = average fixed cost + average variable cost

Fig. 2.1. Perfect competition as the best of possible worlds?

at which AR = MR = MC, as shown in Figure 2.1, and each firm's optimal profits are zero.

In this shaping of the cost curve, organization—in this case, the relation between the entrepreneur as manager and the work force that he employs—is central to the neoclassical theory of the firm and places a limit on the firm's growth. In rendering this optimizing firm as the foundation for perfect competition, neoclassical economists simply assume that increasing cost sets in at a very low level of output so that the firm is very small relative to the size of the industry, and hence its decision on the level of its output does not affect the price at which it can sell its product. Why increasing cost should afflict firms at such a low level of output is not explained.[6] It is only assumed that *the entrepreneur passively accepts this condition of increasing cost, and optimizes subject to it as a constraint.*

"Perfect competition" therefore becomes a state of economic affairs in which there are very large numbers of very small identical firms, each of which has a small share of the total industry output. Being very small, a firm can sell all of the products it wants at the going market price without in any way influencing that price. One might question, as Schumpeter did, why such an industry structure would result in an ideal of economic efficiency. After all, these numerous identical firms in perfect competition are assumed to be so small *because they are so unproductive,* their growth being limited because at a very low level of output each one experiences increasing average total unit cost—or what economists also call "diminishing returns." Yet the claim made by neoclassical economists is that taken together these highly unproductive firms somehow constitute a "model of ideal efficiency." If that sounds like an illogical conclusion, that is because it is an

---

[6] We are grateful to Jamee Moudud for raising this point.

illogical conclusion. Yet it is the foundation of the neoclassical economic theory that it is markets, not firms, that, for the sake of economic efficiency, should allocate resources in the economy.

What led to such an illogical conclusion is not hard to discover. To make the case for perfect competition as the most efficient possible state of economic affairs, neoclassical economists have put forth the "monopoly model" as the analytical basis for assessing the performance of "big businesses." Indeed, in the post-World War II decades, the monopoly model became the theoretical foundation of the "structure–conduct–performance" school of industrial organization, a neoclassical perspective rooted in the "ideal" of perfect competition.[7] According to the monopoly model, a firm that dominates its industry will raise its product price and restrict output of its product compared with price and output under perfectly competitive conditions. If one accepts this comparison of two different structures of industrial organization as valid, then obviously perfect competition outperforms monopoly in terms of economic efficiency (Figure 2.2).

The comparison of perfect competition and monopoly under constrained optimization contains, however, *a fundamental flaw*. The problem is not with the internal logic of the constrained optimization model per se. Rather *the problem is with putting the monopoly model into the logic of the competitive model of constrained-optimization*. If technological and market conditions lead the market to perfect competition, how can one firm (or even a small number of firms) come to dominate an industry?

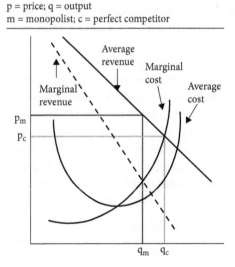

p = price; q = output
m = monopolist; c = perfect competitor

Fig. 2.2. Theory of monopoly?

---

[7] For instance, see Weiss (1979).

To explain the *emergence* of monopoly, the economist would have to assume that the monopolist somehow differentiated itself from other competitors in the industry. But the neoclassical comparison argues that both the monopolist firm and perfectly competitive firms *optimize subject to the same cost structures* that derive from given technological and factor-market conditions.[8] Indeed, except for the assumption that, in one case, the firm can make its profit-maximizing output decision as if it can sell all of its output at a constant price (according to the perfectly elastic demand curve shown in Figure 2.1) and that, in the other case, the firm is so large that it can sell more output only at a lower price (according to a downward-sloping demand curve), there is absolutely nothing in terms of the structure or operation of the firm that distinguishes the perfect competitor from the monopolist! So how would monopoly ever emerge under such conditions?

To repeat, under monopoly, according to the neoclassical model, product prices are higher and product output lower than under the perfectly competitive ideal. The problem is that the comparison is not valid because the neoclassical theory of monopoly contains a fundamental error of logic; it posits that *the monopolist maximizes profits subject to the same cost structure as perfectly competitive firms*! But, if that were to be the case, how could the monopolist become a monopolist? Indeed, given the derivation of the U-shaped cost curve, neoclassical economic theory posits the most unproductive firm as the foundation for most efficient economy.[9] If that sounds like nonsense, it is called neoclassical economics.

2.3 The Theory of Innovative Enterprise and Social Conditions for Value Creation

The solution to this conundrum—self-imposed on economic thinking by neoclassical illogic—is the Theory of Innovative Enterprise, with its recognition that a firm grows large *by transforming its cost structure* as it generates a product that is higher quality and lower unit cost than products previously available. The innovative enterprise invests in *collective and cumulative learning* processes to develop a product that is *higher quality* than those of its competitors. Then, if it is successful in so doing, precisely because buyers view its product as higher quality, the innovative enterprise is able to access a larger portion of the product market

---

[8] Figure 2.2 compares output and price of monopoly and perfect competition along the same industry supply curve, demonstrating that, comparatively, monopoly lowers output and raises price. Of course, if perfect competition could actually exist in this industry, the entry of perfectly competitive firms would expand output and lower price even more until the industry equilibrium is reached with price at the lowest point of the average cost curve. But the logic of the argument to demonstrate the inferiority of monopoly remains nonsensical; if one firm can dominate the industry, why would one assume that it has the same cost structure as would be the case if the industry were characterized by perfect competition?

[9] Lazonick (2017b).

for which it competes. This proportion of the markets spreads its fixed cost of production over more units of sold output, thereby transforming the high fixed cost of developing its higher-quality product into a low unit cost.[10] As a result of this innovation process, the innovative enterprise outcompetes the unproductive firms operating in so-called perfect competition. As Schumpeter correctly claimed, perfect competition is indeed inferior and "has no title to being set up as a model of ideal efficiency."

What makes an enterprise innovative? A business enterprise seeks to transform productive resources into goods and services that can be sold to generate revenues. A theory of the firm must, therefore, at a minimum, explain how this productive transformation occurs and how revenues are obtained. Such explanations must focus on three generic activities—*strategy*, *organization*, and *finance*—in which the business enterprise engages. And the ways in which the innovative enterprise must conduct these three generic activities derive directly from the *uncertain*, *collective*, and *cumulative* characteristics of the innovation process.

- Innovation is *uncertain* because, when investments in transforming technologies and accessing markets are made, the financial returns cannot be known, even probabilistically. Hence the need for *strategy*.
- Innovation is *collective* because, to generate a higher-quality, lower-cost product than was previously available, the business enterprise must integrate the skills and efforts of large numbers of people with different hierarchical responsibilities and functional capabilities into the organizational-learning processes that are the essence of innovation. Hence the need for *organization*.
- Innovation is *cumulative* because collective learning today provides the foundation for collective learning tomorrow, and these organizational-learning processes must be sustained over time until, through the sale of a higher-quality, lower-cost product, financial returns can in fact be generated. Hence the need for *finance*.

We identify three "social conditions of innovative enterprise" that enable a business to generate a higher-quality product at a lower unit cost than that which had previously been available. These social conditions are *strategic control*, *organizational integration*, and *financial commitment*.

- *Strategic control*: Innovation requires the strategic allocation of resources to developing and utilizing productive resources. The social condition that can transform strategy into innovation is *strategic control*: a set of relations that

---

[10] Lazonick (2015b).

gives decision-makers the power to allocate the firm's resources to confront the technological, market, and competitive uncertainties that are inherent in the innovation process. For innovation to occur, those who occupy strategic decision-making positions must have both the *ability* and *incentive* to allocate resources to innovative investment strategies. Their ability to do so will depend on their knowledge of how the current innovative capabilities of the organization over which they exercise strategic control can be enhanced by investments in new, typically complementary, capabilities. Their incentive to do so will depend on the alignment of their personal interests with the objective of the business organization over which they preside in attaining and sustaining its competitive advantage.

- *Organizational integration*: The implementation of an innovative strategy requires organization. The social condition that can transform organization into innovation is *organizational integration*: a set of relations that creates incentives for people with different hierarchical responsibilities and functional capabilities to apply their skills and efforts to strategic objectives. The need for organizational integration derives from the complexity of the innovation process combined with the imperative to secure high levels of utilization of innovative investments if the high fixed costs of these investments are to be transformed into low unit costs. Modes of compensation in the form of work satisfaction, promotion, remuneration, benefits, and participatory management are important instruments for integrating individuals into the organization. To generate innovation, however, a mode of compensation cannot simply manage the labor market by attracting and retaining employees. It must also be part of a reward system that manages the learning processes that are the essence of innovation. Specifically, the compensation system must motivate employees as individuals to engage in collective learning.

- *Financial commitment*: This collective learning, moreover, cumulates over time, thus necessitating the sustained commitment of financial resources to keep the learning organization intact. The social condition that can transform finance into innovation is *financial commitment*: a set of relations that ensures the allocation of funds to sustain the cumulative innovation process until it generates financial returns. What is often called "patient" capital enables the capabilities that derive from collective learning to cumulate over time, notwithstanding the inherent uncertainty that the innovation process entails. Strategic control over internal revenues is a critical form of financial commitment, but such "inside capital" must often be supplemented by external sources of finance such as bond issues, bank debt, and stock issues that, in different times and places, may be more or less committed to sustaining the innovation process.

The "social conditions of innovative enterprise" perspective asks how and under what conditions the exercise of strategic control can ensure that the enterprise will seek to grow using collective processes and along cumulative paths that may become the foundations of distinctive competitive success.[11] Of central importance to the accumulation and transformation of capabilities in knowledge-intensive industries is the *skill base* in which the firm invests in pursuing its innovation strategy.

At any point in time, a firm's functional and hierarchical division of labor defines its skill base.[12] In the effort to generate collective and cumulative learning, those who exercise strategic control can choose how to structure the skill base, including what types of employees (e.g. white-collar versus blue-collar) are integrated into the organizational-learning processes and how employees move around and up the enterprise's functional and hierarchical division of labor over the course of their careers. At the same time, however, the organization of the skill base and its integration will be constrained by both the particular learning requirements of the industrial activities in which the firm has chosen to compete and the alternative employment opportunities available to the personnel whom the firm wants to employ. The innovative enterprise requires that those who exercise strategic control be able to recognize the competitive strengths and weaknesses of their firm's existing skill base and, hence, the changes in that skill base that will be necessary for an innovative response to technological opportunities and competitive challenges. These strategic decision-makers must also be able to mobilize committed finance to sustain investment in the productive capabilities of the skill base until it can generate higher-quality, lower-cost products than were previously available.

In the Theory of Innovative Enterprise, the uncertainty inherent in fixed costs is central to the analysis, whereas, in the neoclassical theory of the optimizing firm, fixed costs are given and hence certain. The investments that the innovative firm makes must be developed and utilized over time as the firm transforms technologies and accesses markets, before returns from those investments can be generated, or indeed before the rate of return can even be known. The problem is not whether the prevailing return on investment provided by existing technological and market conditions will continue in the future. Since the return on investment depends on the extent of the market that the innovating firm ultimately attains, and since that extent of the market is inherently uncertain, a return on investment *does not even prevail* at the time when the investments in innovation are made.

Yet investments in innovation must be made despite the existence of uncertainties concerning prospective returns. The distinguishing characteristics of a particular industry derive from its particular technologies, markets, and competitors.

---

[11] Lazonick (2002).   [12] Lazonick (1998, 2005, 2010).

As a result, any executive who allocates resources to an innovative strategy faces technological, market, and competitive uncertainties concerning the eventual success of the strategy.[13] Therefore, the amount of fixed costs that that executive's company incurs reflects its innovative strategy, rather than being fixed by factors external to the firm. Neither indivisible technology nor the "entrepreneur" as a fixed factor dictates this "fixed-cost" strategy.

Within the neoclassical theory of the optimizing firm, the constraining assumption is that *the entrepreneur passively accepts this condition of increasing cost, and optimizes subject to it as a constraint.* In sharp contrast, in the theory of the innovating firm, the experience of increasing cost provides the firm's strategic decision-makers with an understanding of *the limits of the initial investment strategy,* and with that information they adopt a high-fixed-cost strategy by making additional new investments for the strategic purpose of *taking control* of the variable factor that was the source of increasing cost. This strategy appears less efficient than the profit-maximizing strategy of the optimizing firms because it initially increases unit cost. However, if successful, it "unbends" the U-shaped cost curve, i.e., it results in a lower unit cost by, as illustrated in Figure 2.3, internalizing the development and utilization of the cost-increasing variable factor.

The level of fixed cost that an innovation strategy entails partly depends on the assessment by the firm's strategic decision-makers of the quality and quantity of productive resources in which the firm must invest to *develop* higher-quality processes and products than those previously available or that may be developed by competitors. It is this development of productive resources internal to the enterprise that creates the *potential* for an innovative enterprise to gain a sustained advantage over its competitors and emerge as dominant in its industry.

The *development* of productive resources, when successful, becomes embodied in products, processes, and people with productive capabilities superior to those that had previously existed. But an innovative strategy that can eventually enable the firm to develop superior productive capabilities may place the innovating firm at a *competitive disadvantage* because such strategies tend to entail higher fixed

---

[13] *Technological uncertainty* exists because the firm may be incapable of developing the higher-quality processes and products envisaged in its innovative investment strategy; if one already knew how to generate a new product or process at the outset of the investment, the company would not be engaged in innovation. *Market uncertainty* exists because, even if the firm is successful in its development effort, future reductions in product prices and increases in factor prices may lower the returns that can be generated by the investments. Moreover, the innovative enterprise must access a large enough extent of the product market to transform the fixed costs of developing a new technology into low unit costs. Like transforming technology, accessing the market is an integral part of the innovation process. At the time when resources are committed to an innovative strategy, it is impossible to be certain, even probabilistically, about the extent of the market that will be accessed. Finally, even if a firm can overcome technological and market uncertainty, it still faces *competitive uncertainty*: the possibility that a competitor will have invested in a strategy that generates an even higher-quality, lower-cost product. Nevertheless, if a firm is to have the opportunity to profit and grow through innovation, it must invest in the face of uncertainty.

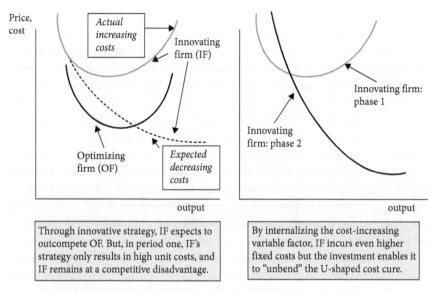

Fig. 2.3. Innovation strategy and the reshaping of the cost curve

costs than the fixed costs incurred by rivals that choose to optimize subject to given constraints. As an essential part of the innovation process, the innovating firm must access sufficient markets for its products to transform high fixed cost into low unit cost, and, thereby, to transform competitive disadvantage into competitive advantage.

These higher fixed costs derive from both the *size* and the *duration* of the innovative investment strategy. Innovative strategies entail higher fixed costs than those incurred by the optimizing firm that takes technology and markets as given constraints if the innovation process requires the *simultaneous development* of productive resources across a broader and deeper range of integrated activities than those undertaken by the optimizing firm. But in addition to, and generally independent of, the size of the innovative investment strategy at a certain point in time, high fixed costs will be incurred because of the length of time that is required to develop productive resources until the time when they result in products that are of sufficiently high quality and low cost to generate returns. If the level of investment in physical capital tends to increase the fixed cost of an innovative strategy, so too does the duration of the investment required for an organization of people to engage in the collective and cumulative—or organizational—learning that is the central characteristic of the innovation process.

The high fixed cost of an innovative strategy creates a necessity for the firm to achieve a high level of *utilization* of the productive resources that it has developed. The innovating firm may experience increasing costs because of the problem of maintaining the productivity of variable inputs as it employs larger quantities of these inputs in the production process. But rather than, as the optimizing firm would do, taking increasing cost as a given constraint, the innovating firm will attempt to transform its access to high-quality productive resources at high levels of output. To do so, it invests in the *development* of that productive resource whose *utilization* as a variable input has become a source of increasing cost.

The development of the productive resource adds to the fixed cost of the innovative strategy. Previously this productive resource was utilized as a variable factor that could be purchased incrementally at the going factor price on the market as extra units of the input were needed to expand output. Now, as a result of the innovation strategy, the development of that particular productive resource has become integrated into the firm's operations. Having added to its fixed costs in order to overcome the constraint on enterprise expansion posed by increasing variable costs, the innovating firm is then under even more pressure to expand its sold output in order to transform high fixed cost into low unit cost.

The innovative enterprise establishes itself as innovative only when it sells its product to buyers who are willing and able to pay for it. The dynamics of the innovation process depend, therefore, on the evolution of not only product costs but also product demand. Indeed, the two are interdependent because the attainment of a low unit cost depends on the extent of the market that the firm accesses, and the extent of the market that the firm is able to access depends on the quality of the product that the firm develops. At any given point in time, there exists a *potential* demand for a good or service that is dependent on both the incomes and wants of buyers. The innovative firm, however, must *access* these markets, a process that generally entails considerable and enduring investments in its sales force, distribution and servicing facilities, advertising, and branding.

These investments, which add to the fixed costs of the innovative investment strategy, are necessary because of the need to inform and convince potential buyers that the product is in fact of higher quality than alternative goods or services that might satisfy their particular wants or needs. Indeed, through its sales efforts, the innovating firm will often learn from actual and potential buyers what can make their product a higher-quality product. These investments put into accessing markets can shift the demand curve for the firm's product by increasing the quantity of the product that buyers will demand at a given price. To some extent, this demand will become "dedicated" as buyers come to view the firm's product as being of higher quality than those of its competitors; that is, buyers— now called "customers" or "clients"—will be willing to pay a premium price for the firm's brand. Market investment can also shape the price elasticity of demand for the firm's product, as buyers' perception of its higher quality makes them less willing than they would otherwise have been to reduce the quantity demanded in response to an increase in price.

What, then, determines output and price in a theory of innovative enterprise? The answers are not straightforward because the innovating firm's pricing strategy and its investments, which will affect market demand, are endogenous to the innovation process itself.[14] The innovating firm will have a strong interest in increasing the extent of the market to which it has access. Greater market share not only lowers unit costs but also increases the learning experience of the innovating firm; moreover, it helps to prevent rivals from gaining access to buyers, not just in the present but into the future, as buyers become customers who continue to purchase the innovating firm's products.[15] For the innovating firm, output and price are variables that are determined by its competitive strategy—a strategy that entails transforming technologies and accessing markets as the firm strives to differentiate itself from its competitors.

Technological transformation and market access require not only strategy, but also organization and finance. The revenues that the innovating firm generates can be critical to sustaining its success. When an innovating firm generates revenue, it has financial resources that can be allocated in a number of ways. If the gains from innovation are sufficient, the firm's revenue creates the possibility for self-financing. The firm may leverage this financing with bonded and bank debt on favorable terms, depending on its relations with the financial sector and its need for finance. Financial resources not only fund the innovating firm's new investment but also enable the firm to keep its learning organization intact. The firm can use the gains of innovative enterprise to reward its employees for their skill and effort in transforming technology and accessing markets.

It may be that, as a result of sharing the gains of innovative enterprise with its employees, the firm's wage bill is higher than would be dictated by labor markets. Yet, depending on the extent of the changes in the supply and demand curves that result from the innovation process, its profits may be higher *because of* its higher wage bill. The gains of enterprise that the innovating firm has shared with its employees may have been critical inducements for gaining their cooperation in implementing its innovative investment strategy. The innovating firm's high wages may be integral to its "dynamic capabilities" that generate competitive advantage.[16]

2.4 The Innovative Enterprise and its Societal Institutions

If one accepts that business enterprises are social structures that are in turn embedded in larger (typically national) institutional environments, one must recognize that a theory of innovative enterprise must itself be embedded in a model of the relations among *industrial sectors*, *business enterprises*, and *economic institutions*. These in turn can support the processes that transform technologies

---

[14] Spence (1981); Moudud (2010).   [15] Christensen (1997).
[16] See Teece (2011, 2012). See also Lazonick (2018d).

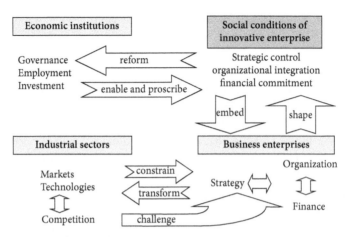

Fig. 2.4. Social conditions of innovative enterprise

and access markets to generate products that are higher quality and/or lower cost than those that had previously existed. Figure 2.4 provides a schematic perspective on the interactions among sectors, enterprises, and institutions that shape the social conditions of innovative enterprise.

Innovation differs across industrial sectors (lower-left section of Figure 2.4) in terms of the technologies that are developed and the markets that are accessed. In the theory of the optimizing firm, business enterprises take technologies and markets as given: they constrain the "strategy" of the business enterprise to be like that of each and every other firm in the industry. In the theory of the innovating firm, in contrast, enterprise strategy seeks to transform technology and access markets. In doing so, strategy confronts technological uncertainty—the possibility that an innovative investment strategy will fail to develop higher-quality products or processes—and market uncertainty—the possibility that the strategy will fail to access a large enough extent of the market to transform the high fixed costs of developing these products and processes into low unit costs. But, as indicated in the lower part of Figure 2.4, the innovating firm must also confront competitive uncertainty—the possibility that even if the firm is successful in transforming technology and accessing markets to develop a higher-quality, lower-cost product than those previously available, competitors will do it better and cheaper.

The rise of new competition poses a challenge to the innovating firm. It can seek to make an innovative response or, alternatively, it can seek to adapt on the basis of the investments that it has already made by, for example, obtaining wage and work concessions from employees, debt relief from creditors, or tax breaks or other subsidies from the state. An enterprise that chooses the adaptive response in effect shifts from being an innovating to an optimizing firm. Not only will the abilities and incentives of those who exercise strategic control determine how the enterprise responds, but also crucial will be the skills and efforts that can be integrated into its organization and the committed finance that, in the face of competitive challenges, can be mobilized to sustain the innovation process.

If and when innovation is successful in a particular nation over a sustained period of time, the types of strategic control, organizational integration, and financial commitment that characterize the nation's innovating firms will constitute distinct social conditions of innovative enterprise. But why, one might ask, would the social conditions of innovative enterprise exhibit similar characteristics across firms within a nation, particularly when they are engaged in different industries? And why, for a given industry, would the social conditions of innovative enterprise differ across nations?

The answer to both questions is that, historically, nations differ in their institutions. At any point in time these institutions both enable and proscribe the activities of firms, while over time distinctive elements of these institutions become embedded in the ways in which firms function. Of particular importance in influencing the social conditions of innovative enterprise are *economic* institutions related to *governance, employment,* and *investment.* Through a historical process, the strategic, organizational, and financial activities of a nation's innovative enterprises shape the characteristics of these economic institutions. However, these institutions also exist and persist independently of the enterprises as part of the "social fabric"—the rules and norms of the nation applicable to economic activity that find application in the social relations of that nation's firms.

Governance institutions determine how a society assigns to different groups of people rights to and responsibilities for the allocation of its productive resources, and how it imposes restrictions on the development and utilization of these resources. Employment institutions determine how a society develops the capabilities of its present and future labor forces as well as levels of employment and conditions of work and remuneration. Investment institutions determine the ways in which a society ensures that sufficient financial resources will be available on a continuing basis to sustain the development of its productive capabilities. These economic institutions both enable and proscribe the strategic, organizational, and financial activities of business enterprises, thus influencing the conditions of innovative enterprise that characterize social relations within any given firm at any point in time. As these business enterprises succeed at innovation, they may reshape the conditions of innovative enterprise; for example, their strategic decision-makers, acting collectively, may take steps to reform these institutions to suit the new needs of their enterprises.

This highly schematic perspective, therefore, posits a dynamic historical relation between organizations and institutions in the evolution of the social conditions of innovative enterprise, while recognizing that industrial sectors differ in terms of their technological, market, and competitive conditions. To go beyond this schema requires the integration of the Theory of Innovative Enterprise with comparative research on the evolution of the conditions of innovative enterprise in different times and places—an exercise in comparative political economy. To study the innovative enterprise in abstraction from the particular social conditions that enable it to generate higher-quality, lower-cost products is to forgo an understanding of how a firm becomes innovative in the first place and how its innovative capabilities may be rendered obsolete. A comparative-historical analysis enables us to learn from the past and provides working hypotheses for ongoing research. This approach also opens the door to an analysis of how political movements might operate at the intersection between economy and society to shape social institutions that, with innovative enterprise as a foundation, can achieve stable and equitable economic growth.

The objectives of government economic policy should be to support stable and equitable economic growth.[17] Growth is stable when employment opportunities enable members of the labor force to engage in collective and cumulative learning processes on a continuing basis. Growth is equitable when those who contribute to the growth process receive a commensurate share of the gains. The equitable sharing of the gains from growth should occur at the level of the enterprise through its relations with employees, suppliers, distributors, and financiers. Tax policy should be designed to ensure that the government secures an equitable return from the business sector on government investments in infrastructure and knowledge as well as government subsidies that companies use to generate innovation and growth.

We can understand the working of what is widely referred to as the "developmental state" in this context of the social conditions of innovative enterprise. The concept of the developmental state came into academic use in the early 1980s to explain the rise of Japan to a position of international industrial leadership[18] and was subsequently invoked as an explanation of the successful growth of follower East Asian nations, in particular South Korea and Taiwan.[19] The general assumption in this literature is that, in comparative perspective, the role of the state in the United States has been regulatory, but not developmental. Yet the historical record strongly supports the view that in terms of government investment in the physical infrastructure and human knowledge that business enterprises need to implement their innovative investment strategies, the United States has had the most formidable developmental state in history.[20] To promote the sustainable prosperity of a national economy, it is generally required that the state be developmental.

Before turning to a brief history of U.S. government investment in physical infrastructure and human knowledge, let us take a quick look at three other,

---

[17] See Lazonick and Mazzucato (2013).   [18] Johnson (1982).
[19] Woo-Cumings (1999).
[20] Block (2009); Block and Keller (2010); Lazonick and Mazzucato (2013); Hopkins and Lazonick (2014).

more indirect, ways in which the U.S. government has supported industrial development: through tariffs, patents, and the law.

In 1841, after the British industrial revolution of the previous 60 years had greatly increased that nation's wealth, the German economist Friedrich List published *The National System of Political Economy* to counter British arguments that all nations of the world would be better off moving to a system of international free trade. List observed "it is a very common clever device that when anyone has attained the summit of greatness, he kicks away the ladder by which he climbed up, in order to deprive others of the means of climbing up after him."[21] Drawing inspiration from Alexander Hamilton, a founding father of the United States, who published his *Report of Manufactures* in 1790, and American economist Daniel Raymond, whose 1823 book *Elements of Political Economy* advocated tariffs to support industrial development, List articulated the "infant industry" argument for tariff protection.[22] Tariff protection, justified by this argument, was fundamental to nineteenth-century U.S. industrial development, although tariffs were also used to generate government revenue. It was not until after World War II, when the U.S.-led restructuring of the international economic order included the General Agreement on Tariffs and Trade, that the United States ceased to use tariff protection as an important policy tool.

The infant-industry argument posits that it requires time for a manufacturing industry in a less-developed nation to attain the productivity levels of existing competitors in an already-developed nation and that, to permit this "growing-up" process to take place, the less-developed nation must give its domestic industry privileged access to the domestic market. In this regard, the Theory of Innovative Enterprise outlined in this chapter is highly relevant. The high fixed cost of an innovative investment strategy places the innovative enterprise at a competitive disadvantage at a low level of output compared with established competitors. It takes time for the innovative enterprise to transform technologies and access markets so that these high fixed costs are transformed into a high-quality product at a low unit cost. So too for a young industry in a less-developed nation. In fact, a national manufacturing industry that engages in learning with the benefit of protected markets may go beyond merely imitating the production methods of the world leader to engaging in "indigenous innovation" that, once the learning has been done, can give it a distinct competitive advantage on global markets.[23] It is also possible that tariff protection will enable companies in an industry to charge domestic buyers higher prices without investing in innovation—but it requires a theory of innovative enterprise to analyze whether that is in fact the case.

---

[21] List (1885); Lazonick (2011b).   [22] Chang (2002).
[23] Lazonick and Mass (1995); Lazonick (2004).

Tariff protection applies to whole industries, whereas patent protection applies to a particular inventor or, more usually, a company that purchases the patent and exploits it. The economic logic of patent protection is that it gives a company time to transform an innovative idea into a higher-quality, lower-cost product than would otherwise be available. That is, in terms of delivering economic benefit to society, and not just to the patent holder, patent protection implicitly assumes a theory of innovative enterprise. Beginning with the passage of the first Patent Act of the U.S. Congress in 1790, the U.S. government used patent protection to "promote the useful arts." From 1860 to 1995, the patent life was seventeen years from the grant date, but, as a result of lobbying from the pharmaceutical industry, it was subsequently extended to twenty years. Today, patents proliferate in the U.S. economy, although, in the current age of "patent trolls"—entities who file patents or buy up patent rights for the purpose of demanding licensing fees—and patent price-gougers such as pharmaceutical companies that use patents to restrict output and raise prices, there is evidence that patents may in fact undermine innovation. But, again, one needs a theory of innovative enterprise to investigate this possibility.

Given that most of the land mass of the continental United States was appropriated from the indigenous peoples (also known as "Native Americans"), it is not surprising that the legal system's common-law interpretations of property rights favor developmental uses of natural resources over the pre-existing property rights of individuals. An important historical case was the granting of riparian rights in the 1820s to a group of Boston merchants (who later became known as "the Boston Associates") who wanted to divert river flows away from the existing farming population so that they could use water power to drive the machinery of a cotton-textile manufacturing complex that they planned to build in Lowell, Massachusetts. This complex did indeed become the site of the nation's first industrial revolution.[24] Citing many other legal cases, in *The Transformation of American Law, 1780–1860*, Morton Horwitz shows more generally how the courts in the United States interpreted common law such that it enabled the property rights of business interests with projects that promised to develop the economy to supersede the existing property rights of individuals.[25] This approach to the use of land remains enshrined in the United States under the laws of "eminent domain," whereby the government can appropriate, with compensation, individual real estate for the sake of development projects. A theory of innovative enterprise permits the analysis of whether the transfer of existing property rights from individuals to business corporations or government agencies for developmental purposes is in fact justified.

Historically, however, U.S. government policy to support an innovative economy has gone far beyond tariff protection, patent rights, and developmental law.

---

[24] Steinberg (1991).   [25] Horwitz (1979).

Since the late nineteenth century, the U.S. government has invested directly in physical infrastructure and human knowledge, without which innovative business strategies would not have been possible.[26]

U.S government investments in physical infrastructure included:

- *The Pacific Railroad Acts of 1862–1866*: The U.S. government gave railroad companies 103 million acres of public land that could be sold or used as loan collateral to finance the construction of transcontinental railroad lines. These land grants to railroads were equivalent to 5.34 percent of the area of the continental United States, which is also greater than the area of California. The transcontinental railroads vastly extended the United States as a nation, permitting the western states to be populated with settlers. Under the Homestead Act of 1862, the U.S. government offered each citizen who was twenty-one years of age or older and the head of a household a grant of 160 acres in a western state on the condition that he or she farmed the land for at least five years. This national expansion resulted in massive increases in agricultural production, which by 1880 accounted for 56 percent of U.S. exports, and vastly heightened domestic demand for U.S. manufactured goods.

- *The AT&T regulated monopoly*: From 1913 to 1984, the U.S. government made American Telephone and Telegraph, operating as a publicly listed business corporation, a regulated monopoly in the provision of telephone services. In return for its monopoly status, AT&T agreed to extend telephone service to every household in the United States, no matter how remote or sparsely populated the location might be. Under this agreement, revenues from long-distance telephone calls, mainly used by business enterprises and government agencies, subsidized local telephone services to households. AT&T's wholly owned subsidiary Western Electric had a monopoly on the production of telephone equipment, and in 1925 the two companies joined together to create Bell Laboratories, which became the world's greatest corporate research facility.

- *The domestic airline network*: The U.S. government, under Republican administrations and through the Postmaster-General's Office, took the lead in structuring a transcontinental airline system.[27] Under the Contract Air Mail Act of 1925, the Postmaster General gave subsidized airmail contracts to selected commercial airline companies operating as regional monopolies, with the explicit intent of encouraging the airlines to demand that aircraft manufacturers develop safer, quieter, and larger planes so that passenger travel would increase. Five years later, when little progress in

---

[26] The following material draws heavily on Hopkins and Lazonick (2014).

[27] Ferleger and Lazonick (2002), and bibliographic references therein.

the development of these passenger-friendly aircraft had been made, the Air Mail Act of 1930 changed the basis of the subsidy to the same set of airline monopolies *from the amount of mail carried on a plane to the size of the plane in which mail was carried,* even if the plane carried only one letter. This industrial policy worked, as, for the sake of the postal subsidy, the airline companies looked to aircraft manufacturers to build large passenger planes. By 1933, aircraft manufacturers Boeing and Douglas, in intense competition with one another, had each developed the modern all-metal, two-engine monoplane for the airlines, and passenger air travel took off.

- *The interstate highway system*: After Dwight Eisenhower became President of the United States in 1953, he nominated Charles E. Wilson, CEO of General Motors, to be Secretary of Defense. At the confirmation hearing, Sen. Robert Hendrickson (R-NJ) asked Wilson whether he would have a conflict of interest in making a decision that was in the interest of the U.S. government but promised extremely adverse consequences for Wilson's shareholdings in GM or other companies, or for GM itself. Wilson replied: "I cannot conceive of one [i.e., a conflict of interest] because for years I thought what was good for our country was good for General Motors, and vice versa. The difference did not exist. Our company is too big. It goes with the welfare of the country. Our contribution to the Nation is quite considerable."[28] During Wilson's tenure as Defense Secretary (1953–57), Congress passed the Federal-Aid Highway Act of 1956, under which the government committed to pay for 90 percent of the cost of building 41,000 miles of interstate highways. President Eisenhower justified this federal expenditure on the grounds that the highways were needed to deploy defense equipment to strategic positions in case of a military attack on U.S. soil. In fact, the interstate highways have provided essential infrastructure for the growth of the U.S. economy. They were also a boon to General Motors, which increased its worldwide employment from 599,000 in 1956 to a peak of 877,000 in 1986, before losing ground to Japanese competition, and eventually in 2009 needing the U.S and Canadian governments, along with the United Auto Workers, to bail the company out of bankruptcy.

- *The Internet*: A 1999 study, *Funding a Revolution: Government Support for Computing Research*, stated, "Federal funding not only financed development of most of the nation's early digital computers, but also has continued to enable breakthroughs in areas as wide ranging as computer time-sharing, the Internet, artificial intelligence, and virtual reality as the industry has matured."[29] Among other things, the study details the now well-known role

---

[28] Terrell (2016).   [29] National Research Council (1999: 1).

of the U.S. government in developing the ARPANET and the NSFNET for over three decades before the services they pioneered became available commercially as the Internet in 1993. As lucrative as the Internet has been for companies such as Intel, Microsoft, Apple, Cisco, Amazon, Google (now Alphabet), and Facebook, it was the U.S. government (with some collaboration in Europe), not these or any other companies, that put the foundational physical infrastructure and knowledge base in place that made the digital revolution in information and communication technology possible.

In addition, and of no less consequence, the U.S. government made investments in the nation's knowledge base that have formed fundamental foundations for organizational learning within innovative enterprises. These investments include:

- *Land-grant colleges:*[30] The Morrill Land Grant College Act of 1862 gave each state in the nation 30,000 acres of land (or land scrip) for each U.S. senator or representative. This land could be sold to fund "the endowment, support, and maintenance of at least one college where the leading object shall be, without excluding other scientific and classical studies, and including military tactics, to teach such branches of learning as are related to agriculture and the mechanic arts, in such manner as the legislatures of the States may respectively prescribe, in order to promote the liberal and practical education of the industrial classes in the several pursuits and professions in life."[31] The Morrill Act carried the condition that the college or colleges being endowed had to be launched within five years of the land grant. In some states, private money supplemented the land grant; for example, in New York State, Ezra Cornell stepped forward with a large donation and had the university named after him. In Massachusetts, the land grant was divided between the University of Massachusetts in Amherst for agricultural education and Massachusetts Institute of Technology for mechanical arts education. A second Morrill Act in 1890 added annual cash support for the land-grant colleges, stipulating that any state in which the existing university barred admission to blacks had to set up a separate black college. In the last decades of the nineteenth century, therefore, the United States created a national system of public higher education that provided scientists, engineers, and administrators who could contribute to the development of agriculture and industry. In agriculture, they tended to find employment in the vast complex of federal and state agencies coordinated by the U.S. Department of Agriculture (USDA). In industry, they tended to find employment in the corporate laboratories and administrative hierarchies that enabled the managerial

---

[30] Ferleger and Lazonick (1993, 1994).   [31] Morrill Act (1862).

revolution in American business between the 1880s and the 1920s. In the early decades of the twentieth century, the public land-grant institutions also put pressure on the elite private universities such as Harvard and Yale to eschew a "pure science" mentality by adding engineering education to their curricula.

- *Agricultural experiment stations:*[32] The USDA was founded in 1862, the same year as the first Morrill Act, for the purpose of increasing crop productivity and disseminating new scientific research of relevance to agriculture. Productivity in agriculture was important to both the American standard of living and the U.S. balance of trade. As late as 1929 food absorbed 23 percent of the personal disposable income of Americans; the figure is now about 11 percent, and Americans have the cheapest food in the world.[33] Food exports (crude and manufactured) represented 56 percent of total U.S. merchandise exports in 1880, 42 percent in 1890, and still stood at 40 percent in 1900.[34] In 1887, with the natural productivity of once-fertile land reaching its limits as the frontier disappeared, Congress passed the Hatch Act to fund agricultural experiment stations throughout the nation to be operated in conjunction with the land-grant universities. Subsequent Congressional legislation increased federal government funding of the experiment stations, with the Smith-Lever Act of 1914 financing cooperative extension services through which agricultural experts, known as "county agents," could both disseminate new knowledge to farmers and collect data from farms that were relevant to the experiment stations' research programs. In the early 1920s there were about 2,100 counties with agricultural-extension agents.[35] Equipped with this institutional structure that integrated basic research with agricultural production through the medium of public state universities, the United States became the world leader in agricultural science.

- *National Institutes of Health:* The agricultural knowledge base helped to provide a foundation more generally for life-sciences research, which from the 1930s has been under the jurisdiction of the National Institute of Health or its multipartite successor, the National Institutes of Health (NIH). In 1936 the initial National Institute of Health employed 177 people in some capacity and had 21 major research projects under way. In 1937 Congress established the National Cancer Institute alongside the National Institute of Health. In 1938 and 1939 the combined annual budget of these two research facilities was $464,000, and by 1945 it had increased by almost five times in real terms to a still-modest $2.8 million.[36] In 1948, with the creation of the National

[32] Ferleger and Lazonick (1993, 1994).   [33] U.S. Department of Agriculture (2016).
[34] U.S. Census Bureau (1976).   [35] Lloyd (1936).
[36] National Institutes of Health (2019).

Heart Institute, the National Institutes of Health was established in its current form, encompassing all of the specialized research institutes. In the six years immediately following World War II, the NIH budget exploded, reaching $65 million in 1951, twenty-three times its 1945 level in real terms. By that time there were five separate research centers within the NIH. Between 1998 and 2003 the NIH budget doubled in real terms, driven largely by the promise of the Human Genome Project. In 2018 there were twenty-seven specialized institutes within the NIH with a budget of $34.1 billion, just below $34.2 billion in 2017 and up from $32.3 billion in 2016 and $30.3 billion in 2015. From 1938 through 2018, total NIH funding in 2018 dollars was just over $1 trillion. Most of this budget funds research labs in universities and hospitals, with the results flowing to life-sciences business enterprises for further development into commercial medical products.[37] It is safe to say that without the NIH, the modern medical-technology industry, including drugs, devices, and equipment, would not exist.

- *Aeronautics*: During the 1920s and 1930s, the new discipline of aeronautics was another major area for U.S. government investment in the high-tech knowledge base. From the founding of the National Advisory Committee for Aeronautics (NACA) in 1915, the U.S. government played a role in supporting aeronautics research. In the 1920s NACA did pioneering wind-tunnel research that resulted in the development of low-drag cowlings for aircraft engines. In the 1930s NACA focused on the design of airfoils, above all wings, as part of an effort to increase the lift of aircraft. In 1958 NACA was absorbed into the National Aeronautics and Space Administration (NASA), created in response to the successful launch by the Soviet Union of Sputnik, the first artificial satellite to reach space. In the twenty-first century, the United States remains the world's aeronautics leader, in large part because of the collaboration of government agencies with corporate research labs that took place from the 1940s to the 1980s. For example, during World War II Raytheon, founded in Cambridge, Massachusetts, in 1922 as the American Appliance Company, played a central role in advancing radar technology, while Motorola, founded in Chicago, Illinois, in 1928 as the Galvin Manufacturing Company, was in the forefront of the introduction of mobile radio communications—technologies of critical importance across a whole range of industrial applications, including aeronautics. A British Royal Air Force Officer, Frank Whittle, invented the modern jet engine in Britain in 1930,[38]

---

[37] Tulum and Lazonick (2019).

[38] Keeper (2006). Whittle first patented his engine in 1930, and, over the next decade, sought to produce a usable technology, founding Power Jets Limited in 1936. In August 1944, the Whittle engine produced by Power Jets powered the Gloster Meteor, although it was the Germans, with the Messerschmitt Me232, who could lay claim to bringing the first jet plane into service. We are grateful to Martyn Roetter for this reference.

but during the war the British transferred the Whittle engine to the U.S. government, which turned it over to General Electric (GE) for product development.[39] At that time GE, one of the world's leading electrical power companies, had no experience in aeronautics research, but it had been carrying out research on gas-turbine engines in its corporate lab since 1903. GE's jet engines did not enter use during World War II, but after the war GE was the leader in developing the technology for the U.S. military. Then, in 1974, GE entered the civilian jet-engine industry through CFM International, a joint venture with the French state-owned company SNECMA (now part of Safran), producing mid-sized turbojet engines for the A300, the first generation of Airbus planes. Building on the correlated successes of Airbus and CFM, GE moved into the production of higher-thrust engines on its own, emerging as the world leader in the jet-engine industry.[40]

- *Integrated circuits:*[41] The technology that launched the microelectronics revolution was the transistor, invented at Bell Labs in 1947 by John Bardeen, Walter Brattain, and William Shockley. All three had worked in military research during World War II, and the knowledge accumulated in those years set the stage for this technological breakthrough.[42] In 1956 Bardeen, Brattain, and Shockley won the Nobel Prize in Physics for their invention. Meanwhile, in 1955, Shockley had sought to work out a deal to start his own semiconductor laboratory at Raytheon, but when that fell through, he secured backing from a Los Angeles-based medical-device firm, Beckman Instruments, to set up a lab in Palo Alto, home of Stanford University. Shockley recruited about fifty young scientists and engineers to work in his Palo Alto lab, but by 1957, with the backing of an East Coast company, Fairchild Camera and Instrument, eight of them, including Gordon Moore and Robert Noyce, left to form Fairchild Semiconductor in nearby Mountain View, California. Then, from 1959, Fairchild's engineers and managers started leaving to form their own startups. From 1959 through 1970, forty-two new semiconductor firms—twenty-one in 1968 and 1969 alone—were launched in the vicinity of Fairchild. By 1985 the number of Silicon Valley semiconductor startups launched since the founding of Fairchild totaled 125. Of these 125 firms, 32 were founded by at least one person who had left employment at Fairchild for that purpose, while another 35 companies were offspring of these "Fairchildren" (especially of National Semiconductor, Intel, Signetics, and Synertek). Fairchild was important to the emergence of Silicon Valley not only because it drew people and knowledge from the established R&D labs of electronic-tube companies such as GE, RCA, Westinghouse, and Sylvania, but also because it invested heavily in

---

[39] Jones (n.d.); GE Report (2012).   [40] Lazonick and Prencipe (2005).
[41] See Lazonick (2009a: ch. 2).   [42] Riordan and Hoddeson (1997).

research, especially research related to manufacturing processes for the mass production of diffused-silicon transistors. The first wave of Silicon Valley semiconductor startups that followed the founding of Fairchild consisted of ten firms oriented toward military markets that were launched between 1959 and 1964. Between 1955 and 1963, the annual value of total U.S. semiconductor production rose from $40 million to $610 million, with the proportion for the U.S. military varying between 35 percent and 48 percent. In 1968, when the value of U.S. semiconductor production stood at $1.2 billion, military production still made up 25 percent of the total. By that time, integrated circuits accounted for 27 percent of the value of all U.S. semiconductor production, up from less than 3 percent five years earlier. Military demand represented 94 percent of integrated-circuit production in 1963 and 37 percent in 1968. Meanwhile, the price per integrated circuit declined from $31.60 in 1963 to $2.33 in 1968, thus dramatically increasing the economic viability of using integrated circuits for cost-conscious civilian markets.[43] It was only when Moore and Noyce founded Intel to produce memory chips that could replace the magnetic-coil memories then in use that they specifically declined to create a separate R&D lab, and refused to accept contracts, for government research.[44]

As exemplified by the cases of the life sciences, aeronautics, and integrated circuits, the success of the United States in high-tech industries since the early twentieth century has depended on the interaction of business and government spending on R&D that has been carried out in a complex of government, civil-society

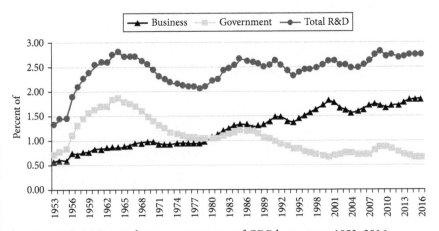

Fig. 2.5. U.S. R&D spending as a percentage of GDP by sources, 1953–2016
Source: National Science Board, *Science and Engineering Indicators 2018*, National Science Foundation.

[43] Tilton (1971).   [44] Bassett (2002).

(especially university), and business facilities. Figure 2.5, using data collected by the National Science Foundation from 1953 to 2016, shows that in the first decade of the twenty-first century total U.S. R&D spending as a percent of GDP has remained high by historical standards, and that business-funded R&D makes up a greater part of the total than does government-funded R&D.[45]

If there is a problem with investment in the high-tech knowledge base in the United States in recent decades, it is not apparent in the statistics on R&D spending. The fundamental problem of achieving sustainable prosperity in the U.S. economy is concerned, as we shall show in the following chapters of this book, with the increasing power of predatory value extractors to reap the benefits of value creation, and in the process to undermine the productivity of R&D investments, even when these investments are made.[46]

---

[45] See Hopkins and Lazonick (2014) for an analysis of these data.
[46] See Hopkins and Lazonick (2014); Lazonick et al. (2017); Tulum and Lazonick (2019).

3

The Stock Market as a Value-Extracting Institution

Conventional wisdom has it that the primary function of the stock market is to raise cash that companies use to invest in productive capabilities: that is, that the stock market provides finance to support value creation. This, like much conventional wisdom, is wrong. Academic research on corporate finance has established that, in advanced countries, the stock market is insignificant as a supplier of capital to corporations and is, in fact, a net extractor of value from corporations. Between 1970 and 1985 the net contribution of the stock market to new capital financing was minus 3 percent in the United Kingdom, 1 percent in the United States, 3 percent in Canada, 3 percent in Germany, and 5 percent in Japan.[1] Over the same time period, the level of investment funds raised from the stock market as a percentage of total funds was minus 10 percent in the United Kingdom, minus 9 percent in the United States, 1 percent in Germany, 4 percent in Japan, and 6 percent in France.[2] In both the United States and the United Kingdom, in aggregate, companies funded the stock market rather than vice versa, as is conventionally assumed. These facts are passed over by neoclassical economists who, in keeping with the ideology of the market economy, simply assume, without empirical support, that the function of the stock market is to fund corporate investment.

As we saw in Chapter 1 and will see in more detail in Chapter 4, in the United States for the first three decades after World War II net equity issues were moderately positive in the corporate economy as a whole, but, in the following decades, became increasingly negative. Over the three most recent decades, U.S. stock markets, of which the New York Stock Exchange (NYSE) and the National Association of Securities Dealers Automated Quotation (NASDAQ) exchange are by far the most important, have in aggregate extracted trillions of dollars from business corporations in the form of stock buybacks. The U.S. stock markets have become the foremost institutions for creating the growing imbalance between value creation and value extraction. Yet underpinning the dominant corporate-governance ideology that, for the sake of superior efficiency, a company should "maximize shareholder value" (MSV) is the mistaken belief that by

---

[1] Mayer (1988); see also Corbett and Jenkinson (1996).   [2] Allen and Gale (2001).

Predatory Value Extraction: How the Looting of the Business Corporation Became the U.S. Norm and How Sustainable Prosperity Can Be Restored. William Lazonick and Jang-Sup Shin, Oxford University Press (2020).
© William Lazonick and Jang-Sup Shin.
DOI: 10.1093/oso/9780198846772.001.0001

supplying companies with investment capital the stock market is a prime value creator. In this chapter, we present the history and theory of the stock market as primarily a value-extracting institution, and we expose fallacies inherent in MSV ideology, a perspective that has inflicted immense damage on the economy and that severely distorts the economic thinking of policy-makers, academics, and the public.

3.1 The Separation of Ownership and Control

Looking back at the rise of big business in the United States in the late nineteenth century, we see that the primary function of the stock market was *not* to raise cash for corporate investment. Rather, it was to enable the owner-entrepreneurs and their venture-finance partners who had led the building of major business enterprises *to exit their investments* through what we now call an "initial public offering" (IPO). This process separated the ownership of corporate shares from managerial control over the allocation of corporate resources and brought about the concurrent emergence of liquid public stock markets and managerial capitalism.[3]

Central to the process of separating share ownership from managerial control in the rise of big business in the United States was the Great Merger Movement of the 1890s and early 1900s. The most enduring mergers proved to be in those industries in which continuous product and process innovation and high-speed utilization of production and distribution facilities were most important for sustaining competitive advantage. And the most successful combinations were ones in which the owner-entrepreneurs of the leading firms had invested in superior managerial capabilities for developing and utilizing productive resources. When the original owner-entrepreneurs retired from the industrial scene, there was an experienced and committed corps of senior executives ready, willing, and able to take their place.

This is how it worked: Wall Street investment banks—J. P. Morgan foremost among them—underwrote the merger of a group of firms within an industry to create a business entity with a large market share that could be floated on the New York Stock Exchange (NYSE). The underwriting syndicate issued corporate bonds to pay the owner-entrepreneurs and their venture-finance partners for their ownership stakes, then sold the corporation's listed shares to the public over time as it saw fit. The result was the transfer of ownership of corporate shares from the original owner-entrepreneurs to an increasingly widely distributed population of shareholders. As a result, beginning in the 1890s a national market

---

[3] For an elaboration of this argument and bibliographic references, see Lazonick (2012: 361–84).

in industrial securities emerged.[4] Contrary to conventional wisdom, the rise of the large-scale industrial corporation created the liquid stock market, not vice versa.

The market dominance of the new combinations, enhanced by the backing of Wall Street, encouraged private wealthholders to invest in industrial stocks. By the 1920s, the NYSE had become a highly liquid market in industrial securities, thus making shareholding attractive to households that simply wanted to place their savings in financial securities that promised an income and, if and when a household should decide to sell its shares, a capital gain.[5] Beyond the opportunity to purchase stock at the market price, public shareholding offered limited liability and did not require the shareholder to make any further commitments of time, effort, or finance to the firms in which he or she had bought shares. And, of utmost importance, the existence of a liquid stock market meant that, at any time, these shareholders could easily monetize this financial asset by instructing a broker to sell some or all of their shares—which became known as the "Wall Street walk."

By instilling confidence in shareholders, the NYSE's listing requirements, stringent with regard to profitability record and capital assets, increased the market's liquidity. Yet underpinning the liquidity of the NYSE in the 1920s, and rendering volatile the prices of even the most profitable and dominant companies' stocks, was the existence of the call-loan market, which enabled stock-market speculators to buy shares on margin, putting up only 5 percent of their own funds while borrowing the rest. It was during the speculative boom of the late 1920s, which culminated in the Great Crash in October 1929, that the term "blue-chip company" came into use. Taken from the color of the most valuable counter in a gambling casino, the name was reserved for the most profitable and best-financed companies listed on the NYSE—companies such as DuPont, General Electric, and General Motors—and served as a reminder that holding shares in even the best companies listed on the stock exchange remained a gamble.

Then as now, public shareholders placed their money in shares that were already outstanding on the market. Unlike the owner-entrepreneurs and their private-equity partners who, as direct investors, had financed the companies from startups into going concerns by reinvesting a high proportion of the companies' profits, the new public shareholders did not invest in the productive capabilities of the companies that issued the shares. Once a company had gone public, it could pay shareholders dividends. However, if growing the firm through investments in innovation was an objective, distributions to shareholders had to leave the firm with sufficient retained earnings to invest in the productive capabilities required to generate the next round of competitive products. These corporate retentions also provided a financial foundation for long-term borrowing to leverage the funds available for investment in productive capabilities. Indeed, in the 1920s, a prime

---

[4] Navin and Sears (1955).   [5] O'Sullivan (2007, 2016).

role of Wall Street in financing major U.S. corporations was to float long-term bond issues to augment the financial commitment of companies to their innovative investment strategies.[6]

The separation of ownership from control not only resulted in the growth of the U.S. public stock markets but also gave birth to "managerial capitalism," a system of strategic control that was responsible for sustained industrial expansion and the emergence of the American middle class during the larger part of the twentieth century.[7] Those companies that had a sufficient financial track record to go public on the NYSE had already grown by building managerial organizations that could take over strategic control when the owner-entrepreneurs withdrew. By reducing the possibility of nepotism in top-management succession, the removal of family control opened up new opportunities for promotion to career managers, which helped to ensure the commitment of managers to the long-run performance of their particular firms.[8]

Over the course of their careers, these salaried managers—increasing numbers of whom, in the first decades of the twentieth century, held university degrees in engineering or business—developed intimate knowledge of their firms' technological and organizational capabilities. With their upward mobility unimpeded by family control, a small subset of the managers rose to senior executive positions in major industrial firms. Not coincidentally, the first decades of the twentieth century also saw the dramatic transformation of the U.S. system of higher education away from the elite British model, with its aristocratic pretensions, to one that serviced the growing needs of U.S. industrial corporations for professional, technical, and administrative personnel.[9]

From the perspective of sustained industrial innovation, therefore, the key impact of the separation of ownership from control in the United States was to overcome the *managerial constraint* on the building of organizational capabilities and the growth of the firm. Moreover, by fragmenting shareholding among a dispersed population with little influence over management, the separation of ownership from control enhanced the access of these firms to long-term finance that was rooted in retained earnings and supplemented by bond issues. In short, professional managers as "organization men" made long-term commitments to their corporations, establishing and maintaining the "retain-and-reinvest" regime that made innovative value creation the corporation's top priority. The managerial revolution in American business was a powerful engine of economic growth, especially in corporations that built deep organizational capabilities.

Even during the Great Depression of the 1930s, when, for lack of product demand, major industrial corporations laid off masses of production workers,

---

[6] Carosso (1970).
[7] Lazonick (1992); Lazonick and O'Sullivan (1997); O'Sullivan (2000, 2007, 2016).
[8] Lazonick (1986).   [9] Noble (1979); Lazonick (1986); Ferleger and Lazonick (1994).

these companies continued to augment their research capabilities by expanding their employment of scientists and engineers.[10] During World War II and the post-war decades, investment in research capabilities enabled U.S. industrial corporations, with support from the U.S. developmental state, to make the U.S. economy the largest and most powerful in the world.[11] Through its "retain-and-reinvest" allocation regime, the managerial corporation contributed to more stable employment and a more equitable income distribution than had been the case before the 1940s and also more stable and equitable than would be the case after the 1970s.

In effect, the managerial revolution overcame the management constraint on the growth of the U.S. industrial enterprise.[12] Yet the conventional wisdom was, and remains, that the separation of ownership and control occurred because of a *capital constraint*, not a managerial constraint, on the growth of the business enterprise. In the late nineteenth and early twentieth centuries, so the story goes, what led to the separation of ownership and control was that the increasing capital requirements of companies in high-fixed-cost industries—steel, oil refining, electric power, farm equipment, and automobiles, to name a few—outstripped the financial capacity of family proprietors and partnerships, thus necessitating the raising of capital on the stock market. In *The Modern Corporation and Private Property*, the classic 1932 study of the separation of ownership and control, Adolf Berle and Gardiner Means made this "capital constraint" argument, and they continued to do so in their later writings. For example, in his 1954 book *The 20th Century Capitalist Revolution*, Berle states that the separation of stock ownership from managerial control "was inevitable, granting that modern organizations of production and distribution must be so large as to be incapable of being owned by any individual or small group of individuals."[13]

As previously indicated, the historical facts do not support this argument. The work of Alfred D. Chandler and other historians of the managerial revolution in American business shows that the critical constraint on the growth of major industrial enterprises was not access to finance, but rather the availability of organizational capabilities that could develop high-quality products and access shares of the product markets large enough that they allowed the companies to transform high fixed costs into low unit costs.[14] By enabling professional managers to assume positions of strategic control, the separation of ownership from control underpinned a critical social condition of innovative enterprise.

It is also important to pay attention to the financial and regulatory environment that enabled managerial capitalism to thrive during this period. Public shareholders were mostly retail portfolio investors who were neither interested in

---

[10] Mowery and Rosenberg (1989).   [11] Eisenhower (1961).
[12] Penrose (1959); Chandler (1962, 1977); Lazonick (2012, 2018e).
[13] Berle and Means (1932); Berle (1954); Means (1983).   [14] Lazonick (2012).

intervening in resource-allocation decisions of corporations nor strong enough to do so. The situation was quite different from that of today, in which the absolute majority of publicly traded shares is held by a small number of strong institutional investors, as we will discuss further in Chapter 5. Moreover, with the rise of the managerial corporation, financial authorities discouraged institutional investors from exerting influence over corporate management. The Securities and Exchange Commission (SEC) even testified before Congress that a mutual fund's only positive function was to provide diversification and that any extension of that function risked thievery.[15] This situation was quite different from the current one, in which financial authorities actually encourage institutional activism, a subject we will take up again in Chapters 5 and 6.

3.2 The Five Functions of the Stock Market

An understanding of the historical origins of the separation of ownership and control transforms the way in which we view the role played by the stock market in the growth and performance of the business corporation. An analysis of the functions of the stock market is, moreover, essential to explain the relation between value creation and value extraction in the corporate economy, whether in connection with the achievement of a certain creation–extraction balance in the United States in the post-World War II decades or the descent into a growing creation–extraction imbalance over the past four decades.

The preceding discussion has argued that the main function of the stock market in the rise of U.S. industrial corporations to positions of dominance was "control," not "cash." The stock market enabled professional managerial employees to exercise strategic control over the allocation of corporate resources while turning the owners of the company's shares into *rentiers* who had neither the capability nor the disposition to participate in corporate decision-making. For a company with the stringent qualifications to be listed on the NYSE, the cash required to sustain investment in the productive capabilities of the company came from prior capital accumulations and current retentions out of profits. By and large, the cash that provided the foundation for this financial commitment did not come from the stock market.

But "control" and "cash" do not exhaust the possible functions of the stock market for the business corporation. Our research has identified three others: "creation," "compensation," and "combination."[16] An understanding of the ways in which these five functions are performed, individually and interactively, is critical to an analysis of whether and to what extent the stock market is an

---

[15] Roe (1991: ch. 5).   [16] Carpenter et al. (2003: 963–1034); Lazonick (2009a, 2009c).

institution that supports the processes of value creation or whether, alternatively, it is an institution that empowers the processes of value extraction.

The following definitions of the five functions of the stock market—control, cash, creation, combination, and compensation—raise questions about their various roles in influencing the relation between value creation and value extraction:

- *Control*: A stock-market listing affects the relationship between share ownership and managerial control over the allocation of resources. A listing of stock on the market usually results in the separation of ownership and control, but it also provides the possibility for their reintegration through the accumulation of shares with voting rights, either directly or through proxies. While the separation of ownership and control provides conditions for the long-term growth of the firm, it also opens up the possibility that professional managers will abuse their positions of control for their own personal benefit through value extraction rather than use those positions for the sake of enterprise growth through value creation.

- *Cash*: The stock market can be a source of corporate finance through new share issues, at the IPO or subsequently in a secondary issue. Once a company has transformed from a new venture into a going concern, the cash function of the stock market requires that dividends to shareholders be limited to an amount that enables the company to retain sufficient earnings from profits to reinvest in productive capabilities and thus support value creation. In the presence of stock buybacks, however, the cash function may be negative, with buybacks joining dividends as a mode of value extraction.

- *Creation*: Since the stock market can provide private equity with a means to exit an investment in the productive capabilities of a company, the prospect of a listing can induce venture capital to support new-firm creation and growth. But in a highly speculative stock market such as the NASDAQ, a young firm with no record of substantial profits, or even a commercial product, may be able to issue an IPO, raising the possibility that the exit of private equity may occur before the company has accumulated the productive capabilities and financial assets to ensure its sustained growth as a value-creating entity. So while an atmosphere of intense stock-market speculation may incline private equity to invest in the creation of new firms, a stock-market listing—amidst this same speculation, in combination with hyping of the market and other forms of manipulation—may permit these shareholders to extract value even in the absence of value creation.

- *Combination*: A stock-market listing makes the company's shares a currency that can be used as payment, partially or wholly, for another company's shares in mergers and acquisitions (M&A). An M&A deal may enable the new combination to build productive capabilities that support value creation. But, with the added cash flow that an acquisition brings to the acquiring enterprise, those who control the new combination will have much greater scope for value extraction. Indeed, it may be control over that cash flow for the purpose of value extraction that was the purpose of the acquisition, with the acquirer's elevated stock price enabling the acquisition.

- *Compensation*: Similarly, a stock-market listing makes the company's shares a currency that can be issued to employees as a form of remuneration, with stock options and stock awards as prime examples. In principle, stock-based pay should motivate employees to work harder and smarter so that, through the value-creating success of the firm, they will be rewarded by higher stock prices in the future, when the options are exercised or the awards vest. Depending on the distribution of options and awards among employees, higher stock prices driven by innovation, which reflect contributions of employees to the process of value creation, may enable them to share equitably in the gains from that innovation. But a stock market that is driven by speculation and manipulation, rather than by innovation, may disrupt the relation between value creation and value extraction delivered through stock-based pay, undermining the stable and equitable remuneration structures that sustained value creation generally requires.

The analysis of the five functions that the stock market performs is central to understanding whether the stock market supports the process of value creation or enables the process of value extraction, and hence the extent to which value creation and value extraction are, or are not, in balance. There are two ways by which shareholders can extract value from a company via the stock market: cash dividends and stock repurchases. These two modes of value extraction are not equivalent ways in which a shareholder can realize a yield. The difference between dividends and buybacks as modes of distributing cash to shareholders is important for understanding the relation between value creation and value extraction.

Dividends accrue to shareholders for *holding* shares. If dividends are too high, corporate retentions from profits may be too low to fund the investments in productive capabilities that can enable a company to grow and, possibly, generate new innovative products, which, in turn, can generate the profits from which dividends can be paid later. That would be a problem for shareholders who, as savers rather than speculators, want to hold shares for the sake of a reliable stream of dividend income. The shareholder who thinks that reinvestment of earnings by the company is insufficient—or too ineptly managed—to generate an acceptable level of profits in the future should, and in a liquid market easily can, take the "Wall Street walk," selling the shares before the stock price enters into a long-term decline.

Buybacks are not the same as dividends because, whereas dividends reward shareholders for holding shares, the only way for a shareholder to make money from stock repurchases is by *selling* shares; that is, by ceasing to be a share*holder* and becoming a share*seller*. Moreover, in selling shares, the timing of the sale determines the amount of the gains that are made. In the case of a buyback that takes place through a tender offer, shareholders are given a window of opportunity to sell the shares to the company at a stipulated price that remains constant for the offer's duration. In open-market stock repurchases, which represent the vast majority of buybacks in the United States and are the subject of our discussion here, the increased demand for a company's shares will lift the stock price immediately, perhaps setting off increased speculation—in some cases fomented by the manipulative activities of Wall Street traders—that raises the stock price further. In the United States, public shareholders who are simply savers are ill-positioned to take advantage of these speculative and manipulative boosts to a company's stock price because, under prevailing SEC rules, a company is not required to make public the trading days on which open-market repurchases take place. Companies need not disclose at the time of the buyback, or, even after the fact, the days on which open-market repurchases are executed. Certain insiders do, however, possess this information, and major Wall Street players who are in the business of timing stock transactions know how to access this information and make use of it to enrich themselves.

How, then, over the course of the past century have the changing functions of the stock market in the United States affected the balance between value creation and value extraction? In Section 3.3, we summarize the evolution of the stock market's five functions and of their impact on the creation–extraction relation. This discussion in turn provides the historical context for understanding how and why the ideology that a company should be run to maximize shareholder value (MSV) became full-blown and dominant during the 1980s, and how and why MSV ideology is fundamentally flawed as an approach to the governance and performance of the modern business corporation.

3.3 The Changing Functions of the Stock Market as Influences on the Creation–Extraction Imbalance

3.3.1 Control: From "Retain-and-Reinvest" to "Downsize-and-Distribute"

In the 1920s, when the NYSE emerged as a well-developed stock market, it was largely unregulated, except by the NYSE's governing body itself. In the mid-1920s, concerned that the holders of corporate shares were being harmed by the separation of managerial control and equity ownership, economist William Z. Ripley, in lectures, articles, and his book *Main Street and Wall Street*, decried shareholders' lack of power and their abuse by managers, who exercised control over the allocation of corporate resources. Specifically, some corporations had created "management shares"—or what today would be called "dual-class shares"—with disproportionate voting rights that gave their holders *de jure*, rather than just *de facto*, control over the allocation of corporate resources. Indeed, some companies were even issuing common shares with no voting rights at all.[17] In response, the NYSE insisted that all common shares have equal voting rights. On the surface, this change shifted power to public shareholders, but in practice, by inspiring confidence in the governance of the NYSE, the reform further fragmented shareholder power, with public shareholders remaining content to leave corporate decision-making under the control of senior executives.

When the stock-market boom of the late 1920s resulted in the Great Crash—which, as it turned out, was the opening act of the descent of the U.S. economy into a deep depression—the U.S. government responded with the Securities Act of 1933, regulating new share issues, and the Securities Exchange Act of 1934, regulating the trading of outstanding shares. Together, these laws were designed to eliminate fraud and manipulation from the stock markets, and from other financial markets as well. The 1934 Act established the SEC to carry out this regulatory role.

It was the control function of the stock market, aided by the SEC's efforts to reduce fraud and manipulation, that helped to keep major U.S. business corporations focused on investment in innovation and balancing value creation and value extraction into the 1980s. The separation of equity ownership and managerial control left professional managers in positions of strategic control. That having been said, the adherence of top executives to a retain-and-reinvest allocation regime in the post-war decades reflected the fact that their own career success within the corporation was closely bound up with the success of the business organization as a whole. Coming up through the ranks of the organization, senior executives typically accumulated a deep knowledge of the capabilities of the company and of the business sectors in which it operated, and hence had the ability to make investment decisions concerning the company's strategic direction.

Their own career experience also led them to adopt and respect the career-with-one-company norm for the "organization men" whom they led.[18] In the post-World War II decades, top executives accepted the need to train and retain growing numbers of professional, technical, and administrative personnel, who came to constitute the white-collar labor force. Given the size of the corporate human-capital investment this entailed and the productive capabilities of these personnel, it became the norm that such employees could expect to be with the company until the end of their careers and to retire with a defined-benefit pension

---

[17] Ripley (1927).

[18] Lazonick (2009c: ch. 3). For a more general discussion, see Hopkins and Lazonick (2014) and Lazonick et al. (2014).

funded by the company, its value based on years of service. Leading companies also provided these employees with medical coverage, thus making health insurance a responsibility of business rather than of government.

As for the blue-collar labor force, across a wide range of industries New Deal legislation compelled senior management to engage in collective bargaining over wages and benefits with mass-production unions, for which seniority was a fundamental principle of job security. Although blue-collar workers were known as "hourly" employees, making them potentially eligible under the Fair Labor Standards Act of 1938 for payment of "time-and-a-half" wages for hours worked overtime, the institutionalization of seniority in effect gave the blue-collar employee a career with one company that could last for decades. Some workers with substantial seniority might be laid off in a deep downturn, but they would be re-employed in order of seniority in the next upturn. As long as senior executives accepted the career-with-one-company norm for a broad base of employees, they had the incentive to adhere to a retain-and-reinvest resource-allocation regime.

Retain-and-reinvest did not mean that the company should—or could—grow larger and larger in a single line of business. In most industries, the innovative enterprise had to assume that over time competitors would learn how to produce an equally high-quality, or even superior, product for a market in which it had been an innovator. Those exercising strategic control would want to reallocate the company's capabilities—first and foremost, its human resources—to new lines of business in which developing new technologies or accessing new markets could make use of these capabilities. Retained earnings provided the financial foundation for exercising such strategic investments in the growth of the firm.

It was this type of strategic control that underpinned the prominence of what in his 1962 book, *Strategy and Structure*, Alfred Chandler called the "multidivisional structure."[19] At about the same time, the economist Edith Penrose sought to discover the theoretical principles of a business that, through diversification, could build on its competitive advantage to sustain its growth. In her classic contribution *The Theory of the Growth of the Firm*, published in 1959, Penrose portrayed multidivisionalization as the process through which those in positions of strategic control reallocated unused capabilities accumulated in the old lines of business to new lines of business.[20] Moving around and up a company's managerial hierarchy over the course of a career, the professional manager who attained a position of strategic control had the ability to make these strategic decisions because he had developed a deep understanding of the firm's productive capabilities and the new types of products to which they could be allocated. Given the prevailing norm of a career with one company, his income and prestige generally

---

[19] Chandler (1962).   [20] Penrose (1959, 1960).

benefited from the growth of the firm. Hence his personal incentives were aligned with the objective of making innovative use of the company's productive resources. There was a close integration of strategic decision-making with the processes of organizational learning.

There was also the potential, however, for this integration of strategy and learning to break down, undermining the value-creation process and creating conditions for predatory value extraction.[21] The seeds of imbalance were sown in the 1950s, when one of the oldest and strongest corporations, General Electric (GE), promulgated the ideology that "a good manager could manage any type of business."[22] In the 1960s, this ideology became standard fare in U.S. graduate business schools. It was used to justify the diversification of the U.S. industrial corporation into a conglomeration of different markets and locations, even if many of the different businesses into which the corporation moved had no technological or market relation to one another. GE itself diversified into hundreds of lines of business, emerging by the 1970s as an unwieldy conglomerate. The job of top executives at the corporate office, lacking knowledge of the technological and organizational capabilities of the increasing number of business units, was reduced to "managing by the numbers," which tended to favor cost-cutting over investments in innovation.[23]

During the 1960s what has become known as the "conglomerate movement" significantly reshaped patterns of strategic control within the U.S. industrial corporation. Unlike the case of GE, most of the conglomerates were constructed not by incumbent executives but by outsiders, who, having acquired control of one company through ownership stakes, used that corporation's stock and added to its debt to buy other companies. As many among the largest manufacturing corporations came to be run by executives whose only interest was in acquiring more companies to build these corporate empires, the mean number of lines of business of the top 200 ranked by sales rose from 4.76 in 1950 to 10.89 in 1975. For the 148 corporations of the 200 largest by revenue in 1950 that still existed in 1975, the mean number of lines of business had risen from 5.22 to 9.74. During the conglomerate movement of the 1960s, the number of M&A announcements increased from an average of 1,951 per year in 1963–67 to 3,736 in 1968–72, hitting a peak of 5,306 in 1969.[24] Between 1950 and 1978 Beatrice Foods made 290 acquisitions; W. R. Grace, 186; IT&T, 163; Gulf and Western, 155; Textron, 115; Litton Industries, 99; and LTV, 58.[25] One analysis revealed that, of assets that large manufacturing and mining companies acquired when they bought other companies, the "pure conglomerate" category—that is, assets unrelated to the company's established

---

[21] O'Sullivan (2000); Lazonick (2006).   [22] O'Sullivan (2000).
[23] On this problem more generally at the end of the 1970s, see Hayes and Abernathy (1980).
[24] Merrill Lynch Advisory Services (1994).   [25] Ravenscraft and Scherer (1987).

businesses—represented 10.1 percent in 1948–55, 17.7 percent in 1956–63, 34.8 percent in 1964–71, and 45.5 percent in 1972–79.[26]

With the downturn in the U.S. economy in the early 1970s, it became apparent that resource allocation in many U.S. industrial corporations had become over-centralized. The problem was not size per se but rather a failure of the conglomerateurs who exercised strategic control to comprehend what the businesses they had acquired actually needed for investments in productive capabilities.[27] In addition, particularly by the end of the 1960s, the growth of conglomerates through M&A had been debt-financed; the debt–equity ratio in U.S. manufacturing rose from 0.40 in 1960 to 0.48 in 1965 and to 0.72 in 1970.

Conglomeration generally undermined the innovative capabilities of the constituent businesses, and when the 1960s stock-market bubble burst in 1970, there was mounting financial pressure on the corporations to shed some of the businesses that they had taken on. The conglomerate movement of the 1960s turned into the deconglomeration movement of the 1970s. The annual average number of divestiture announcements had been 207 in 1963–67 (10.6 percent of the corresponding number of M&A announcements) but rose to 1,290 in 1968–72 (34.5 percent) and to 1,266 in 1973–77 (85.9 percent). Thereafter, the absolute number of average annual announced divestitures declined somewhat, to 789 (57.0 percent of M&A announcements) in 1978–82, 1,023 (61.4 percent) in 1983–87, and 953 (74.6 percent) in 1988–92, but the undoing of the conglomerate movement continued.[28]

By the mid-1980s, many divestitures were occurring in the aftermath of hostile takeovers. Corporate raiders looked for companies that were undervalued in the stock market relative to the "breakup" value of their various lines of business, used debt issues to acquire the companies, and then sold off corporate divisions to pay down the debt and generate cash that they could extract.[29] The "junk bond" was widely favored as a debt instrument in hostile takeovers.[30] Initially, junk bonds were previously issued investment-grade corporate securities the ratings of which had been lowered. Since these downgraded bonds could be bought at a deep discount, they offered a high, if risky, yield. In the first half of the 1970s, Michael Milken of the Wall Street firm Drexel Burnham Lambert in effect made a market in junk bonds by convincing institutional investors, particularly mutual funds and insurance companies, to include these high-yield securities in their investment portfolios.[31] Liquidity was thus bestowed on the junk-bond market, and, in a period in which escalating inflation was eroding real interest rates, institutional investors welcomed the higher risk-adjusted yields that these securities offered.

---

[26] Scherer and Ross (1990).   [27] Holland (1989).
[28] Merrill Lynch Advisory Services (2002).   [29] Long and Ravenscraft (1993).
[30] Taggart (1988).   [31] Bruck (1989).

By the late 1970s, with the junk-bond market well developed, it became possible to issue new junk bonds—as distinct from those "fallen angels" that had previously been investment grade—to finance leveraged buyouts (LBOs). Most of these LBOs were divisional buyouts in which the top managers of a business unit took that unit private with a view to recapturing strategic control over resource allocation. Specialized Wall Street LBO firms, of which KKR was the most prominent, would finance the LBO with the prospect of reaping returns when the newly formed private firms could issue an IPO. In 1980 there were 47 divisional LBOs at an average value (in 1988 dollars) of $34.5 million rising to a peak of 144 divisional LBOs in 1986 at a real average value of $180.7 million.

In 1987 and 1988, however, whole-company LBOs became more prevalent; there were 47 in 1987 and 125 in 1988 at an average value in 1988 dollars of $480 million, with the most famous being the KKR buyout of RJR Nabisco for $24.5 billion.[32] The purpose of these LBOs—also known as "hostile takeovers"—was usually to take over companies in order to sell them off in pieces while, at the same time, extracting value by downsizing the labor force and ramping up distributions to shareholders in the form of dividends and buybacks. By the last half of the 1980s, the era of "downsize-and-distribute" had clearly arrived.

3.3.2 Cash: Finance for Value Creation or Booty for Value Extraction?

The use of the stock market to buy and sell companies in the conglomerate movement of the 1960s undermined the integration of strategic control with the processes of organizational learning, opening the door for financial interests that had played little if any role in contributing to value creation to attain positions of strategic control. Increasingly, they used this power to drain cash from companies in the form of executive pay, management fees, interest payments, cash dividends, and stock buybacks. From the mid-1980s, as we have seen, buybacks emerged, on top of dividends, as a leading mode of value extraction, incentivized from within the corporate suite by stock-based executive pay. In the process, the stock market began to perform a *negative* cash function that has increased from decade to decade.[33]

As mentioned above, the stock market performs a *positive* cash function when a company issues shares at its IPO or in a subsequent, secondary stock offering. The funds that are raised may be used for investment in productive capabilities or retained to solidify the corporate balance sheet, possibly providing the capitalization that permits a company to take on debt with little risk of being forced into

---

[32] Jensen (1989); Gaughan (1999).
[33] Lazonick (2014c: 46–55); Lazonick (2015a, 2016b).

bankruptcy if business temporarily goes bad. In the Old Economy corporation, funds raised by the IPO were relatively unimportant to corporate finance because companies going public on the NYSE, being subject to its listing requirements, would have already had to accumulate cash reserves and to achieve a level of profits sufficient to fund internal investments on an ongoing basis. If a company needed to leverage these retentions, its NYSE listing gave it access to the corporate bond market at favorable rates. Once listed on the stock market, these companies sought to pay stable dividends in order to meet the income expectations of their "loyal" shareholders. Until companies started to do large-scale stock buybacks in 1984, profits retained after the payment of dividends formed a firm foundation of financial commitment.

In general, NYSE-listed companies did not do secondary stock offerings— with one notable period during which the exception proved the rule. In the late 1920s many publicly listed companies that had salaried executives at the helm did large-scale share issues on the NYSE, even as, by lending on the call-loan market, these corporations were channeling large sums of surplus cash to speculators. These speculators were buying corporate shares on margin with funds borrowed on the call-loan market at interest rates of 10 percent to 15 percent. The purpose of such corporate share issues was *not* to raise funds for new investment in productive capabilities; rather, it was to take advantage of high stock prices driven by market speculators to secure an influx of cash that could be used to pay off debt or bolster the corporate treasury.[34] The results of such financial engineering would stand these companies in good stead at the beginning of the 1930s, after the economy had moved from boom to bust.

In retrospect, this financial behavior also contrasts dramatically with major U.S. corporations' practice over the past two decades of doing large-scale stock repurchases when stock prices are high—for the purpose of pushing their own stock prices even higher. In the current era, as we document in Chapter 4, senior executives have done large-scale stock buybacks in booming stock markets to fatten up their pay packages, larded as they are with gains from exercising stock options and the vesting of stock awards. In the late 1920s, in contrast, with the managerial revolution intact, senior executives sold the corporation's shares on the speculative market to improve the financial condition of the companies over which they exercised strategic control, not for the sake of increasing their own compensation. The growing importance over the past three decades of stock buybacks, which have been especially large and widespread during boom periods, manifests a dramatic transformation of the thrust of U.S. corporations' behavior from retain-and-reinvest to downsize-and-distribute—and hence from a balance to an imbalance in the relation between value creation and value extraction.

[34] Smiley and Keehn (1988).

3.3.3 Creation: The Role of the Stock Market
in New-Firm Creation

The 1971 launch of the National Association of Security Dealers Automated Quotation electronic exchange, better known as NASDAQ, created a highly liquid stock market with listing requirements far less stringent than those of the NYSE.[35] By making it much easier for a young company to execute an IPO a scant few years after its founding, the existence of NASDAQ induced private equity to flow to startups. The first company to list on NASDAQ was Intel, founded in 1968 and publicly listed in 1971. When Intel sought startup funding, before NASDAQ was in place, the money was secured because of the reputation of founders Gordon Moore and Robert Noyce and their connection with a pioneer venture capitalist, Arthur Rock. But with NASDAQ in operation, a specialized venture-capital industry dedicated to new-firm creation in high-tech fields rapidly emerged in the 1970s, especially in the region south of San Francisco, centered on Stanford University. It was also in 1971 that a local journalist dubbed this blossoming industrial district "Silicon Valley."

In 1975, the SEC barred stock exchanges from charging fixed commissions on stock-trading transactions, ending a practice that had prevailed on Wall Street since 1796. This change reduced the cost of buying and selling shares in pursuit of capital gains as an alternative to sitting back and collecting dividends, and thus it facilitated early IPOs of new ventures that were not yet profitable enough to pay dividends. It also favored the subsequent growth of the firm as a publicly listed company because of the willingness of capital-gains-oriented stockholders to forgo dividends, thus leaving more earnings with the company for internal investment.

In 1978–79, in response to intensive lobbying led by the American Electronics Association and the National Venture Capital Association, both of which were dominated by Silicon Valley interests, the U.S. Congress reduced the capital-gains tax rate from a maximum of almost 40 percent to a maximum of 28 percent, thus reversing a 36-year trend toward higher capital-gains taxes.[36] In 1981, the capital-gains tax rate was further reduced, to a maximum of 20 percent. Venture capitalists saw lower capital-gains taxes as encouraging both entrepreneurial investment in new companies and portfolio investment by individuals in the publicly traded stocks of young, potentially high-growth firms.

During the 1970s, however, venture capitalists still faced constraints on the amount of money that they could raise for venture funds, mainly because of restrictions on their access to the vast accumulation of household savings held by pension funds. In the early 1970s there was only a trickle of institutional money

---

[35] Lazonick (2009a: ch. 2).   [36] Tax Foundation (2010).

invested in venture capital, and even that flow dried up when the passage of the Employee Retirement Income Security Act (ERISA) in 1974 made corporations responsible for underfunded pensions and pension-fund managers personally liable for breaches of their fiduciary duty to use the "prudent man" rule when allocating pension funds to investments in securities. Under these circumstances, pension-fund managers, who controlled the allocation of an ever-increasing share of U.S. household savings, avoided investment in venture-capital funds.

On July 23, 1979, however, the U.S. Department of Labor decreed that, under ERISA, pension-fund money could be invested not only in listed stocks and high-grade bonds but also in more speculative assets, including new ventures, without transgressing the prudent man rule. As a result, pension-fund money poured into venture-capital funds. Independent venture partnerships of the type that prevailed in Silicon Valley increased their access to the capital of pension funds from, measured in 1997 dollars, $69 million in 1978—just 15 percent of all funds raised—to $1,808 million in 1983. Throughout the 1980s and 1990s, pension funds provided anywhere from 31 percent to 59 percent of the funds raised by independent venture-capital partnerships, which in turn increased their share of all venture funds raised from 40 percent in 1980 to 80 percent a decade later.[37]

Apple Computer's highly successful IPO in December 1980 is generally credited with setting off the startup and IPO booms of the early 1980s. After achieving spectacular returns on its investments, averaging around 35 percent per year between 1978 and 1983, the venture-capital industry was punished for overinvesting, with returns averaging less than 10 percent in the last half of the 1980s. After 1990 annual returns rose once again, soaring to almost 150 percent at the peak of the Internet boom before turning negative in the crash of 2001 and 2002.[38]

The Silicon Valley venture-capital model spread to other parts of the United States, especially during the 1990s, with investments made in many different locations and a wide range of industries. Measured in 2000 dollars, total venture-capital investment in the United States per annum rose from $9.1 billion in 1995 to $22.3 billion in 1998 before skyrocketing to $55.9 billion in 1999 and $105.0 billion in 2000. After falling to $39.5 billion in 2001, venture-capital investment averaged $21.4 billion per year from 2002 to 2007, including $25.3 billion in 2007. In current dollars, however, venture-capital investment declined from $30.5 billion in 2007 to $28.3 billion in 2008. After a sharp slump in 2009 and 2010, the industry recovered, reaching $73.3 billion in 2015 and $59.0 billion in 2016. Silicon Valley remains by far the world's most important location for venture capital.[39]

The centrality of a rapid stock-market listing to the creation function under the New Economy business model meant that from a very early stage in the growth of

---

[37] Gompers and Lerner (2002).   [38] Lerner (2002).   [39] PricewaterhouseCoopers (2019).

the firm, those who exercised strategic control in these New Economy companies had a deep concern with the company's stock price. Indeed, in a speculative stock market, the IPO itself created opportunities for value extraction without value creation. In the dot.com boom of the late 1990s, companies without a single commercial product could do an IPO that brought in billions of dollars, netting fortunes for senior executives and venture capitalists even if the company was eventually to fail.[40] In the biopharma industry, in which developing an effective new drug can require billions of dollars and a decade or two, product-less IPOs on NASDAQ are the rule in the United States. Through the National Institutes of Health, the taxpayer funds scientific discovery and in many cases even clinical trials, while countless scientists in government and university research labs contribute to the drug-development process. Yet it is financial interests that reap the lion's share of the gains by selling stock on a market that is speculative and, often, manipulated. In the world of product-less IPOs, those who contribute most to the collective and cumulative process of value creation often share least in the process of value extraction. And the very process of funneling financial resources into the hands of the value extractors often cuts short or dooms to failure the process of value creation.[41]

3.3.4 Combination: Stock as a Currency for M&A

Since the Great Merger Movement of the 1890s and early 1900s, there have been a number of waves of M&A activity in the United States, most notably in the mid-1920s, 1960s, 1980s, and 1990s. An M&A deal can be carried out with cash, with stock, or with some combination of the two. While stock has often been used as a currency to fund combinations, it was in the 1990s that its use was most pronounced.[42]

In their *Harvard Business Review* article entitled "Stock or Cash?" published in 1999, at the peak of the Internet boom, Alfred Rappaport and Mark Sirower argue:

> The legendary merger mania of the 1980s pales beside the M&A activity of this decade. In 1998 alone, 12,356 deals involving U.S. targets were announced for a total value of $1.63 trillion. Compare that with the 4,066 deals worth $378.9 billion announced in 1988, at the height of the 1980s merger movement. But the numbers should be no surprise. After all, acquisitions remain the quickest route companies have to new markets and to new capabilities. As markets globalize, and the pace at which technologies change continues to accelerate, more and

---

[40] Gimein (2002); Lazonick (2016a).
[41] Lazonick and Sakinç (2010); Sakinç and Tulum (2012).
[42] Carpenter et al. (2003); Lazonick (2006).

more companies are finding mergers and acquisitions to be a compelling strategy for growth. What is striking about acquisitions in the 1990s, however, is the way they're being paid for. In 1988, nearly 60% of the value of large deals—those over $100 million—was paid for entirely in cash. Less than 2% was paid for in *stock*. But just ten years later, the profile is almost reversed: 50% of the value of all large deals in 1998 was paid for entirely in *stock*, and only 17% was paid for entirely in cash.[43]

An advantage of using stock as a combination currency was that, under accounting rules in place in the United States, it enabled a company to treat an acquisition as a "pooling of interests": the enlarged entity accounted for its additional assets at the book value of the acquired company, and thus avoided recording goodwill—the difference between the market value and the book value of the acquisition—as an intangible asset on its balance sheet. By not having to amortize goodwill, the enlarged company would show higher earnings on its profit-and-loss statement over subsequent years than if it had recorded the acquisition at its purchase price. During the conglomerate boom of the 1960s, many pooling-of-interests acquisitions were made with debt or with a combination of securities and cash.[44] In 1970, in response to abuses of pooling-of-interests accounting during the conglomeration era, the Accounting Principles Board (replaced in 1973 by the current Financial Accounting Standards Board [FASB]) ruled, among other things, that only acquisitions made entirely with common stock could use pooling-of-interests accounting.[45]

The New Economy boom of the 1990s raised the value of shares and made stock a relatively more attractive combination currency than cash. Pooling-of-interests accounting made stock-based acquisitions especially advantageous to reported earnings when established companies were bidding for relatively young companies—indeed, in some cases revenue-less startups—with low book values. It may well have been for this reason that the use of stock instead of cash as an acquisition currency was much more prevalent in the United States in the late 1990s than it had been during the late 1980s.[46] The collapse of stock prices that occurred in late 2000 and the first half of 2001 led to widespread criticism of pooling of interests, and in July 2001 FASB banned the further use of this method of accounting for acquisitions.

An exemplar in the use of stock as a combination currency in the 1990s was Cisco Systems. Founded in 1984 in the heart of Silicon Valley, Cisco grew from $70 million in sales and 254 employees in 1990, the year of its IPO, to $18.9 billion in sales and 34,000 employees a decade later. By that time, Cisco had come to

---

[43] Rappaport and Sirower (1999).   [44] Fortune (1970); Brooks (1973).
[45] Rayburn and Powers (1991); Seligman (1995: 419–29); Wallman et al. (1999).
[46] Tufano (1993); Rappaport and Sirower (1999).

dominate the market for internetworking equipment, and it was entering the more-complex market for service-provider (or carrier-class) communication technology.

Key to Cisco's growth from 1993 were acquisitions of numerous other technology companies. From 1993 through 2000, Cisco did 60 acquisitions valued at $32.5 billion, of which 98 percent was paid in Cisco's shares.[47] On the strength of this "growth-through-acquisition" strategy, by the late 1990s Cisco could claim to have been the fastest-growing company in U.S. history.[48] Meanwhile, during the Internet boom two of Cisco's Old Economy competitors—U.S.-based Lucent, the largest communication-equipment company in the world in 2000, and Nortel, based in Canada but with its largest footprint in the United States—destroyed themselves by emulating Cisco's growth-through-acquisition model, using massive amounts of stock as the acquisition currency. The hype surrounding their acquisitions gave the two companies' stock prices a boost in the Internet boom but left them with massive losses and junk-bond ratings in the bust.[49]

Given the centrality of its equipment to the growth of the Internet economy, Cisco would have shown substantial profits in the last half of the 1990s under any circumstances. But its use of pooling-of-interests accounting helped increase its reported profits even more, adding to the speculative fervor over its stock. In March 2000, Cisco had the highest market capitalization in the world. A *Barron's* editor calculated that to justify Cisco's stock price of 130 times estimated earnings per share for 2000, Cisco's earnings, which stood at $2.5 billion in 1999, would have to reach $2.5 trillion in 2010![50]

With the bursting of the Internet bubble in September 2001, Cisco's stock price fell to just 15 percent of its March 2000 peak. At that point, Cisco began doing stock buybacks to boost its share price. Its buybacks escalated from $1.9 billion in its fiscal year 2002 (ended July 31, 2002) to $5.9 billion in fiscal 2003, $9.1 billion in fiscal 2003, and $10.2 billion in fiscal 2004. In all, from 2002 through 2018 Cisco did $118.7 billion in buybacks, equal to 106 percent of its net income, on top of which it distributed $29.5 billion in dividends from 2011 through 2018. By 2004 Cisco was doing its acquisitions in cash, and in the case of its largest, Scientific Atlanta for $6.9 billion in 2005, it took on debt, largely because it was doing buybacks to boost its stock price and did not want to dilute its shareholding using its stock as an acquisition currency.

Our detailed research on Cisco reveals that as it dramatically ramped up its spending on stock buybacks in the first half of the 2000s, it eschewed making deep investments in carrier-class communications equipment, a segment that, as a result of acquisitions made in the previous boom, it was positioned to enter. Instead, most of Cisco's acquisitions during the 2000s brought the company

---

[47] Carpenter et al. (2003).   [48] O'Reilly (2002).
[49] Carpenter et al. (2003); Lazonick and March (2011).   [50] Donlan (2000: 31–4).

products that turned out to be commodities. Given its dominant position in enterprise-communication equipment, the growth of data centers and cloud computing enabled Cisco to increase its sales from $22 billion to over $49 billion from 2004 to 2018, and its employees from 34,000 to over 74,000. But, with an obsessive focus on manipulating its stock price, Cisco ceased to be an innovative enterprise.[51] Today, the world leader in communication technology, with large market shares in service-provider equipment, enterprise equipment, and consumer devices—the company that, in our view, Cisco could have been—is the Chinese company Huawei, founded in the then-unsophisticated city of Shenzhen in 1987, three years after Silicon Valley's Cisco emerged out of Stanford University. Owing to a retain-and-reinvest allocation regime, by 2018 Huawei had $107 billion in revenues and 180,000 employees. Huawei does not do stock buybacks because, as a 100 percent employee-owned company, it is not listed on a stock market.[52]

3.3.5 Compensation: Stock as a Currency for Employee Pay

The stock market can perform a compensation function by enabling a company to use its own shares to pay a substantial portion of the remuneration of employees, among whom the greatest beneficiaries are the senior executives who exercise strategic control over the allocation of corporate resources.[53] It was in the 1950s that stock-based compensation first became a source of additional income for senior executives of major companies. While taxing personal income in excess of $200,000 at a rate of 91 percent, the Revenue Act of 1950 gave senior executives the alternative of paying the capital-gains tax of 25 percent on their gains from exercising "qualified" stock options, provided that the eligible stock was held for at least two years from the grant date and six months from the exercise date. From the late 1950s, there was a public backlash against this tax privilege of executives, leading the U.S. Congress to pass legislation that made it more difficult for executives to take advantage of the capital-gains loophole, and the Tax Reform Act of 1976 closed it completely. In 1978 Graef Crystal, an executive-compensation consultant who would later become a vocal critic of excessive executive pay, stated that qualified stock options, "once the most popular of all executive compensation devices, . . . have been given the last rites by Congress."[54]

From the beginning of the 1980s, however, executive stock options, with the gains now taxed at the *ordinary income-tax rate*—which declined dramatically with the coming of Reaganomics—re-emerged with a vengeance, incentivizing

[51] Bell et al. (2014); Carpenter and Lazonick (2017).
[52] Huawei Investment & Holding Co., Ltd. (2016); Li (2017: ch. 5).
[53] Hopkins and Lazonick (2016).   [54] Crystal (1978, 1991).

value extraction rather than value creation. The driving force for the return to stock options as a form of compensation was the rapid growth in the 1980s of the New Economy business model, as startup companies sought to use stock options to induce professional, technical, and administrative personnel to abandon the career-long employment security they enjoyed at Old Economy companies. As startups, the New Economy companies could not hold out the Old Economy promise of a career with one company with a defined-benefit pension in retirement. As New Economy companies such as Oracle, Microsoft, and Cisco grew to employ tens of thousands of people in the 1990s, they continued to use stock options as partial remuneration for most of them. By the 2000s, the career-with-one-company norm was largely gone, exposing even college-educated workers to high levels of employment insecurity and, often, truncated careers when the senior executives for whom they worked deserted the operating principle of retain-and-reinvest and embraced downsize-and-distribute.

But granting broad-based stock options proved to be a problematic mode of employee remuneration at the New Economy companies as well. In the Internet boom of 1996–2000, at certain technology companies the gains from exercising stock options were so high that they fostered a hypermobility of labor incompatible with the commitment of employees to engage in the collective and cumulative learning processes that are central to innovation. For example, at Microsoft the employee's average gain from the exercise of stock options was—leaving the CEO and other four highest-paid executives out of the calculation—$79,000 across 19,200 employees in 1996. This number then soared to $369,700 across 29,200 employees in 1999, and peaked at $449,100 across 35,200 employees in 2000, before falling back to $80,300 across 52,800 employees in 2003. It is said that, in 2000 alone, Microsoft created 10,000 millionaires, large numbers of whom became angel investors, founded or joined startups, or retired at an early age. This hypermobility of labor disrupted projects at Microsoft Research, which had been founded in 1991, and helped to ensure that the company would not be a leader in innovation in the 2000s and beyond.[55]

During the 1980s, as broad-based stock-option programs became a widespread mode of remunerating rank-and-file high-tech employees, senior executives of these companies received stock options in abundance as part of special compensation packages meted out by their boards. As they saw top executives of New Economy companies receiving unprecedented levels of stock-based remuneration, the senior executives of Old Economy companies clamored for this mode of compensation as well. In the process, a distinctive procedure emerged for rewarding top executives that had a "ratchet effect"—the mechanics of which we detail in Chapter 4—in pumping up executive pay over time, severing any plausible

---

[55] Lazonick (2009c).

relation between the executives' contributions to value creation through their strategic decision-making and their value extraction through remuneration. Indeed, as we also detail in Chapter 4, in the United States executive stock-based pay incentivizes those who exercise strategic control to adopt a downsize-and-distribute resource-allocation regime.

The result has been an ongoing explosion of executive pay since the 1980s. The average total compensation of the 500 highest-paid executives listed in the Execu-Comp database for each year from 2008 through 2017 ranged from a low of $15.8 million in the post-crash year of 2009, with stock-based pay making up 60 percent of the total, to a high of $34.1 million in 2015, with stock-based gains making up 83 percent of the total. U.S. corporate executives are incentivized to boost their companies' stock prices and are amply rewarded for doing so. In SEC-approved stock buybacks, they have at their disposal an instrument to enrich themselves. In their massive, widespread, and ubiquitous use of this instrument, they have been participating in the looting of the U.S. business corporation.[56]

3.4 Maximizing Shareholder Value as an Ideology of Value Extraction

Legitimizing the looting of the U.S. industrial corporation has been the ideology that a company should be run to "maximize shareholder value" (MSV). From this perspective, the main problem of large corporations is the alleged tendency of managers, in control of the allocation of vast corporate resources, to "build empires" by investing in wasteful projects for their personal aggrandizement. The proponents of MSV argue that hostile takeovers, more generally known as "the market for corporate control," can force managers to stop dissipating corporate resources but distribute cash to shareholders instead. The MSV proponents also argue that making stock-based pay a major proportion of executive compensation will cause the incentives that corporate managers respond to in the allocation of resources to align with those of public shareholders.[57] Only when corporations "disgorge" their "free cash flow" to shareholders in the form of cash dividends and stock repurchases, they contend, are the economy's resources being allocated to their most efficient uses.[58]

MSV ideology is rooted in two misconceptions of the role of public shareholders in the U.S. business corporation. The most fundamental error is the assumption that public shareholders actually invest in the productive assets of the corporation. That error is then compounded by the assumption that it is *only* public shareholders who make risky investments in the corporation's productive

---

[56] Hopkins and Lazonick (2016); Lazonick (2016a).
[57] Jensen and Murphy (1990).   [58] Jensen (1986).

assets, and hence that it is only shareholders who have a legitimate claim on the corporation's profits. Once the flaws in these assumptions are recognized, the factual foundation for MSV ideology falls apart.

Central to the MSV argument is the assumption that, of all participants in the business corporation, shareholders are the only economic actors who make productive contributions *without a guaranteed return.* All other participants— among them, creditors, workers, suppliers, and distributors—allegedly receive a market-determined price for the goods or services that they render to the corporation, and hence take no risk on whether the company makes or loses money. On this assumption, "free cash flow" by definition simply includes corporate earnings that under a retain-and-reinvest resource-allocation regime the corporation would have invested in training, retaining, and rewarding employees. Also, on this assumption, only shareholders have an economically justifiable claim to any "residual" of revenues over costs that exists after the company has paid all other stakeholders their (supposedly) guaranteed contractual claims for their productive contributions to the firm.

By the MSV argument, shareholders are the only stakeholders who need to be incentivized to bear the risk of investing in productive resources that may result in superior economic performance. As the only "residual claimants," the MSV story goes, shareholders are the only stakeholders who have an interest in monitoring managers to ensure that they allocate resources efficiently. Furthermore, by buying and selling corporate shares on the stock market, public shareholders, it is argued, can directly reallocate resources to uses that are more efficient than investments within the corporation.

As already stated, there are two fundamental flaws in this argument.[59] The first flaw is the contention that, via the stock market, public shareholders allocate resources to more efficient uses. As a general rule, they do not. *Passive* shareholders provide their savings to the stock market to seek yields on their savings. But these funds simply increase the demand for already-outstanding shares of companies that—through the value-creation process, which combines strategic control, organizational integration, and financial commitment—have themselves already determined the most "efficient" uses of productive resources, typically making little if any use of the stock market as a source of financial commitment. In contrast, in the name of MSV, *active* public shareholders seek to extract value from companies that, even without their participation in the value-creation process, have been successful in generating high-quality, low-cost products. Most representative today of active public shareholders are hedge-fund activists, formerly known as corporate raiders and better described as corporate predators, who seek to extract value from companies by pressuring CEOs and their boards to

---

[59]   See Lazonick and O'Sullivan (2000b); Lazonick (2014a, 2015d).

downsize and distribute, and where possible to engage in price gouging. Their business model is to sell their shares at higher prices and thereby build their hedge-fund "war chests," thus increasing their financial power so that, in turn, they will be able to extract even more value from companies as time goes on.[60] MSV is the ideology that legitimizes this looting of the industrial corporation.

The second flaw in MSV lies in the erroneous assumption that shareholders are the only corporate participants who bear risk. Taxpayers, through government agencies, and workers, through the firms that employ them, make risky investments in productive capabilities on a regular basis. From this perspective, households as *taxpayers* and as *workers* may have "residual claimant" status: that is, they may have an economic claim on the distribution of profits.

Through government investments and subsidies, taxpayers regularly provide productive resources to companies without being guaranteed a return. To cite an important example, already encountered in Chapter 2, the 2018 budget of the U.S. National Institutes of Health (NIH) was $34.1 billion, making the NIH's investments in life-sciences research from 1938 through 2018 just over a total of $1 trillion in 2018 dollars.[61] Businesses that make use of life-sciences research benefit from the public knowledge that the NIH generates. As risk bearers, taxpayers who fund such investments in the knowledge base, or in physical infrastructure such as roads, have a claim on corporate profits if and when they are generated. Through the tax system, governments, representing households as taxpayers, seek to extract this return from corporations that reap the rewards of government spending. However, tax revenues from prospective gains from innovation depend on the success of innovative enterprise while at the same time, through the political process, tax rates on those gains are subject to change. Hence, for both economic and political reasons, the returns to taxpayers whose money has been invested for the benefit of business enterprises are by no means guaranteed.

Workers regularly make productive contributions to the companies for which they work through the exercise of skill and effort that goes beyond that level required to lay claim to their current pay but that carries no guaranteed return.[62] Any employer who is seeking to generate a higher-quality, lower-cost product knows the profound productivity difference between employees who just punch the clock to get their daily pay and those who engage in learning to make productive contributions through which they can build their careers and thereby reap future returns in work and in retirement. Yet neither these careers nor the returns that they can generate are guaranteed,

---

[60] As an example, see Lazonick and Mazzucato (2013); Lazonick et al. (2016a); Lazonick et al. (2016b).

[61] National Institutes of Health (2019). See also Lazonick and Tulum (2011).

[62] Lazonick (1990, 2015c).

and, under the downsize-and-distribute resource-allocation regime that MSV ideology has helped put into place, these returns and careers have, in fact, been undermined.

As risk bearers, therefore, taxpayers whose money supports business enterprises and workers whose efforts generate productivity improvements have claims on corporate profits if and when they occur. MSV ignores the risk–reward relation for these two types of economic actors in the operation and performance of business corporations and erroneously assumes that shareholders are the only residual claimants.

The irony of MSV is that the public shareholders whom it holds up as the only risk bearers rarely, if ever, invest in the value-creating capabilities of the company at all. Rather, they purchase outstanding corporate equities with the expectation that while they are holding the shares, dividend income will be forthcoming, and with the hope that when they decide to sell the shares, the stock-market price will have risen to yield a capital gain. Following the directives of MSV, the executives who control corporate resource allocation employ a prime tool for fueling this hope: allocating corporate cash to stock buybacks in order to pump up their company's stock price. Yet those who are best positioned to gain from these manipulative price increases are the senior executives themselves. Senior executives cause the company to "disgorge" cash flow not for the sake of efficient resource allocation, but rather for the sake of increasing their own stock-based pay.[63] Since the early 2000s, the growing power of hedge-fund activists, currently the most conspicuous corporate predators, has supported senior executives and their boards in accelerating this looting of the U.S. business corporation.

In the process, the triumph of MSV has been eroding the social conditions of innovative enterprise: strategic control, organizational integration, and financial commitment. This chapter concludes with brief descriptions of how, legitimized by MSV, the current operation of U.S. stock markets as value-extracting institutions has been undermining innovative enterprise.

3.4.1 Strategic Control

Senior executives who are willing to waste hundreds of millions or billions of dollars annually on buybacks in order to manipulate their companies' stock prices are likely to lose the judgmental capacity to comprehend the types of investments in organization and technology that are required to remain innovative in their industries. Executives' use of financial tools to determine whether the "relevant cost of capital," as Jensen put it in an essay on "agency costs,"[64] justifies investment

---

[63] Hopkins and Lazonick (2014).   [64] Jensen (1986).

in innovation reflects, in our view, this loss of judgmental capacity.[65] Indeed, the current structure of stock-based executive remuneration creates incentives for senior executives to allocate resources in ways that achieve "timely" boosts to stock prices that help to increase their take-home pay.[66] There are other ways in which, depending on the industry in which the company operates, an executive can generate manipulative increases in stock prices; a prominent example is price-gouging in the pharmaceutical industry.[67] More generally, however, the stock buyback is a powerful tool at the disposal of corporate executives for manipulating the stock market for their personal gain. Yet buybacks manifest precisely the "disgorging" (as if it had been ill-gotten by the corporation) of "free cash flow" that agency theory prescribes. So too, agency theory advocates stock-based pay to incentivize senior executives to engage in this financialized behavior.[68]

3.4.2 Organizational Integration

Collective and cumulative, or organizational, learning about the technologies, markets, and competitors relevant to a particular industry is the foundation for generating the higher-quality, lower-cost goods and services that result in pro-ductivity growth.[69] Productivity is collective because one learns through the interaction with others that takes place in a hierarchical and functional division of labor. Productivity is cumulative because what the collectivity learns today provides the foundation for what it is capable of learning tomorrow. What we call "collective and cumulative careers" are essential for organizational learning, especially in industries that are technologically and organizationally complex.[70] It is the higher levels of productivity generated by organizational learning that enable business enterprises to pay their valued employees higher wages on a sustainable basis. Organizational learning in turn depends on a "retain-and-reinvest" corporate resource-allocation regime in which senior executives make corporate resource-allocation decisions that, by retaining people and profits in the company, permit reinvestment in the productive capabilities that can generate competitive products.[71] Our research into the dynamics of innovative enterprise supports the hypothesis that stock buybacks, an element of a corporate resource-allocation regime that downsizes the U.S. labor force and distributes corporate cash to shareholders, are done at the expense of investments in collective and cumulative careers. The disappearance of this career employment in major busi-ness enterprises is central to the erosion of the American middle class over the

---

[65] Baldwin (1991); Christensen et al. (2008).
[66] Hopkins and Lazonick (2014); Lazonick (2014c).   [67] Lazonick et al. (2016b).
[68] See Jensen and Murphy (1990).   [69] Lazonick et al. (2014); Lazonick (2015c).
[70] Lazonick et al. (2014).   [71] Lazonick and O'Sullivan (2000b); Lazonick (2015d).

past three decades.[72] By legitimizing massive distributions of corporate cash to shareholders, MSV directly undermines the building of the organizational capabilities that are the essence of innovative enterprise.

3.4.3 Financial Commitment

The loss of the cash flow that MSV calls "free" can deprive the business enterprise of the foundational finance for investment in innovative enterprise. Stock buybacks represent a withdrawal of internally controlled finance that could be used to support investment in the company's productive capabilities. In the case of many of the largest repurchasers, it is dominant product-market positions based on past investments in innovation that generate the stream of profits that makes it possible to do billions of dollars in buybacks year after year without running low on cash. The ability of some companies to use their cash reserves, often leveraged by borrowed funds, cost-cutting, and tax breaks, to manipulate their stock prices places pressure to do large-scale buybacks on other companies whose success is measured by stock-price performance but whose cash flow is insufficient to support their buyback habits. Every once in a while, as documented in our research, a company that has done massive buybacks over a period of years has hit a financial wall, as the billions of dollars it had wasted on buybacks were not available to support the restructuring of its accumulated capabilities that it would have needed to become innovative once again.[73] The process of predatory value extraction that destroys innovative enterprise is irreversible. It must be stopped before it starts.

---

[72] Lazonick (2015e); Lazonick et al. (2016b).
[73] Lazonick (2008, 2009c, 2013, 2015e).

4

The Value-Extracting Insiders

As we have seen in Chapter 3, the irony of MSV is that the public shareholders whom it posits as the only risk bearers typically never invest in the value-creating capabilities of the company at all. Rather, they purchase outstanding corporate equities, prompted by the expectation that dividend income will be forthcoming while they are holding the shares, and by the hope that by the time they have decided to sell the shares, the stock-market price will have risen so that the sale will yield a capital gain. A prime way in which the executives in control of corporate resource allocation fuel this hope, and one perfectly in line with the precepts of MSV and agency theory, is by pouring corporate cash into stock buybacks in order to pump up their company's stock price. And, indeed, it is the senior executives themselves who are best positioned to gain from these manipulative price increases.

Beginning in the 1980s senior executives of major U.S. corporations, armed with MSV as a legitimizing ideology and incentivized by stock-based pay, transformed themselves from leaders of processes of value creation to perpetrators of processes of value extraction. Rather than engaging in a corporate resource-allocation process of "retain-and-reinvest," they engaged in one of "downsize-and-distribute." Senior executives "disgorged" the corporate cash flow, not for the sake of efficient resource allocation, but rather for the sake of increasing their own stock-based pay.[1]

4.1 Corporate Resource Allocation and Productive Capabilities

A company's senior executives, with the advice and support of the board of directors, are responsible for allocating corporate resources to investments in productive capabilities. Senior executives also advise the board on the extent to which, given the need to invest in productive capabilities, the company can afford to make cash distributions to shareholders. Motivating corporate resource-allocation decisions are the modes of remuneration that incentivize and reward a company's top executives. Although CEOs may also be motivated by non-pecuniary

---

[1] Lazonick (2016a).

Predatory Value Extraction: How the Looting of the Business Corporation Became the U.S. Norm and How Sustainable Prosperity Can Be Restored. William Lazonick and Jang-Sup Shin, Oxford University Press (2020). © William Lazonick and Jang-Sup Shin. DOI: 10.1093/oso/9780198846772.001.0001

objectives in making these decisions, a sound analysis of the operation and performance of the U.S. economy—or any modern economy—requires not merely knowing how much these executives are paid; it additionally requires an understanding of the ways in which the prevailing system of executive pay influences their allocation decisions.

Modes of compensation, characterized by an array of different pay components, ostensibly incentivize senior executives to behave in ways that improve corporate performance and reward them for achieving performance goals. But what is the performance measure upon which their rewards are based? As we saw in Chapter 3, since the last half of the 1980s the overriding goal of U.S. corporations has been to "maximize shareholder value" (MSV), with corporate performance measured by a company's "total shareholder return": percentage stock-price appreciation plus dividend yield. Also since the 1980s, the most important components of senior executives' total compensation have been modes of *stock-based pay* in the form of stock options and stock awards. This stock-based pay is structured to incentivize executives to make corporate-allocation decisions that will boost the stock prices of the companies that employ them and reward them for achieving this objective.[2]

Whether one admires or abhors the current system of executive compensation in the United States, one can scarcely deny the breadth of the consensus that the achievement of a high and rising company stock price is the paramount corporate-performance objective.[3] But does a rising stock price truly reflect superior corporate performance? Possibly, but by no means necessarily. As we discuss in Section 4.2, there are three drivers of stock prices: *innovation, speculation,* and *manipulation.* Only a stock-price rise rooted in "innovation" reflects superior economic performance, and the stock-market registers the impact of innovation *only after it has occurred.* In any given instance, the first critical question to address is: *Which of these drivers, individually or in combination, has contributed to a company's stock-price performance?*

Then we can ask the second critical question: *Does executive compensation reflect the success of the company in value creation, or the power of senior executives to engage in value extraction?* Based on intensive research into these questions for the U.S. case, our short answers are that (a) the stock-price performance of major U.S. companies increasingly reflects manipulation, and (b) given the preponderance of stock-based pay in the total compensation of the senior executives of major U.S. business corporations, what their remuneration reflects is their power to extract value far in excess of the value they help to create in the companies that they control.

---

[2] Lazonick (2014a); Hopkins and Lazonick (2016).   [3] Biden (2016).

As outlined in Chapter 2, *innovation* is the process by which a company, embedded in a particular economic and political context, generates a product that is of higher quality and lower cost than those products previously available. When a company invests in productive capabilities, it creates the possibility, although by no means the certainty, that, through the development and utilization of its productive capabilities, it will be able to generate an innovative (higher-quality, lower-cost) product. As the innovative enterprise expands its market and becomes more profitable, stock-market traders will tend to bid up its stock price to a level justified by *the gains from innovation that the company has already achieved.*

At that point, stock-market *speculation that future gains from innovation will occur* can drive the company's price still higher. Under certain conditions, this speculation may continue at a rapid pace for an extended period of time, with the stock price propelled to new heights by speculative traders' adherence to the "greater fool theory": traders buy a company's shares at prices that they think are unduly high on the assumption that there remain greater fools in the market who will be willing to buy the shares at even higher prices. At some point, however, as increasing numbers of traders lose their speculative optimism, the greatest fools are left holding the overvalued shares, and the stock price declines, often precipitously, as they seek to cut their losses.

Hence, as we observe in practice, stock prices can go through highly volatile booms and busts. Meanwhile, however, certain actors in the stock market may have *the power to manipulate stock prices*, both to foment speculation that generates further price boosts on the upswing and to limit or offset stock-price declines in the downturn. Alternatively, short-sellers who have sufficient financial power to manipulate the market may deliberately exacerbate stock-price declines. A major reason for the passage of the U.S. Securities Exchange Act of 1934, which established the Securities and Exchange Commission (SEC) as the federal government's regulator of the stock market, was to prevent manipulation of stock prices. Senior corporate executives are often in a position to engage in stock-price manipulation by disseminating false or misleading financial information and by engaging in monopolistic product-pricing behavior. Since the early 1980s, however, the most widespread, systemic, and direct way in which senior executives have been able, legally, to manipulate their companies' stock prices has been through stock repurchases, also known as stock buybacks. As we have seen in Chapter 1, large U.S. companies often spend billions of dollars per year on buybacks.

The stock-based compensation of senior corporate executives incentivizes these massive buybacks. We rely on senior corporate executives to make, in the face of uncertainty, the value-creating resource-allocation decisions that can result in innovation. But, in the financialized business enterprise, these corporate executives may be incentivized to make value-extracting resource-allocation decisions that encourage stock-price speculation and implement stock-price manipulation, both of which inflate their stock-based pay. The "value-extracting CEO" hypothesis posits that, in the United States, a significant portion of senior executives' compensation is rewarding them for making decisions that foment speculation and manipulate stock prices, thereby enabling them to extract value for their own personal gain. In support of this hypothesis, we present data on the total compensation of the 500 highest-paid corporate executives in the United States, which show the magnitude of their total pay and the proportions of their average annual pay that have been in the form of realized gains from stock options and stock awards. In 2017, the annual total compensation of the 500 highest-paid executives averaged $32.1 million, with gains realized from the exercise of stock options accounting for 46 percent and gains from the vesting of stock awards accounting for another 35 percent.

4.2 The Changing Drivers of the Stock Market: Innovation, Speculation, and Manipulation

Underpinning the "value-extracting CEO" hypothesis is our analysis of the evolution of the drivers of the U.S. stock market from innovation to speculation to manipulation. Stock-based executive compensation encourages senior corporate executives to participate in the transformation from innovation to manipulation, manifested at the company level by a change from "retain-and-reinvest" to "downsize-and-distribute." There is always speculation at play on the stock market, and the potential for speculation was greatly increased from 1971 with the creation of NASDAQ as a highly liquid electronic "Over-the-Counter" market, with its lax listing requirements. In the 1980s the growth of New Economy companies engaged in the microelectronics revolution enhanced the importance of innovation as a driver of the stock market. Meanwhile, however, from the mid-1980s, with the SEC having given corporations license to do large-scale open-market repurchases with the adoption of Rule 10b-18 at the end of 1982 and with MSV ideology becoming prominent in business schools and boardrooms, buy-backs brought a new form of manipulation into the stock market, with stock buybacks becoming more systemic and large scale over time.

During the 1980s and into the 1990s, all three drivers of the stock market were at work, but speculation would become much more pronounced in the dot.com boom of the late 1990s. After the Internet bubble burst in 2000 and the stock market declined in 2001 and 2002, the widespread use of stock buybacks to manipulate the market accelerated. Of course, these drivers are not mutually exclusive. Innovation can be combined with speculative bubbles and speculation can be combined with manipulation. But since the early 2000s manipulation has tended to trump innovation. The speculation phase of the late 1990s was important because it created the expectation of extraordinary gains from stock-price increases that since the early 2000s has encouraged manipulation at established companies, as top executives, in collaboration with shareholder activists, have sought to recreate the stock-market gains of the Internet boom.

Consider Cisco Systems, which made its initial public offering (IPO) on the NASDAQ stock exchange on February 16, 1990. A holding in Cisco bought for $1,000 at the IPO had a market value of $389,000 at the end of 2015. Meanwhile, however, as can be seen in Figure 4.1, during that quarter-century Cisco's stock price underwent dramatic fluctuations, driven in different periods by a combination of innovation, speculation, or manipulation.

One can posit that during the first seven to eight years of Cisco's existence as a public company *innovation* was the primary driver of the increase in its stock price, as stock-market traders observed, after the fact, that the company was generating high levels of profit by becoming the dominant competitor in the new and booming Internet-equipment market. In October 1998, at the end of this innovation phase, Charles O'Reilly, a professor at Stanford Business School, published a case that began with the statement, "Cisco is a $6 billion high

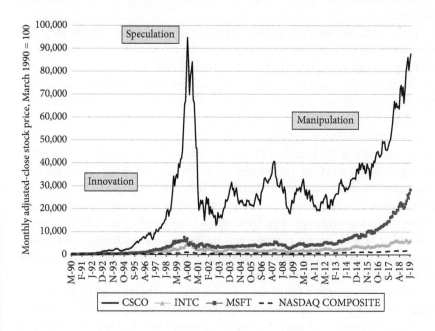

Fig. 4.1. Prime drivers of stock prices: Cisco, Intel, Microsoft, and NASDAQ Composite Index (March 26, 1990 = 100)

Note: CSCO (Cisco), INTC (Intel), and MSFT (Microsoft).

Source: Yahoo! Finance, daily data, adjusted close. (March 26, 1990–November 12, 2018)

technology stealth company, largely unknown to the general public."[4] Yet at that point Cisco was already the fastest-growing company in history, with a share bought for $1,000 at the company's IPO worth $185,000 at the beginning of October 1998.

From November 1998 to March 2000, however, this "largely unknown" company was the focus of intense stock-market *speculation*, with its stock price rising almost sevenfold, giving Cisco the highest market capitalization in the world in March 2000. At its all-time stock-price peak, reached on March 21, 2000, those $1,000 shares bought at the IPO were worth over $1 million. This speculation had a profound impact on stock-based pay. Cisco CEO John Chambers received total compensation of $121.7 million in 1999 and $156.3 million in 2000, with over 99 percent in each year consisting of gains realized from exercising stock options. Cisco's other four highest-paid executives averaged $25.9 million in 1999 (96 percent from options) and $38.0 million in 2000 (97 percent from options). Indeed, with its broad-based stock-option plan, the average realized gains from exercising stock options at Cisco (not including those of the five highest-paid executives, whose incomes we know) were an estimated $193,500 across an average of 18,000 employees in 1999, and $290,900 across an average of 27,500 employees in 2000.[5]

Then, with the bursting of the Internet bubble, between March 2000 and September 2001 Cisco's stock price plunged by 85 percent, at which point the company began doing stock buybacks, therewith entering into the *manipulation* phase of stock-price determination. Cisco repurchased $1.9 billion worth of shares in fiscal year 2002 (ending July 27, 2002), $6.0 billion in 2003, $9.1 billion in 2004, and $10.2 billion in 2005. From then through 2016, Cisco's buybacks ranged from a high of $10.4 billion in 2008 to a low of $3.1 billion in 2013. From 2002 through the first quarter of 2019 (ending October 27, 2018), Cisco expended $123.8 billion on repurchases, equal to 107 percent of its net income, while since 2011 the company has also paid shareholders $31.0 billion in dividends. The purpose of these massive buybacks was mainly to manipulate the company's share price. Those executives who have been able to take advantage of the price boosts through the timing of their option exercises and stock sales, and by hitting stock-related performance targets that trigger vesting of stock awards, have enhanced their realized gains from stock-based pay.

The dramatic rise and fall of Cisco's stock price in the Internet boom and bust make the stock-price movements of Intel, Microsoft, and the NASDAQ Composite Index, as shown in Figure 4.1, appear as mere blips. In Figure 4.2, however, if we apply a more limited stock-price scale, the price movements of Intel and Microsoft, and the NASDAQ Index (in which Cisco, Intel, and Microsoft are

---

[4] O'Reilly (2002).   [5] Lazonick (2009a).

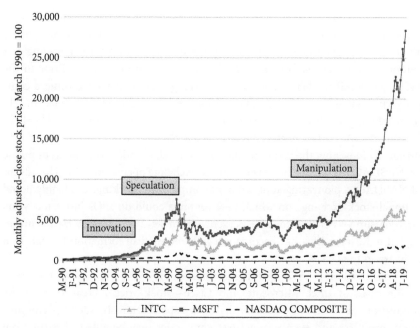

Fig. 4.2. Prime drivers of stock prices: Intel, Microsoft, and NASDAQ Composite Index (March 26, 1990 = 100)

Note: INTC (Intel), and MSFT (Microsoft).

Source: Yahoo! Finance, daily data, adjusted close. (March 26, 1990–November 12, 2018)

included), look similar, in terms of boom and bust, to that of Cisco. We posit that over the past quarter-century the stock prices of Intel and Microsoft have also followed a sequence of innovation, speculation, and manipulation phases. One difference is that, with speculation in its stock rampant, Cisco executed no buybacks in 1998–2000, whereas Intel spent $15.4 billion and Microsoft $10.3 billion in those years. Like Cisco, however, both Intel and Microsoft have undertaken massive buybacks to manipulate their stock prices since the Internet boom turned to bust: $98.6 billion (65 percent of net income) by Intel from 2001 through the third quarter of its fiscal year 2018 (ending September 29, 2018), and $195.9 billion (69 percent of net income) by Microsoft from 2001 through the first quarter of its fiscal year 2019 (ending September 30, 2018).

More generally, the transformation of the stock market enabled by NASDAQ's allowing the listing of "unproven" companies has strengthened the role of speculation and manipulation as price drivers. The stock market traditionally rewarded innovative enterprise only *after the fact*, once the innovations proved successful. However, it has now become possible for the stock market to reward executives and shareholders *before the fact*, even though the success of a business's innovative investment strategy is still uncertain. In the case of startups, venture capitalists can use the stock market to do an IPO and thereby, with the company listed on the stock market, "exit" their investments by selling on the market part or all of their shareholdings. The brevity of the time period from the founding of a company to its IPO is of prime importance to venture capitalists. Prior to the 1970s the dominant NYSE had stringent listing requirements regarding a company's profitability record and capitalization level that generally precluded an IPO from taking place just a few years after the founding of a company. The 1971 launch of NASDAQ dramatically truncated the lag from startup to IPO by drastically loosening the listing requirements. Intel, founded in 1968, went public on NASDAQ as soon as the new electronic exchange opened in 1971. The advent of NASDAQ, a pioneering application of computer networking, as a highly liquid national stock exchange on which new ventures could do IPOs just a few years after startup was critical to the emergence from 1972 of the organized venture-capital industry, which has become integral to new-firm formation in high-tech industry in the U.S. economy.[6]

As occurred on NASDAQ in the last half of the 1990s—and as we have seen in the cases of Intel, Microsoft, and Cisco—stock-price increases driven by innovation can turn into bubbles driven by speculation. In such an environment, profitless and even product-less companies may be able to benefit from speculation to raise substantial amounts of cash on the stock market, making their shareholders super-rich. In some cases, such as that of Amazon, which was unprofitable at the time of its IPO in 1997, successful companies may eventually emerge from these speculative IPOs. But considering that there have been numerous failures, some of them spectacular, speculative funding of the young companies that NASDAQ permits to list may represent a major misallocation of resources.[7]

A case in point was Sycamore Networks, an optical-networking company founded in February 1998 and located in Boston's Route 128 high-tech district.[8] With a single customer (whose executives were given Sycamore shares), in its first year Sycamore had revenues of $11 million and losses of $19 million, and only 155 employees. Yet Sycamore was able to do its IPO in October 1999 and translate the "New Economy" hype of the time into a $284-million infusion of cash for less than 10 percent of its shares. In December 1999 Sycamore ranked 117th in market capitalization in the United States, just behind Emerson Electric, a company founded in 1890 that had revenues of $14.3 billion and 117,000 employees![9] Sycamore then made a secondary offering in March 2000, at the

---

[6] Lazonick (2009a).   [7] Cassidy (2002); Gimein (2002).   [8] Lazonick (2007a).

[9] In 2015, with 110,800 employees, Emerson was in the identical 118th place in market capitalization, while Sycamore had been liquidated three years earlier. Online Investor (2015). See also Fortune (2016).

very apex of the boom, with its stock price at $150, and netted another $1.2 billion for its corporate treasury.

At the same time, top executives and board members of Sycamore sold a portion of their own stockholdings for $726 million.[10] By September 2001 the company's stock price had plunged to as low as $3.80, and it never recovered to any significant extent. In that year Sycamore achieved what turned out to be peaks of $375 million in revenues and 944 employees, but it never became profitable. After distributing $470 million in dividends in 2010 and 2011—money still remaining as the result of its March 2000 secondary issue—Sycamore went out of business in 2012, having racked up losses of $875 million over its 14-year history as a public company.[11] Taken in by the Internet boom, the stock-market speculators who endowed the company with $1.5 billion in 1999 and 2000 were in effect "accidental" venture capitalists who lost their money betting on a company that proclaimed an innovative future but never generated the innovative products to deliver on its promise.

Besides allocating inordinate amounts of resources to unproductive New Economy startups, the speculative boom of the late 1990s helped to inflict even greater damage on the innovative capabilities of some established Old Economy companies whose top executives also got caught up in the New Economy hype.[12] In 2000 Lucent Technologies—formerly Western Electric and then AT&T Technologies, with a history dating back to 1869—was the largest communication-technology company in the world. In 1998 through 2000, its top executives made resource-allocation decisions that contributed to the dramatic post-2000 decline of the company. In particular, they lavished massive amounts of the company's stock on "New Economy" acquisitions that Lucent then failed to integrate into its organization. The most expensive acquisitions, such as Ascend Communications, Chromatis Networks, and International Network Services, were made to convince the stock market that Lucent was an agile New Economy company. It was not. Enriched by their equity stakes in the acquired company, key personnel of the acquisitions exhibited their individual agility by leaving Lucent to launch new companies, become angel investors, take jobs at other hyped startups, or just retire. In the Internet crash of 2001–02, to stave off bankruptcy, Lucent had to sell stock at 1 or 2 percent of the price its shares had commanded during the boom, and by 2006, the vastly weakened company was taken over by its French rival, Alcatel.[13]

While an Old Economy company such as Lucent was destroying itself by using its stock to acquire New Economy startups that lacked proven products at highly

[10] Gimein (2002).   [11] Syre (2012).

[12] Carpenter et al. (2003); Lazonick and March (2011). Also see Lazonick (2009a) that focuses on the information-and-communication-technology industries. For the problem of product-less IPOs in biotechnology, see Lazonick and Tulum (2011).

[13] Lazonick and March (2011).

Table 4.1. Cash distributions to shareholders at HP, IBM, Merck, and Pfizer, 1978–2017

	NI, $m	DV, $m	BB, $m	DV/NI, %	BB/NI, %	(DV+BB)/ NI, %
HP						
1978–1987	4,066	377	889	9.3	21.9	31.1
1988–1997	14,934	2,407	5,456	16.1	36.5	52.7
1988–2007	31,730	7,950	38,788	25.1	122.2	147.3
2008–2017	38,876	9,483	47,254	24.4	121.6	145.9
IBM						
1978–1987	46,070	22,166	4,664	48.1	10.1	58.2
1988–1997	18,574	17,415	21,237	93.8	114.3	208.1
1998–2007	77,328	11,952	76,498	15.5	98.9	114.4
2008–2017	132,371	39,850	100,727	30.1	76.1	106.2
Merck						
1978–1987	3,879	1,718	2,001	44.3	51.6	95.9
1988–1997	26,046	12,157	9,713	46.7	37.3	84.0
1998–2007	57,377	30,518	23,191	53.2	40.4	93.6
2008–2017	61,091	46,770	34,683	76.6	56.8	133.3
Pfizer						
1978–1987	4,138	1,745	253	42.2	6.1	48.3
1988–1997	11,760	5,456	3,675	46.4	31.3	77.6
1998–2007	78,472	40,088	54,544	51.1	69.5	120.6
2008–2017	94,988	68,050	56,178	71.6	59.1	130.8

Notes: NI (net income), DV (dividends), BB (stock buybacks).

Source: Standard and Poor's Compustat database.

speculative prices, other Old Economy companies were making a transition to the "New Economy business model" by deliberately ending the norm of a career with one company, outsourcing manufacturing, and doing large-scale stock buybacks to give manipulative boosts to their stock prices. What occurred were, in fact, transitions from innovation to financialization. In the information-technology industry, the leading Old Economy companies were International Business Machines (IBM) and Hewlett-Packard (HP). In pharmaceuticals, the leading companies were Pfizer and Merck. Table 4.1 shows the distributions these four companies made to their shareholders—in the form of both dividends and buybacks—by decade from 1976 to 2015, in absolute terms and as percentages of net income. Buybacks are by no means new at these companies, but they have become massive over the decades, even as dividends have increased. All four of these companies have made a transition from innovation to financialization— that is, from an orientation toward value creation to an orientation toward value extraction.[14]

---

[14] Lazonick (2009a); Lazonick et al. (2016b).

Companies began to do large-scale buybacks on a persistent basis in the mid-1980s, after the SEC adopted Rule 10b-18 in November 1982.[15] Rule 10b-18 gives a company "safe harbor" immunity to manipulation charges when doing open-market repurchases. Under the rule's safe-harbor provision, a company will not be charged with manipulation if, among other things, the volume of its buybacks on any single day does not exceed 25 percent of the previous four weeks' average daily trading volume (ADTV). Even while remaining within the safe harbor, a large company can often do hundreds of millions of dollars in buybacks per day, and, if its top executives so choose, it can do so repeatedly, trading day after trading day. On December 2, 2016, for example, the safe-harbor daily limits were $142 million for IBM, $54 million for HP, $171 million for Merck, and $290 million for Pfizer. For Cisco, Intel, and Microsoft, discussed previously, these ADTV numbers were $200 million, $167 million, and $435 million, respectively. Moreover, there is no presumption of manipulation under Rule 10b-18 even if a corporation's repurchases do exceed the 25 percent ADTV limit.

From the 2000s, stock buybacks have come to define the "investment" strategies of many of America's biggest businesses. Over the past three decades, in aggregate, dividends have tended to increase as a proportion of corporate profits. Yet in 1997, for the first time, buybacks surpassed dividends in the U.S. corporate economy and, even with dividends continuing to increase, have far exceeded them in recent stock-market booms.

Retained earnings have always been the financial foundation for business investment in innovation and sustained employment in advanced countries. These retentions can fund investment in plant and equipment, research and development, and, of critical importance, training and retaining employees. If dividends alone are too high, investments in the company's productive capabilities will suffer. The addition of buybacks to dividends over the past three decades reflects a failure of corporate executives to develop strategies for investing in the productive capabilities of the companies over which they exercise strategic control.

Dividends are the traditional and legitimate way for a publicly listed corporation to provide income to shareholders. Dividends provide shareholders with an income for, as the name says, *holding* shares. Moreover, if the firm retains enough of its profits to finance further investment in its productive capabilities, there is the possibility, although by no means the certainty, that it will generate competitive products that will help lift its future stock price and the value of the shares held. When, for whatever reason, shareholders who have benefited from a stream of income on their holdings decide to sell some or all of their shares, they stand to benefit from the innovation behind the rise in the stock price by registering a capital gain.

---

[15] Jacobson and Lazonick (2015); Lazonick (2015a).

In contrast, by creating demand for the company's stock that provides an immediate and manipulative boost to its price, buybacks reward those shareholders who *sell* their shares. The most prominent sharesellers are those stock-market traders, including corporate executives, investment bankers, and hedge-fund managers, who are able to time their stock sales to take advantage of buyback activity conducted on the open market. Buybacks also automatically increase earnings per share (EPS) by decreasing the number of shares outstanding. Since EPS has become a major metric by which financial interests evaluate the performance of a company, buybacks tend to increase demand for a company's stock, thus creating opportunities for stock-market traders to sell their shares at a gain even in the absence of increased corporate revenues or profits.

Since the early 1980s major U.S. business corporations have been doing stock buybacks on top of, not instead of, making dividend payments to shareholders. Indeed, many of America's largest corporations routinely distribute more than 100 percent of net income to shareholders, generating the extra cash by reducing cash reserves, selling off assets, taking on debt, or laying off employees.[16] Table 4.2 shows the payout ratios of buybacks and dividends to net income for the twenty-five largest repurchasers for the decade 2008–17.

Figure 4.3 shows data for 1981 through 2017 on 226 companies in the S&P 500 Index in January 2018 that were publicly listed over these 37 years. In 1981–83, buybacks averaged 4.4 percent of their net income and dividends 50.3 percent— and the debate at that time was whether excessive dividend payments were depriving companies of the retained earnings needed for reinvestment in productive capabilities. That discussion has now gone by the board. In 2015–17, buybacks for the same 226 companies averaged 62.3 percent of net income and dividends an additional 54.6 percent!

The buyback portion of net income increased to 17.6 percent in 1984. Then it increased to 25.2 percent in 1986–95, 42.2 percent in 1996–2005 and 50.4 percent in 2006–15. More recently, the buyback ratio rose to 58.8 percent in 2016 and 66.7 percent in 2017. Over the past three decades, in aggregate, dividends have tended to increase as a proportion of corporate profits. Yet in 1997, for the first time, buybacks surpassed dividends in the U.S. corporate economy and, even with dividends continuing to increase, have far exceeded them. The increase in the total payout ratio from the early 1980s to date is almost entirely explained by the increase in the ratio of stock buybacks to net income.

The 466 companies in the S&P 500 Index in January 2018 that were publicly listed over the ten-year period 2008–17 expended $4.0 trillion on stock buybacks,

---

[16] Lazonick (2015b, 2016b).

Table 4.2. Payout ratios of buybacks and dividends for the twenty-five largest stock repurchasers, 2008–2017

Rank	Company Name	BB, $billions	BB/NI%	DV/NI%	(BB+DV)/NI%
1	APPLE	165.7	52	19	71
2	EXXON MOBIL	146.6	51	36	86
3	MICROSOFT	104.6	56	40	96
4	IBM	100.7	76	30	106
5	WAL-MART STORES	67.9	46	36	83
6	ORACLE	67.0	80	21	101
7	CISCO SYSTEMS	60.1	72	28	100
8	PROCTER & GAMBLE	59.3	51	54	104
9	PFIZER	56.2	48	59	107
10	GOLDMAN SACHS	55.1	78	23	102
11	JPMORGAN CHASE	53.2	29	31	60
12	INTEL	52.6	54	43	96
13	WELLS FARGO	50.2	29	34	62
14	GENERAL ELECTRIC	49.4	53	89	143
15	DISNEY (WALT)	48.8	78	23	101
16	AIG	48.0	−69	−9	−78
17	HOME DEPOT	47.8	92	45	137
18	HP	47.3	122	24	146
19	VISA	46.3	112	19	131
20	JOHNSON & JOHNSON	45.4	37	57	94
21	MCDONALD'S	42.3	85	56	141
22	GILEAD SCIENCES	37.9	59	11	70
23	PHILIP MORRIS	37.7	51	75	126
24	BOEING	34.8	80	42	122
25	AT&T	34.7	25	75	101

Notes: NI (net income), DV (dividends), BB (stock buybacks).

Source: Standard and Poor's Compustat database; calculations by Mustafa Erdem Sakınç and Emre Gömeç of the Academic-Industry Research Network.

representing 52.6 percent of net income, plus another 40.6 percent of net income on dividends. Much of the remaining 6.8 percent of profits was held abroad, sheltered from U.S. taxes. Mean buybacks for these 466 companies ranged from $325 million in 2009, when the stock markets had collapsed, to $1,115 million in 2015. Meanwhile, mean dividends declined by 11.3 percent from 2008 to 2009, but then rose from $461 million per company in 2009 to $934 per company in 2017. Buoyed by the Republican tax cuts, dividends of companies in the S&P 500 Index set records in each of the last three quarters of 2018, totaling $454.2 billion for the year, while buybacks set records in each of the four quarters of 2018, for an annual total of $806.4 billion.[17]

---

[17] Yardeni et al. (2019).

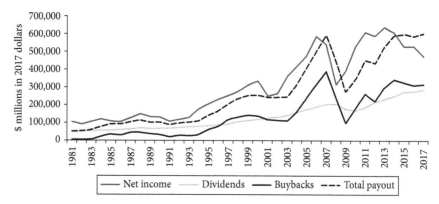

Fig. 4.3. Net income, buybacks, dividends, and total payouts of 226 companies in the S&P 500 Index in January 2018 ($millions in 2017 dollars, 1981–2017)

Note: Data are for 226 companies in the S&P 500 Index in January 2018 that were publicly listed from 1981 through 2017.

Source: Standard and Poor's Compustat database; calculations by Mustafa Erdem Sakinç and Emre Gömeç of the Academic-Industry Research Network.

4.3 The Anatomy of Stock-Based Compensation

In the United States, a company's board of directors can authorize a stock buyback program of a specified value (say, $10 billion) over a specified period of time (say, three years). It is then at the discretion of the CEO, presumably in agreement with the company's chief financial officer (CFO), to do a chosen amount of buybacks on the open market on any given day. Within the scope of the buyback program and subject to the restrictions contained in Rule 10b-18, the CEO and CFO can then implement buybacks either sporadically or for a number of days in sequence as they see fit. Little is known about this decision-making process. Indeed, under Rule 10b-18 a company does not need to disclose, even after the fact, the particular days on which it does stock buybacks as open-market repurchases.

Since 2004, the SEC has required companies to report quarterly on buyback activity in their 10-Q filings, stating the monthly volume and value of buybacks and the weighted average repurchase price. But, even with the advent of SEC Rule 10b5-1,[18] adopted in 2000 to increase disclosure of material information that could be used in insider trading, the failure of the SEC to require reporting of the precise days on which buybacks are done creates opportunities for senior executives who are in the know to trade on this insider information without being detected, unless the SEC chooses to launch a special investigation.[19] And in the almost four decades that Rule 10b-18 has been in force, the SEC has never charged

---

[18] SEC (2000).   [19] Eisinger (2014b).

a company or its senior executives for the use of insider information on the timing of open-market repurchases for personal gain.[20]

Corporate executives and the academics who provide apologetics for them have given two main reasons for doing buybacks, each of which portrays this mode of resource allocation as being in the best interest of the company. These two reasons are, however, deeply flawed:[21]

- Executives often claim that, in repurchasing stock, they are making an investment in the company because the market undervalues its shares. According to this argument, shareholders who are wise enough to hold onto their shares will benefit from higher earnings per share. But even if done when shares are agreed to be undervalued, buybacks are not investments in productive capabilities. Rather, they merely change which shareholders are able *to lay claim to the earnings of existing productive capabilities.* Whether this change in the structure of share ownership will promote or undermine investments in productive capabilities is quite another question. Indeed, buybacks may come at the expense of investments in productive capabilities, thereby causing future earnings to decline. Our company-level research identifies the ways in which buybacks undermine investments in innovative products. We show how buybacks enable top executives and other powerful financial interests to extract from the company value that workers and taxpayers helped to create. Moreover, the justification that the company is getting a bargain by repurchasing shares that are purportedly undervalued is contradicted by overwhelming evidence showing that most buybacks occur when stock prices are high, not when they are low.[22] That is because most buybacks are done in the periods in the stock-price cycle that are most propitious for top executives to reap gains from exercising stock options and the vesting of stock awards.
- Executives sometimes claim that their companies do buybacks to offset dilution of EPS that results when employees exercise stock options that they have received as part of their compensation. But if stock-based pay is supposed to induce employees to work harder and smarter, then those who receive it should be made to wait until their efforts have paid off in higher corporate earnings and stock prices rather than being permitted to gain right away from buybacks that increase EPS by simply reducing the number of shares outstanding. Moreover, research has shown that even at high-tech companies with stock-based compensation programs that extend to a broad base of employees and that, hence, have high levels of dilution, the volume of

---

[20] Baldwin (2015); Dayen (2015).   [21] Lazonick (2014b).
[22] See, for example, Birstingl (2016).

shares repurchased tends to be a multiple of the volume of shares that employees receive from options and awards.[23]

The only logical explanation for the prevalence of buybacks is that stock-based pay gives executives ample incentive to do them.[24] How bounteous the gains from stock-based pay are depends in large part on a process of CEO-pay determination that produces a "ratchet effect" that, across booms and busts in the stock market, inflates the general level of CEO pay over time. Here is a five-step guide to how U.S. CEOs manage their way to higher executive pay:

1. The CEO appoints a *compliant board of directors*, with the most prominent and influential members being other CEOs, all of whom have an interest in increasing the "benchmark" level of executive compensation. It has long been known that, whatever the formalities of the election of the directors of a U.S. corporation, it is really the CEO who chooses the board members.[25] A CEO does not want to be evaluated by directors who fail to appreciate his or her talent to run the company. Occasionally, the disastrous performance of a company or a scandal might result in a previously compliant board ousting a CEO. Hedge-fund activists, eager to loot an established company, sometimes see fit, and garner the proxy votes, to oust the CEO.[26] In general, however, when a board keeps a CEO and his or her top people in place, it confers generous compensation packages as a stamp of approval.

2. The CEO *hires compensation consultants* at company expense to benchmark his or her pay to the pay of comparable firms' CEOs—who, as if by coincidence, hire the same group of consultants to benchmark their pay by the same method. In recommending pay packages for the CEOs who hired them, as well as for the members of the CEOs' teams of senior executives, consultants will almost invariably recommend that a CEO be paid well above the median of the other CEOs surveyed—the 75th percentile is a common rating. This is meant as a sign that their client is no ordinary executive and, in fact, it is the role of compensation consultants to justify the remuneration that the board bestows on its CEO and his or her senior executive team. Over time, this benchmarking exercise inevitably ratchets

---

[23] Lazonick (2009a).   [24] Lazonick (2014a).

[25] Lorsch and MacIver (1989). For a recent discussion of CEO power vis-à-vis the board, and its decline in the face of hedge-fund activism and certain regulatory changes, see Kahan and Rock (2010). This alleged decline in CEO power manifests itself in top executives becoming ever more committed to "maximizing shareholder value," which in turn gets translated into increases in their stock-based pay. The reason why the "hostile" takeovers that marked the late 1980s have largely disappeared is because there is no longer any hostility between what used to be called corporate raiders and top corporate executives; both parties stand ready to disgorge cash to shareholders through stock buybacks and dividends. On the rise and dominance of shareholder value ideology and its implications for corporate resource allocation and executive pay, see Lazonick (2014c).

[26] See discussions in Chapter 6.

up the pay of all CEOs. Given that CEOs are key members of each other's boards, they rarely complain that a fellow CEO is being overpaid.[27]

3. The CEO and his or her senior executive team get paid in a currency—the company's shares—that the board can dole out abundantly in *stock options and stock awards*. Boards have shown a tendency to sweeten the pot whether the share price rises or falls. In the latter case, an increased number of shares may be stuffed into new options and awards to offset a drop in the price; in the former case, additional shares are often granted as a reward for hitting financial targets when existing stock awards vest. Although some of these devices may be illegal, executives and their boards can further influence potential gains from stock options by securing more favorable exercise prices through "repricing" or "backdating" options and through timing options issues ahead of favorable corporate news ("spring-loading") or following unfavorable corporate news ("bullet-dodging").[28] Unlike stock options, which have no value if the market price of the stock remains below where it was when the option was granted (the exercise price), stock awards always have some value because they are bestowed on the executive at no cost. It is often the case, however, that stock awards vest only if the company's stock price or earnings per share reaches a stipulated level. As a rule, the higher the price of a company's stock—even if the price turns out to have been driven up by a temporary spike—the more both options and awards can contribute to raising executive pay.

4. The CEO and other high-level executives can benefit from SEC Rule 10b-18, which, as we have seen, permits a corporation to give manipulative boosts to its stock price through large-scale open-market stock repurchases. In the early 1980s, the corporate-finance debate among academics, regulators, and executives centered on the amount of dividends a company could distribute to shareholders while still retaining sufficient earnings to invest in its productive capabilities.[29] Since then, however, encouraged by the regulatory authority itself, buybacks have become not only enormous in volume but also pervasive among companies. According to the consulting company FactSet, from the second half of 2011 through the first half of 2016, with the stock market booming, between 360 and 390 of the companies in the S&P 500 Index executed stock buybacks in any particular quarter.[30] Companies

---

[27] Crystal (1991); Bebchuk and Fried (2004); Martin (2011); Desai (2012); Foroohar (2014); Nocera (2014).

[28] Hopkins and Lazonick (2016).

[29] Williams (1981). Harold Williams stressed the problem of excessive dividends in "The Corporation as a Continuing Enterprise," his final speech as chairman of the SEC before resigning his position in view of the election of Ronald Reagan to the U.S. Presidency. Williams had previously been a corporate lawyer, business executive, and dean of the UCLA business school.

[30] Birstingl (2016).

deploy buybacks in a competition to boost their stock prices, with corporate executives realizing the gains from their stock-based pay.

5. The CEO and his or her senior executive team can benefit from a 1991 reinterpretation of Section 16(b) of the 1934 Securities Exchange Act that enables top executives to profit from the immediate sale of stock acquired through exercising stock options, erasing the six-month waiting period that had been in force since 1934. Reflecting the permissive attitude toward stock buybacks it had adopted in 1982, the SEC smoothed the way through this reinterpretation for top executives who are privy to a company's repurchasing activity to boost their pay by using this insider information to time their option exercises and stock sales. Prior to the 1991 change, if an insider sold shares acquired by exercising stock options within six months of the exercise date, the gains, considered "short-swing profits," had to be forfeited to the corporation. Arguing in 1991 that a stock option is a derivative, the SEC ruled that, henceforth, the six-month waiting period would no longer begin at the option's exercise date, but at its grant date. Since the option grant date is always at least one year before the option vesting date, top executives, as company insiders, could now sell the shares acquired from stock options immediately upon exercise.[31]

The result has been an ongoing explosion of executive pay since the 1980s that has vastly increased the representation of senior executives among the top one-tenth of 1 percent of households in the U.S. income distribution. In Figure 1.2 we showed the data on the income shares of the top 0.1 percent of U.S. households for 1916 to 2011, collected from tax returns by Thomas Piketty, Emmanuel Saez, and their colleagues.[32] The largest component of the pay of the top 0.1 percent over the past quarter-century has been "salaries," supplemented by spikes in capital gains at the peaks of the stock-market booms in 2000 and 2007. It is in part because these "salaries" include substantial components of stock-based pay, which is taxed at ordinary rates, that the spikes are so pronounced.

The Piketty–Saez data, collected from personal income-tax returns filed with the Internal Revenue Service, do not separate out the stock-based components of executive pay.[33] But knowledge of the extent to which executives gain from stock-based pay is critical if the question of why companies do buybacks is to be answered. It is the stock-based components of executive pay—gains from the

---

[31] Gould (1989); Rosen (1991).   [32] World Wealth and Income Database (2017a).

[33] Almost all gains from exercising employee stock options and the vesting of employee stock awards are taxed at the ordinary income-tax rate, not at the capital-gains tax rate, with taxes withheld by the employer at the time that options are exercised or awards vest. Hence these stock-based gains are reported as part of "wages, tips, other compensation." IRS Form 1040 for individual income-tax returns has the line item (no. 7): "Wages, salaries, tips, etc. Attach Form(s) W-2," in which realized gains from stock-based pay are included but not shown separately from other forms of compensation. On Form W-2, the corresponding item is (no. 1) "Wages, tips, other compensation."

exercise of stock options and the vesting of stock awards—that incentivize and reward the value-extracting behavior of senior executives. And as we shall see, these stock-based components are far and away the largest components of executive pay.

Federal tax returns include information on a filer's occupation and, through an employer identification number (EIN) on Form W-2, the business sector of the entity that provides the taxpayer with his or her primary employment income. Accessing federal tax-return data for selected years from 1979 to 2005 to analyze the occupations of federal taxpayers at the top of the U.S. income distribution, Jon Bakija, Adam Cole, and Bradley Heim found that "executives, managers, supervisors, and financial professionals account for about 60 percent of the top 0.1% of income earners in recent years, and can account for 70 percent of the increase in the share of national income going to the top 0.1% of the income distribution between 1979 and 2005."[34]

For 2005 they found that executives, managers, and supervisors in non-finance businesses made up 41.3 percent of all taxpayers whose incomes, with capital gains included, placed them in the top 0.1 percent, while financial professionals, including management, accounted for another 17.7 percent. Of the 41.3 percent who were non-finance executives, managers, or supervisors, 19.8 percent were salaried and the rest were in closely held businesses.[35] After the 6.2 percent of the top 0.1 percent who were "not working or deceased," the next-largest occupational groups were lawyers at 5.8 percent, real estate professionals at 5.1 percent, and medical professionals at 4.1 percent.

We can use the Standard & Poor's ExecuComp database, which compiles data on executive pay disclosed in SEC Form DEF 14A—the proxy statement that a company files prior to its annual general meeting of shareholders—to get an idea of the representation of highly paid corporate executives among the top 0.1 percent of households in the income distribution. In 2012, for example, the threshold income, including capital gains, for inclusion in the top 0.1 percent was $1,906,047.[36] ExecuComp's 2012 proxy-statement data for "named" top executives—the CEO, CFO, and three other highest-paid in any given company—shows that 4,339 executives, 41 percent of those in that year's database, had total compensation greater than this threshold amount. Of their average income of $7,524,168, 64 percent represented gains realized from stock-based compensation, with 32 percent derived from the exercise of stock options and the other 32 percent from the vesting of stock awards.

The number of corporate executives who were members of the top 0.1 percent club in 2012 was, however, far higher than 4,339 for two reasons. First, total corporate compensation of the named executives does not include other forms of

---

[34] Bakija et al. (2012). The quote is from the paper's abstract.
[35] Bakija et al. (2012).   [36] World Wealth and Income Database (2017b).

non-compensation income—from securities, property, fees for sitting on the boards of other corporations, etc.—that would be included in their federal tax returns. If we assume that named executives whose corporate compensation was below the $1.91 million threshold were able to augment that income by, say, 25 percent from other sources, then the number of named executives in the top 0.1 percent in 2012 rises to 5,095.

Second, included in the top 0.1 percent of the U.S. income distribution were a potentially large, but unknown, number of U.S. corporate executives whose pay was above the $1.91 million threshold but who were not named in proxy statements because they were not among the five executives named in their companies' proxy statements. For example, of the highest-paid executives named in IBM's 2012 proxy statement, the lowest-paid had a total compensation of $9,177,663. There were presumably many other IBM executives whose total compensation was between this amount and the $1.91 million threshold for inclusion in the top 0.1 percent in the income distribution.

Therefore, top executives of U.S. business corporations—industrial as well as financial—are very well represented among the top 0.1 percent of the U.S. income distribution, with much, and often most, of their corporate pay coming from the gains realized from exercising stock options and the vesting of stock awards. If one keeps in mind that Wall Street has, since the 1980s, judged the performance of corporations by their quarterly stock prices, the impact of stock-based pay on executive behavior is impossible to miss. Stock-based pay gives top executives powerful personal incentives to boost, from quarter to quarter, the stock prices of the companies that employ them. In stock buybacks, these executives have found a potent, and SEC-approved, instrument for stock-market manipulation from which they can personally benefit, even if the stock-price boosts that accompany buybacks are only temporary.

As indicated previously, the ExecuComp database, drawn from the proxy statements that companies submit to the SEC, provides the numbers needed to determine how much money the highest-paid corporate executives in the United States take home in total and the proportion of their total compensation which is stock based. Figure 4.4 shows the average total compensation of the 500 highest-paid executives in the ExecuComp database for each year from 2008 through 2017. Realized gains from stock options and stock awards make up 60 to 81 percent of the total.[37] We repeat what we stated in Chapter 3: U.S. corporate executives are incentivized to boost their companies' stock prices and are amply rewarded for doing so. In SEC-approved stock buybacks, they have at their disposal an instrument to enrich themselves. In their massive, widespread, and ubiquitous use of this instrument, they have been participating in the looting of the U.S. business corporation.

---

[37] Hopkins and Lazonick (2016).

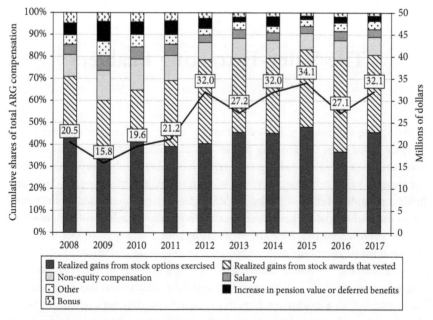

Fig. 4.4. Amount and composition of executive pay, 2008–2017

Notes: ARG (actual realized gains). Figures are for 500 highest-paid executives in each year. The following extraordinarily highly paid outliers, with $1 billion or more in total compensation, have been removed: 2012, Richard Kinder, Kinder Morgan, $1.1 billion, and Mark Zuckerberg, Facebook, $2.3 billion; 2013, Mark Zuckerberg, $3.3 billion.

Source: Standard & Poor's ExecuComp database, retrieved October 11, 2018. Calculations by Matt Hopkins of the Academic-Industry Research Network.

The willingness of senior corporate executives to do stock buybacks to manipulate the stock prices of the companies for which they work is destructive of innovative enterprise, as we have shown in a growing body of empirical research that we have carried out.[38] It is on the basis of this ongoing research that we summarized at the end of Chapter 3 how stock buybacks undermine the three social conditions of innovative enterprise: strategic control, organizational integration, and financial commitment. Value-extracting CEOs tear companies down rather than building them up. These corporate "leaders" have been on the front lines of the transformation of U.S. corporate governance from a regime of retain-and-reinvest to downsize-and-distribute. But, in leading this transformation, they are not acting alone. As we shall see in Chapters 5 and 6, supporting the agenda of predatory value extraction have been institutional investors as "value-extracting enablers" and hedge-fund activists as "value-extracting outsiders."

---

[38] For references to the body of empirical research that has been carried out from the "innovative enterprise" perspective, see Hopkins and Lazonick (2014, 2016); Lazonick et al. (2014); Lazonick (2015b).

5

The Value-Extracting Enablers

Enabling the exorbitant value extraction by corporate executives discussed in Chapter 4 has been the growing power and misguided activism of institutional investors. Instead of supporting long-term value creation by corporations with appropriate value extraction over time, institutional investors—mainly pension funds and mutual funds—deluded by MSV ideology and motivated by their own quest for higher yields, have exercised their rapidly growing voting power to enable corporate raiders, now known as "hedge-fund activists," to loot industrial corporations in an unholy alliance with senior corporate executives.

To understand the role of these value-extracting enablers in historical perspective, it is important to note the fact that institutional activism has only recently been accepted as a normative feature in the relationship between institutional shareholders and corporations. Even in the 1980s, when it became evident that institutional investors would soon hold the majority of corporate shares, it was not clearly established that voting was part of their fiduciary duty, and few institutional investors were interested in exercising the voting rights attached to the common shares in their portfolios. Nor did regulatory authorities encourage them to vote; in fact, they imposed heavy restrictions on communications among the institutions themselves, as well as on their communications with both corporate management and the public. In crusading for their activist agenda, shareholder activists portrayed the traditional financial regulations as outmoded relics that had lost their historical relevance and clamored for the wholesale removal of these regulations in the name of realizing "shareholder democracy." The current rise of hedge-fund activism, anchored in the voting power of institutional investors and the easy aggregation of their proxy votes, is a consequence of the misguided activism of institutional investors. To make sense of this transformation in the relations between business corporations and institutional investors, it is necessary to understand why institutional investors were originally under heavy regulation.

5.1 Origins of Shareholder Democracy and New Deal Financial Regulation of Institutional Investors

When managerial capitalism was taking shape in the early twentieth century, those who came to own public shares were mostly retail investors—that is, individual households. As we discussed in Chapter 2, retail investors had no

Predatory Value Extraction: How the Looting of the Business Corporation Became the U.S. Norm and How Sustainable Prosperity Can Be Restored. William Lazonick and Jang-Sup Shin, Oxford University Press (2020).
© William Lazonick and Jang-Sup Shin.
DOI: 10.1093/oso/9780198846772.001.0001

interest in managing corporations, a fraction of whose shares they had come to own. Their general willingness to leave control to managers stemmed in part from the prior revenue-generating successes of those corporations under managerial control and in part from the trust the shareholders had in financial intermediaries who had persuaded them to buy those corporate stocks. But, more fundamentally, this willingness to abdicate control derived from the confidence of public share-holders that the stocks they held were liquid and that they could therefore sell them on the stock market at any time, a maneuver that became known as "the Wall Street walk." Another reason they were willing to hold public stocks was that their "ownership" stake in a company entailed neither commitment of their time or effort, nor of funds beyond those they had expended to purchase the shares, while their liability was limited only to the cash that they had paid for those shares. They would not have bought the shares in the first place had they been obliged to provide such commitment or to assume the corporation's financial liabilities.[1]

Those who, from the early twentieth century, had embraced and promoted "investor democracy," or "shareholder democracy," were not at all interested in encouraging these public shareholders to influence management decisions, the hallmark of current-day shareholder activism. As Julia Ott has argued in *When Wall Street Met Main Street: The Quest for Investors' Democracy*, the main concern of "intellectual, political, corporate, and financial leaders who embarked on a quest for mass investment" was how to build a stable and prosperous political system in the face of not only public distrust of "corporate power and account-ability" but also of political challenges from "mounting economic inequality, surging immigration, ethnic diversity, Jim Crow segregation, and women's de-mands for suffrage [that] sparked fundamental debates about citizenship." These leaders hoped that "[m]ass investment could shore up the propertied foundations of citizenship, preserve economic mobility and autonomy, enhance national prosperity, and make corporations accord with the will of the people."[2]

The promoters of shareholder democracy of a century ago also made it clear that they did not think of it as being related to raising capital. Ott states that they "did not view mass investment as a particularly efficient or profitable means of raising capital" and points out that the "[c]orporate need for capital did not call forth popular demand for financial securities spontaneously."[3] William Lazonick and Mary O'Sullivan also point out: "The stock market did not serve as a source of

---

[1] Lazonick and O'Sullivan (2000a: 113).
[2] Ott (2011: 4). For instance, Clark (1900) envisioned that the share ownership by workers would "blur, or perhaps disappear...the old line of demarcation between the capitalist class and the laboring class" and argued "The socialist is not the only man who can have beatific visions" (quoted in Ott (2011: 25)). This vision continued into the 1920s with John Raskob, for instance, making his famous statement in 1929, "Everyone ought to be rich," by laying out proposals for working- and middle-class wealth-building in an article in *Ladies Home Journal* (John J. Raskob papers (Accession 0473), Hagley Museum and Library, Wilmington, DE 19807, https://findingaids.hagley.org/xtf/view?docId=ead/0473.xml).
[3] Ott (2011: 4).

funds for long-term business investment. When an enterprise went public, the stock market was the instrument for the separation of stock ownership from strategic control over internally generated corporate revenues."[4]

Being a political project, shareholder democracy was premised on retail investors who had political citizenship in the country. Institutional investors such as investment trusts and mutual funds were not to be part of it because they were fiduciaries, not owners, of shares and did not have the status of citizens. Institutional investors were only beginning to emerge and held only about 5 percent of the market capitalization of the U.S. equity market by 1929.[5] They were simply "money managers" whose basic function was to diversify investments, thereby raising yields on portfolio investments while managing risks, an option that was not available to most retail investors. This function of institutional investors had been well established from the days of the first collective investment trusts that emerged in Scotland and the U.K. in the late nineteenth century.[6]

The regulations on the financial market established during the New Deal era also emphasized the passivity of public shareholders and specifically discouraged institutional activism. As a policy response to the turmoil of the New York Stock Exchange crash of 1929 and the subsequent collapse of economic activity, the Securities Act of 1933 and the Securities Exchange Act of 1934, the second of which established the Securities and Exchange Commission (SEC), sought to regulate financial markets. The specific regulation of mutual funds had to await passage of the Investment Company Act of 1940. The New Deal regulations embodied three enduring principles to guide the relation between shareholders and companies: (1) that "fraud and deceit," including profiting from insider information, be prohibited; (2) that shareholders acting as a group be heavily regulated and the forming of investors' cartels prohibited; and (3) that institutional investors be encouraged to diversify their portfolios and discouraged from exerting influence over management.

Under the first principle, the regulations required public companies to make regular, accurate, and timely public disclosure of financial information to shareholders while barring shareholders and managers from profiting from insider information and misappropriating corporate resources. They specifically prohibited "fraud or deceit" and "manipulative or deceptive devices or contrivances."[7]

---

[4] Lazonick and O'Sullivan (2000a: 112).

[5] Ellen R. McGrattan and Edward C. Prescott, "The 1929 Stock Market: Irving Fisher Was Right," Federal Reserve Bank of Minneapolis Research Department Staff Report 294 (Feb. 2003), cited in Coates (2018: 8).

[6] For instance, the stated goal of the Foreign and Colonial Government Investment Trust established in 1868 was "to give the investor of moderate means the same advantages as the large capitalist in diminishing the risk of investing in Foreign and Colonial Government Stocks, by spreading the investment over a number of different stocks" (Coates 2018: 7).

[7] Blair (1995: 51). See also Parrish (1970); Roe (1990); U.S. Senate Committee on Banking and Currency (2009).

To deter insider trading, they required those who were deemed insiders, whether manager-owners or investors, to "report all purchases and sales of company securities." In addition, they stipulated that, should insiders "profit by buying a company's securities and selling them within six months or by selling and rebuying within six months, they may be required to forfeit those profits to the company."[8]

Under the second principle, the formation of a "voting group" by investors was considered to represent an investor cartel, a practice that was heavily regulated. If the combined shares of a group of investors exceeded a specified threshold, its members were placed under the same regulations as insiders. In view of the fact that investors intending to form a group would need to communicate with one another in advance, communication among investors came in for strict oversight: The Securities Exchange Act of 1934 ruled that "If one institution contacted enough others, the communications would be deemed a proxy solicitation.... Filing would have to be made; the filers would have to give those contacted the information specified in Schedule 14A. Similarly, the securities acts trigger liability of controlling persons for illegal actions by the controlled company. Groups that control could be liable for the misdeeds of the controlled portfolio company."[9]

In line with the third principle, institutional investors were encouraged to diversify their portfolios while being discouraged from seeking to control management. The 1934 Pecora Report, the product of a Senate securities investigation, explicitly walled off institutional investors from management, making clear that mutual funds were allowed to engage in investment only.[10] This principle was also embodied in the Tax Code of 1936: "another safeguard...is to prevent an investment trust or investment corporation [from] being set up to obtain control of some corporation and to manipulate its affairs."[11] Upon enactment of the Investment Company Act of 1940, a high-ranking SEC official even testified that "a mutual fund's *only* positive function was to provide diversification; any extension risked thievery."[12]

This regulation that clearly separated management from institutional investors answered in part to the need to remove the potential for conflict of interest: If institutional investors were allowed to control corporations, they would tend to utilize their position for their own profit at the expense of other shareholders. More important, behind the regulation was a clear understanding that institutional investors and management perform fundamentally different functions: While the former are basically speculators and/or savers who help individuals

---

[8] Blair (1995: 51).

[9] Roe (1990: 17). Blair (1995: 71) points out that this regulation made it "difficult for shareholders to communicate with each other at all...without the approval and support of management."

[10] Roe (1990: 12). For details on the Pecora Report, see U.S. Senate Committee on Banking and Currency (2009); Perino (2010).

[11] Roe (1991: 1483).   [12] Roe (1991: 1488). The emphasis is in the original.

invest in corporate stock through utilizing their size and diversification, the latter creates value in corporations by producing high-quality, low-cost goods and services.[13] The mutual fund industry, therefore, did not oppose the regulations imposed by the government; on the contrary, the industry readily accepted the regulations because it "wanted to sell its products and needed a code of conduct to certify the industry to the public."[14]

These three principles had been well enough established that they went unchallenged until the 1980s. For instance, the same principles were upheld when the Employee Retirement Income Security Act (ERISA) was introduced in 1974 as a policy response to the growing need to regulate pensions. First, ERISA rules prevented self-dealing behavior on the part of employers and fund managers. Second, they discouraged pension funds from taking excessive risks and encouraged them to diversify investment portfolios very broadly. Third, pension funds were requested to refrain from exercising control over companies in their portfolio; if they tried to do so, they could lose their tax-exempt status.[15] In this context, Peter Drucker pointed out that pension funds "have no business trying to 'manage'.... To sit on a board of directors, for instance, and accept the obligations of board membership, is incompatible with duties as 'trustees'... which have been sharply and strictly defined in the Pension Fund Reform Act of 1974 [ERISA]."[16]

Beginning in the 1980s, however, these principles increasingly came under assault. As discussed in Chapter 4, corporate executives were allowed by the adoption of SEC Rule 10b-18 in 1982 to manipulate stock prices through stock buybacks, seriously impairing the first principle. The principles were also encroached upon by attacks from corporate raiders and other shareholder activists, who found ways to leverage the rapidly growing voting power of institutional investors. These actions were legitimized by the broad acceptance of agency theory, which underpinned the ideology that a company should be run to maximize shareholder value. In the next sections, we will chart this transformation and show how it enabled the process of value extraction, contributing to the creation–extraction imbalance.

5.2 The Growing Voting Power of Institutional Investors

The ownership structure of U.S. corporations is conventionally characterized as "dispersed ownership." Since 1932, when Adolf Berle and Gardiner Means offered this classic characterization and pointed out the "separation of ownership and control" as its result, it has been the starting point of the debate on corporate

---

[13] For details on this, see Lazonick (2015c) and Chapter 2 of this book.
[14] Roe (1991: 1489).   [15] Blair (1995: 157).   [16] Drucker (1976: 83).

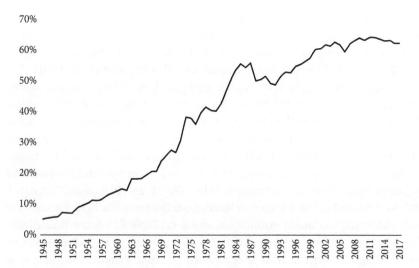

Fig. 5.1. The growth of institutional shareholding in the United States (% of total corporate shares outstanding)

Source: Estimated from Z.1 Statistical Release of Federal Reserve Board, Board of Governors of the Federal Reserve System (2018).

governance and economic performance.[17] There is no doubt that shareholding per se in the United States is still dispersed. However, the characteristics of the dispersion have undergone qualitative changes. If the classic dispersion saw shares in the hands of retail investors who were the actual owners of the shares, the prominent feature of the current-day dispersion is that shares are in the hands of institutional investors, fiduciaries of the savers who are the shares' ultimate owners.

This institutionalization of shareholding progressed through the latter half of the twentieth century and has continued in the twenty-first century. As shown in Figure 5.1, institutional shareholding of U.S. public stocks was at only 7 percent in 1950, but increased to 14 percent in 1960, 26 percent in 1970, 40 percent in 1980, 52 percent in 1990, 61 percent in 2000, and 63 percent in 2017. Note that in Figure 5.1, drawn from the Federal Reserve dataset, hedge funds and private-equity funds are classified as "households," not as "institutional investors," despite the fact that most of them are functioning as institutions by pooling and managing other people's money.[18] If one included hedge funds and private-equity funds as

---

[17] Berle and Means (1932). For criticisms of this kind of characterization, see Pichhadze (2010, 2012).

[18] "Non-profit organizations" such as university endowment funds are also not included here. The apparent slowdown in the growth of institutional shareholding in the 2000s would be mainly due to the explosive growth of hedge funds and private equities. For the growth of hedge funds in the 2000s, see Chapter 6. For the growth of private equities, for instance, see McKinsey (2018).

institutional investors, the actual institutional shareholding would be substantially higher than Figure 5.1 shows. For instance, *Pensions & Investment* estimated institutional holding as 80.3 percent of the market value of the S&P 500 index and 78.1 percent of the U.S. broad-market Russell 3000 index in April 2017.[19]

A notable trend in the institutionalization of shareholding has been shares' extreme concentration in the hands of relatively few large institutional investors despite an explosive growth in the number of institutional investors. In September 2018, for example, the ten largest institutional investors held stock valued at $8.5 trillion, more than half (55.5 percent) of that held by the 100 largest institutional investors. Even among these ten largest institutional investors, the degree of concentration is remarkable. The "Big Three," BlackRock, Vanguard, and State Street, held $5.2 trillion of stock, more than one third (33.8 percent) of that held by the 100 largest institutional investors (Table 5.1). It is estimated that the Big Three "collectively vote about 20% of the shares in all S&P 500 companies."[20] The U.S. stock market is dominated by what Vanguard founder John Bogle called the "King Kong of investment America."[21]

In the conventional characterization of "dispersed ownership," public shareholders are described as powerless "minority shareholders" who have no means to influence the management. "King Kong" institutional investors, however, have amassed unprecedented voting power over individual companies. For instance, BlackRock, currently the largest institutional investor in the world with $6.3 trillion

Table 5.1. Concentration of shareholding among institutional investors, 2018

Rank	Institutional investors	Shareholdings ($ billion)
1	Vanguard Group, Inc.	2,203
2	BlackRock, Inc.	1,894
3	State Street Corporation	1,111
4	Capital Group Companies, Inc.	793
5	Fidelity Investments	672
6	T. Rowe Price Group, Inc.	567
7	Wellington Management Group LLP	371
8	Northern Trust Global Investments	324
9	Geode Capital Management, LLC	307
10	The Bank of New York Mellon Corporation	297
	The "Big Three"	5,207 (33.8%)
	Top 5 Holders	6,672 (43.3%)
	Top 10 Holders	8,538 (55.5%)
	Top 25 Holders	11,065 (71.9%)
	Top 100 Holders	15,395 (100%)

Source: Capital IQ.

---

[19] McGrath (2017).   [20] Bebchuk and Hirst (2018).   [21] Bogle (2005: 76).

Table 5.2. Number of companies in which an institutional investor has a 5% or greater stake, 2018

Institutional investor	Number of global companies
BlackRock, Inc.	2,985
Vanguard Group, Inc.	2,067
Fidelity Investments	1,058
Capital Group Companies, Inc.	468
T. Rowe Price Group, Inc.	451
Wellington Management Group LLP	383
State Street Corporation	217
The Bank of New York Mellon Corporation	75
Northern Trust Global Investments	13
Geode Capital Management, LLC	0

Source: Capital IQ.

of assets under management (AUM), held 5 percent or more of the outstanding shares in each of 2,985 companies around the world in September 2018. Vanguard and Fidelity also held 5 percent or more of the shares in each of 2,067 companies and 1,058 companies, respectively (see Table 5.2). In an article entitled "The Giant of Shareholders, Quietly Stirring," the *New York Times* reported in 2013 that BlackRock was "the single largest shareholder in one of every five U.S. companies including Exxon Mobil and Chevron; AT&T and Verizon; JPMorgan Chase and Citigroup; GE; and more than 800 others. It also holds 5% or more shares of 1,803 U.S.-listed companies, about 40% of roughly 4,300 total U.S.-listed companies."[22]

Their voting power over individual companies is more remarkable when we consider the fact that these largest of institutional investors are the most diversified stock investors in world history. Leading mutual funds and pension funds rely heavily on holdings in index funds and exchange-traded funds (ETFs), by which they effectively "own the market," as the number of portfolio companies in a fund sometimes exceeds 10,000. Even though their portfolios are often criticized for "excessive diversification," they are still the single largest shareholders in a great number of public companies.

A serious problem with the voting power of index funds lies in the fact that they are neither interested in nor capable of voting even if they have already become the most important and powerful shareholders of U.S. public corporations and will become more so in the future. John C. Coates estimated that in 2018 "indexed funds now own more than 20% and perhaps 30% or more of nearly all U.S. public companies."[23] The wide variation of his estimates is understandable. First, official statistics on index funds released by the Investment Company Institute only

---

[22] Craig (2013).   [23] Coates (2018: 13).

include "registered index fund assets." Yet a large and increasing portion of assets held by pension funds, insurance companies, and non-profits are managed in index fashion. Secondly, the statistics do not include foreign funds. Foreign funds hold about 20 percent of all U.S. equities and they are managed in index fashion much more than domestic funds.[24] Thirdly, a large portion of "nominally active funds" are in fact managed in index fashion.[25] Whether one chooses to use the lower bound or the higher bound of the estimates, an inevitable trend is that the dominance of index funds in shareholding of U.S. public corporations is going to be strengthened further for the foreseeable future. Coates estimated, "If current growth rates continued, . . . the entire U.S. market would be held by such funds no later than 2030. But even if the trend flattens, the majority of most companies will soon be owned by indexed funds."[26]

Shareholder activists in the 1980s crusaded to "correct" the perceived "autocratic management" of big corporations by relying on the growing voting power of institutional investors, whom they also further empowered, as will be detailed in Section 5.3. Their actions were quite successful in making institutional investors increasingly active and bringing about major regulatory changes, undermining and eventually obliterating the traditional principles concerning the prohibition of investor cartels and the separation of public shareholding and corporate management.

In arguing for the empowerment of institutional investors, the proponents of shareholder activism characterized them as weak "minority shareholders" who did not have effective means of voicing their concerns to all-powerful corporate management. Shareholder activists sought to strengthen the power of institutional investors against management by changing the rules that had forbidden de facto investor cartels, free communication among shareholders, and "engagement" with management. They argued that deep corporate problems of "creating value for shareholders" could only be resolved by lifting traditional strictures on institutional-investor activism. Meanwhile, in the 1980s institutional investors were concentrating their control over shareholding, surpassing the 32 percent mark of all shares outstanding in 1980 and approaching 45 percent in 1990 (Figure 5.1).

---

[24] Coates (2018: 11) explains this as follows: "Much of that ownership is indexed. While precise data on how much are not available, it is fair to assume that a greater portion of foreign ownership is truly passive than is the case for domestic. That is because foreign investors have good reasons to understand that their knowledge of foreign markets will tend to be worse than for domestic investors, and so attempting to out-guess the markets through market timing or picking stocks will fail."

[25] Coates (2018: 11) elaborates on this as follows: "Active funds commonly minimize management costs by essentially holding an index and selecting a few companies to over- or under-weight. This allows them to distinguish themselves from the index funds, while not attempting to engage in serious analysis of the value of each portfolio company. The 'active share,' as the portion of active funds that is significantly different from what would follow from a passive indexing strategy is commonly estimated to exceed 50% at many funds, resulting in an additional chunk of the market being fairly understood as indexed and truly passive."

[26] Coates (2018: 13).

The regulatory changes introduced at the instigation of shareholder activists in the 1980s and the 1990s served to further increase institutional investors' growing power by removing obstacles to the aggregation of their proxy votes, thus paving the way for hedge-fund activists to roam easily around the corporate world engaging in predatory value extraction.

The proponents of shareholder activism contended that, if empowered, institutional investors would exercise their voting rights for the benefit of their ultimate customers and potentially for the common good of shareholders. Institutional investors have turned out, however, to be susceptible to their own agency problems and conflicts of interest, often to an even greater extent than corporate managers. Moreover, the largest institutional investors have become heavily reliant on index funds, which means that they have little if any interest in keeping up with the management decisions of individual companies or in developing the capability to exercise in an intelligent manner the voting rights attached to the common stocks they hold. One can say, ironically, that the legitimacy of institutional investors' exercise of their voting power has eroded as their voting power over corporations has increased. We will investigate this transformation and its consequences in later sections.

5.3 The Evolution of Institutional Activism

There were various groups of activists who, in the 1980s, pursued corporate reforms to obtain what they considered to be public benefits. At the same time, there were groups of stock-market traders, including corporate raiders, who did not hide their raw intention to profit from the process of "reforming" corporations. In the name of "shareholder democracy" in corporate governance, this coalition of reformers and raiders succeeded in bringing about major changes in the traditional New Deal financial regulations.[27] This section summarizes this process of changing corporate governance and financial regulation, and critically examines its consequences. The upshot of the regulatory changes is shown in Figure 5.2.

5.3.1 Robert Monks: The Inevitability of Institutional Activism?

Robert Monks, later described as "an entrepreneur of the idea of corporate governance" or "an agent of change in corporate governance,"[28] was the principal

---

[27] On the evolution of corporate governance discourse, see Cheffins (2013).
[28] Rosenberg (1999).

The New Deal financial regulations in the 1930s
• Establishing the principle of separation between public shareholding and corporate management

ERISA regulation in 1974
• Maintaining the New Deal principles

Formalizing institutional activism in 1985–86
• Establishment of Council of Institutional Investors (CII) (1985)
• Establishment of Institutional Shareholder Services (ISS) (1985)
• Launch of United Shareholders Association (USA) (1986)

Avon letter and DOL-Treasury directives in 1988
• Compulsory voting for pension funds

SEC proxy rule change in 1992
• Allowing de facto investor cartels
• Unlimited freedom of "communication and engagement"

SEC final rule on proxy voting in 2003
• Compulsory voting for mutual funds and other investment advisors

Fig. 5.2. Changes in regulations on the relation between institutional investors and corporations

ideologue, administrator, and businessman to provide justification for institutional activism, resulting in the empowerment of institutional investors, as Monks himself sought to profit from this transformation. A close consideration of his arguments and his career illuminates the evolution and consequences of institutional activism.

Monks joined the Department of Labor as Administrator of the Office of Pension and Welfare Benefit Programs in 1984, after previously working as a lawyer, businessman, and banker, and having been an aspiring politician. "The only reason Monks took this job was to advance his governance agenda," according to Hilary Rosenberg, his biographer. "His main concern [was] establishing the position that pension funds had fiduciary duties to act as owners of corporations."[29] From the beginning of his tenure, he intended to serve only one year as a

---

[29] Rosenberg (1999: 83–4).

pension administrator and to leverage his experience in government for a business career in corporate governance.[30]

In a speech, "The Institutional Shareholder as a Corporate Citizen," later considered seminal among corporate-governance activists, Monks told pension-plan officers that:

> it seems to me to be a self-evident proposition, that institutional investors have to be activist corporate citizens.... Given the huge blocks of stocks owned by institutions in all of our major companies, it is not always practical to quietly support management or ... sell if you don't approve of management's handling of the company.... I would suggest that it behooves institutional investors, in the exercise of their corporate citizenship, to take the lead in proposing, and passing, provisions.... Even if you wanted to run away from a poorly managed company, you couldn't all do it at once.... So like it or not, ... as a practical business matter, institutional investors are going to have to become more and more active shareholder-owners, and less and less passive investors,...[31]

Two aspects of this speech demand our attention: the call for stronger activism and the use of the term "owners." As to the first point, Monks took for granted, as did later corporate-governance activists, that with the growth of institutional shareholding, it had become more difficult for investors to resort to the "Wall Street walk." The advocacy of stronger institutional activism was a corollary of this growing difficulty.

From the perspective of the traditional regulations on institutional investors that encouraged diversification, however, this argument puts the cart before the horse. Diversification was encouraged not only to spread out risks across a portfolio of assets but also to make it easier for institutional investors to take the Wall Street walk by selling off blocks of shares in a portfolio when the need arose. As institutional shareholding grew, the market for selling blocks of shares became more liquid, actually making it easier for an institutional investor to take the Wall Street walk by selling its shares to other institutional investors. Given the liquid stock market, there are no grounds for saying that any particular institutional investor is "stuck" with certain portfolios. Monks, however, employed the growth of institutional shareholding *in aggregate* as a reason for claiming that their shareholdings are illiquid, and used this assumption of illiquidity as a pretext for justifying the need for stronger institutional activism.

---

[30] Rosenberg (1999: 80), borrowing Monks's own words, details this decision as follows: "On taking the pension job, Monks vowed—to himself and his family—that he would stay in the position for just one year.... he told his wife ... 'Trust me', he remembers saying to her ... 'I know my own temperament in the government. I have a single agenda for this. I'm not going into this because I want to be a career public servant. I'm going into this because it's in aid of my long-term project in trying to create change in the way that corporations function. I can't afford more than a year's time here.'"

[31] Rosenberg (1999: 92–3).

A crucial tactic in advancing this argument for stronger activism is to portray institutional investors as if they are homogeneous. They are, however, a diverse group that includes pension funds, mutual funds, universities and other civil-society organizations, insurance companies, bank trusts, and other investment companies. Even among pension funds, over which Monks had influence as the chief U.S. government pension administrator in 1984–85, the investment objectives and approaches of private pension funds differ from one to another as well as from those of public pension funds. Institutional investors are in general competing fiercely with each other to improve investment performance and attract more customers. Treating them as a group and urging them to strengthen their activism in regard to particular companies is tantamount to asking them to form an investor cartel. Moreover, as the growth of index funds demonstrates, institutional investors in general evolved in the direction of being less interested in getting to know the affairs of individual companies closely. Diversification is still a main concern of most institutional investors. One can even say that, in its investment objectives and approaches, institutional investing has evolved in the direction of being more diversified and passive rather than more focused and active.

As to the second point, it is an intentional misrepresentation to say that large blocks of stock are "owned" by institutions. Institutional investors are fiduciaries or trustees of those households or organizations whose money they are managing. As a law student, Monks himself was clearly aware of this legal situation and used the term "fiduciaries" not infrequently in his writings and speeches. At the same time, however, he often used the term "owners." This rhetorical tactic to portray institutional investors as "owners" has successfully contributed to the broad acceptance of a vertical relation of "owner versus manager"; that is, that corporate managers are agents of institutional investors who "own" the companies. Once it has been incorporated, however, nobody owns a corporation. The corporation, as a legal entity, makes contracts with managers and issues securities to shareholders.[32] Corporate managers are employees of corporations. They are business-managing fiduciaries as much as institutional investors are money-managing fiduciaries, and the relation between corporate managers and institutional investors is a horizontal one between two different fiduciaries. Monks, as well as other shareholder activists, nonetheless distorted this relation in public discourse and increasingly in the minds of policy-makers, academics, and even businesspeople.[33]

---

[32] See Demsetz (1995); Hansmann and Kraakman (2000); Blair (2003b); Klein and Coffee (2004); Stout (2004); Robé (2011).

[33] In a similar vein, Blair (2003a: 57) remarks: "The rhetoric of 'ownership,' however, subtly redefines corporations in terms of the presumed property rights of one class of participants in the firm, thereby adding a tone of moral superiority to the idea that corporations should be run in the sole interest of shareholders."

As we emphasized above, however, institutional investors are money-managing fiduciaries, not "owners" of the stocks they hold. In the same vein, corporate managers are business-managing fiduciaries empowered by the corporate board. To repeat: The relation between institutional shareholders and corporate managers is basically a horizontal one between two different fiduciaries.

5.3.2 Institutional Investors Acting Together: The Leading Role of Public Pension Funds

If Robert Monks was mainly an ideologue who promoted institutional activism through his corporate-governance agenda, public pension funds were its practitioners, taking direct action against corporations. This they did by bringing to bear their rights and influence as shareholders, setting up umbrella organizations for their activism, and lobbying the U.S. government to change regulations in ways that would strengthen activism. They were "the most vocal advocates of corporate governance intervention" in the 1980s, and, conducting themselves as if they were rule-setters, they drafted codes of "best corporate governance practices" for their portfolio firms to adopt.[35]

From the 1950s, pension funds emerged as the biggest group of institutional investors in the United States because of the rapid expansion of business and government defined-benefit pension systems. By 1975, they held 16 percent of U.S. corporate shares, four times more than mutual funds. Among them, private pension funds, although in aggregate a lot larger than public pension funds, were not interested in institutional activism. Most of them were run by business corporations on behalf of their employees, and it was unthinkable for their top managers to take activist positions against their own companies or against other companies in general.[36]

Unlike those of corporate pensions, fund managers of public pensions were not representing pensioners in the business sector and hence were freer to take an activist position regarding their portfolio companies. The retirement benefits of their clients, public-sector workers, were also more or less guaranteed by the state or federal government and they had relatively less sympathy with corporate-sector workers. This fact made them freer to favor shareholder interests over labor interests when the two conflicted, even by advocating corporate restructuring led by corporate raiders that brought about layoffs and divestitures.[37]

---

[35] Cheffins (2013: 55).
[36] Corporate pensions held 13% of the market value of U.S. corporate stocks whereas public pensions held 3% of the stocks in 1975. The corresponding figures were 20% and 5% respectively in 1985 and 18% and 8% in 1994 (Blair 1995: 46, Table 5.1).
[37] Gelter (2013: 40).

Moreover, public pensions mostly held onto defined-benefit (DB) plans and were very slow to move to defined-contribution (DC) plans—a transition that occurred with increasing momentum at business corporations from the 1980s. DB plans expose the employer to the potential for underfunding of their pension plans, whereas DC plans do not. Public-pension fund administrators tried to avert this potential funding shortfall by using their collective shareholding power to seek higher yields from the stock market by strengthening shareholder activism. Public pension funds also had better access to regulatory authorities because they were regulated by states and exempted from the federal ERISA regime regulating private pension funds, and because a larger number of their administrators and board members were local administrators, politicians, labor unionists, and others. It was, therefore, relatively easy for them to effect regulatory changes that would allow them to increase the ratio of stock to other holdings in their investment portfolios and to then use shareholder activism to seek higher yields on their portfolios.[38]

Among public pension funds, the California Public Employees' Retirement System (CalPERS) emerged as the leader in institutional activism in the 1980s. As it was then the largest institutional investor in the world, its size gave it the muscle to exercise its power. Moreover, CalPERS was under pressure to boost its investment yields by expanding its investments in stock and by becoming active in influencing its portfolio companies because it had become one of the most expensive pension systems.[39] Having introduced annual cost-of-living adjustments in 1968, two years later the fund adopted a very generous pension formula under which it paid workers who retire at age 65 90 percent of their final salary for life. Following California voters' approval of a 1966 ballot measure, CalPERS had been allowed to invest up to 25 percent of its portfolio in stock, and in the early 1980s it asked for permission to increase that limit to 60 percent. Although the voters rejected this proposal, they approved a different one in 1984 that, while it "likewise let CalPERS expand its investments [in stock]," refrained from specifying a percentage limit and, for cosmetic purposes, put in "a clause that held CalPERS board members personally responsible if they didn't act prudently."[40] This permissive regime contrasted with the restrictions placed on other public pension funds, many of which had few or even no equities in their portfolios until the mid-1990s.[41]

From 1986 CalPERS started its major shareholder campaigns in close collaboration with the Council of Institutional Investors (CII), which had been set up the year before. It led in drafting the list of companies characterized by "poor

---

[38] See Gelter (2013).

[39] In this context, Strine (2007: 7) observes as follows: "Interestingly, some of the demand for outsized returns has come from institutional investors—such as public pension funds—facing actuarial risks because of underfunding and past investment mistakes."

[40] Malanga (2013).   [41] Gelter (2013: 39).

performance" to make it easy for CII member institutions to identify targets for their activist campaigns.[42] It also created a shareholders' bill of rights establishing the principle that all shareholders have equal voting rights; demanded that corporations seek shareholder approval before paying greenmail or setting up poison pills; and called for a majority of outside directors to approve any extraordinary bonuses or other payments to corporate executives. CalPERS itself initiated, in 1989, a movement to change traditional proxy rules that led to the SEC's landmark proxy-rule amendments in 1992, which will be detailed in Section 5.3.5.

5.3.3 Institutional Investors and Corporate Raiders Acting Together: CII, USA, and ISS

The Council of Institutional Investors (CII), established in 1985 as "the voice of corporate governance," was the first of several formal organizations created to espouse the collective interest of institutional investors. Its founders were twenty-two public and union pension funds, with California State Treasurer Jesse Unruh, New York City Comptroller Harrison J. Goldin, and State of Wisconsin Investment Board Chair John Konrad as founding co-chairs.

Jesse Unruh, California's second-longest serving state treasurer (1975–87), was the principal catalyst in the formation of CII and the fashioning of CalPERS and CalSTRS into the progenitors of institutional activism. Because, under him, California had issued massive quantities of state-backed bonds through Wall Street bankers, Unruh was dubbed "the most politically powerful public finance officer outside the U.S. Treasury" and regarded as having "transformed the job . . . [which] used to garner as much political clout as the director of a local mosquito abatement district . . . into a source of financial and political power that reached from California to Wall Street."[43]

By Unruh's own account, he was outraged that Texaco Inc. and Walt Disney Productions, of which California pension funds were major shareholders, had made greenmail payments in 1984. These actions prompted him to call upon the nation's public pension funds to support a new shareholder organization to

---

[42] Individual activist pension funds also drafted their own list. For instance, CalPERS produced the list of the "Failing Fifty." Firms in the "Failing Fifty" are then analyzed further and the Investment Committee identifies approximately twelve targets and one corporate governance structure issue (for each target) that it will pursue in the form of a shareholder resolution. Shareholder resolutions have included creating shareholder advisory committees, changing the composition of the board of directors and its committees, and restructuring executive compensation. See Smith (1996).

[43] Boyarsky (2007: 221). Uhlig (1987) also observed: 'Because as Treasurer he was *ex officio* member of many California boards and commissions, Unruh oversaw "the raising and expenditure of virtually all the state's money and consolidated his influence over billions of dollars in public investments and pension funds."'

oppose corporate management decisions that would hurt the funds financially. He also closely cooperated with Monks, who in his position at the Labor Department was the chief official regulating private pension plans at the time. Monks agreed with Unruh about "the need for an assembly of large institutional investors" and helped him set up CII as a bipartisan organization.[44] CII later grew into a global organization comprising "more than 125 public, union and corporate employee benefit plans, endowments and foundations."[45]

If CII was crusading for shareholder activism among institutional investors, the United Shareholders Association (USA), launched by corporate raider T. Boone Pickens in 1986 and comprising more than 65,000 members, was ostensibly representing the interests of small shareholders. The USA put pressure on corporations by developing its "Target 50" list of firms with "poor financial performance, top executive compensation plans that were not sensitive to firm performance, and policies that limited shareholder input on governance issues."[46] It attempted to negotiate with target companies to modify their governance structures so that they would be more responsive to shareholder interests. It also mobilized its members' votes to sponsor proxy proposals if the target companies did not come into agreement with its demands. Although the USA claimed to represent retail investors, several large institutional shareholders, such as CalPERS, the College Retirement Equities Fund (CREF), and the New York City Employees Retirement System (NYCERS), sponsored proposals on the USA's behalf. In 1992, not long after the SEC proxy-solicitation rules changed significantly, the USA declared victory, saying "mission accomplished"; it disbanded in 1993.[47]

Immediately after resigning from the Department of Labor (DOL) in 1985, Monks established the proxy advisory firm Institutional Investors Service, which changed its name to Institutional Shareholder Services (ISS) the same year. He had already proposed the idea of ISS while he was the chief pension administrator, arguing in a December 1984 speech: "Current fiduciaries have neither the inclination nor the training to act as proprietors. Either they have to acquire them [capabilities to vote], or a new institution will be developed."[48] He later provided more details regarding this "new institution" at a Labor Department hearing,

---

[44] When Monks met with Unruh in 1984 to discuss the need for an assembly of large institutional investors, he said: "I thought it was a good idea, and I would give any Republican institutional support to the idea of forming an organization of institutional investors, but that…it should be bipartisan." (Rosenberg 1999: 100).

[45] CII website (http://www.cii.org/).

[46] Strickland et al. (1996: 320).

[47] Ralph V. Whitworth, 'United Shareholder Associations: Mission Accomplished," Remarks to Investor Responsibility Research Centre Conference on Shareholder Management and Cooperation, October 27, 1993. Quoted in Blair (1995: 73).

[48] Rosenberg (1999: 102).

saying "[i]t was time ... for corporate, ERISA-covered pension fund sponsors and their managers to assign the vote to a third, neutral party."[49]

Monks was not only a shareholder activist in what he presumed to be the public interest, but also a businessman who wanted to profit by "selling the idea of a company that carried out voting tasks for funds." He had made it clear from the beginning—to his family, at least—that he would stay with DOL for only a year, then pursue his corporate-governance agenda in the business sector. One fund manager directly admonished Monks for his being out for profit when he, as DOL's chief pension official, talked about the need for a "third, neutral party" to advise proxy voting: "Monks, goddamn you. Guys like you, you go into government and start a forest fire and then you come and try to sell us all fire extinguishers."[50]

Monks later employed an analogy based on the double helix to justify his personal profit-seeking as compatible with the public benefit of shareholder activism undertaken by institutional investors. Pointing to the structure of DNA, which consists of two strands of molecules arrayed as a twisted ladder, he argued that one strand represented the "mission" of activism, the other strand "money" to be earned from activism. Monks said he wanted to "pursue the development of corporate governance through the structure of a profit-making business," explaining: "As a business, my idea had to be made relevant to people who were accustomed to paying only for something that was in fact valuable to them. I had to demonstrate that year in and year out good governance was good business.... The parallel spiral forces of the double helix do not touch but are indispensable to each other."[51]

His business ambitions were largely fulfilled. After being investigated by the SEC for potential conflict of interest, he left ISS on paper in 1990, transferring $3 million worth of his shares in the company to an irrevocable trust and making his nephew Nicholas Higgins and his son Robert the trustees.[52] He then continued his corporate-governance activism in the "double-helix" fashion by setting up "corporate-governance funds" like Lens Fund.[53] ISS successfully grew into a global company that currently maintains "1200 employees spread across 19 offices in 13 countries, covering approximately 42,000 meetings in 115 countries yearly, delivering proxy research and vote recommendations ... [for] more than 9.6 million

---

[49] Rosenberg (1999: 103).

[50] Rosenberg (1999: 117) continued to say, "Monks was astonished. Here was someone who saw right through him. He was indeed interested in selling the idea of a company that carried out voting tasks for funds."

[51] Rosenberg (1999: 118). This "double helix" analogy can be also found in public pension funds' justification for combining social objectives with shareholder value. For instance, CalPERS introduced its "Double Bottom Line initiative" in 2000 by claiming that its investment would produce both good returns and good social policy.

[52] Rosenberg (1999: 211–14).

[53] Corporate governance funds aim at increasing investment yields by applying pressure to improve corporate governance of their portfolio companies.

ballots representing 3.7 trillion shares."[54] However, it is extremely questionable whether Monks' attempt to serve the public interest has been fulfilled, as will be detailed in Section 5.3.4.

5.3.4 Imposing Proxy Voting upon Institutional Investors as a Fiduciary Duty

The first major regulatory change that resulted from the growing institutional activism in the 1980s was the so-called "Avon letter" in 1988. The letter was sent by a deputy assistant secretary at DOL to the Retirement Board of Avon Products Inc., to clarify the Department's position on the fiduciary duty of pension funds under ERISA. It marked the first written statement of the DOL position on the fiduciary duty of voting, stating: "The decision as to how proxies should be voted with regard to the issues presented by the fact pattern are fiduciary acts of plan asset management." In a subsequent speech, the then-assistant secretary of DOL asserted that "to meet this obligation, pension plan sponsors under ERISA must draw up detailed policies governing proxy voting and document all votes and the reasons behind them."[55] This position was reiterated in "Statements on Pension Funds Investment" issued by the Department of Labor and the Department of the Treasury in 1989. The Avon letter has thus been "widely cited as the Labor Department's official position on fiduciary obligations of pension fund managers to vote the shares under their management."[56]

Through these administrative directives, proxy voting was established as a fiduciary duty of pension fund managers, and they were required to vote in what they regarded as the "economic best interest of a plan's participants and beneficiaries."[57] This was exactly what Monks endeavored to achieve while he was the chief pension-fund administrator at DOL. Not of their own accord but under the new regulation, pension funds now faced the necessity either of acquiring capabilities to act as proprietors or else of seeking professional advice from a "third, neutral party."

This fiduciary duty of voting imposed on pension funds was later extended to all other institutional investors, including mutual funds, under an SEC regulation. In its ruling on proxy voting in 2003, the SEC made clear that "...an adviser is a fiduciary that owes each of its clients duties of care and loyalty..., including proxy voting" and required advisers "to adopt and implement policies and procedures for voting proxies in the best interest of clients, to describe the procedures to clients, and to tell clients how they may obtain information about how the adviser

---

[54] ISS website, https://www.issgovernance.com/about/about-iss/.
[55] Rosenberg (1999: 165).   [56] Blair (1995: 158).   [57] Blair (1995: 158).

has actually voted their proxies."[58] The spirit of the SEC rule was basically the same as that of the DOL directives to pension funds of about fifteen years before: It represented an attempt to "correct" perceived corporate problems by strengthening institutional activism. Until the SEC rule in 2003, ISS was virtually a monopoly proxy adviser. Glass Lewis, now the second-largest proxy-advisory firm, entered the proxy-advisory market in the same year.[59]

5.3.5 Allowing Free Communication and Engagement

While establishing proxy voting as a fiduciary duty of institutional investors, institutional activists pushed for changes in regulations governing the proxy system that would allow their collective voice to be heard more effectively by both corporate management and the public. It was CalPERS that initiated the move in 1989 by sending a letter to the SEC requesting a comprehensive review of the proxy system. The letter "proposed forty-eight separate changes to the proxy rules," and CalPERS's main purpose, it claimed, was "to even the imbalance between shareholders and management concerning the filing and processing of proxy materials."[60]

The CalPERS petition was followed by those of other groups, including CII and USA. In one instance, the USA sent a similar letter to the SEC arguing that "reform of the proxy process to allow shareholders a meaningful corporate governance role could forge a fundamental realignment of the now conflicting interests of management and shareholders.... [S]uch realignment would maximize value on a constant basis, rather than through one-time restructuring transactions."[61] This proxy-rule change was made during the period when corporate raiders were in retreat owing to the collapse of the junk-bond market, with such prominent figures in the junk-bond market as Ivan Boesky and Michael Milken being jailed. State governments had passed regulations limiting hostile takeovers and, with devices such as the "poison pill," corporations had strengthened their defenses against corporate raiders. The sudden change in the market for corporate control in the late 1980s made institutional activists vigorous in lobbying to change the federal proxy regulations, as "one of the few remaining venues for effecting corporate management."[62]

After over three years' deliberation, during which the SEC made two proposals and received comments from various groups and individuals in response, the SEC

---

[58] SEC (2003).
[59] http://www.glasslewis.com/company-overview/; https://en.wikipedia.org/wiki/Glass_Lewis.
[60] Sharara and Hoke-Witherspoon (1993: 336).
[61] Sharara and Hoke-Witherspoon (1993: 337).
[62] Calio and Zahralddin (1994: 466).

finalized the watershed amendments to its proxy regulations in 1992.[63] The fact that, as we have seen, in 1993 immediately following the amendments' adoption, the USA declared "mission accomplished" and disbanded testified to the significance of this change for institutional activists and, especially, corporate raiders. Why were the amendments so important?

It should be noted that traditional regulations on institutional investors were unambiguous about prohibiting the formation of investor cartels, defining communication among investors as a "proxy solicitation."[64] It was therefore illegal for any shareholder to discuss company matters with more than ten other shareholders without first filing with, and obtaining the approval of, the SEC. The 1992 amendments, however, largely deregulated proxy communication, not only among investors but also with company management and the public. This change flew in the face of the whole spirit of the New Deal regulations, overturning them in the name of allowing "market forces to restore a better sense of balance to America's board rooms" through the freer flow of communication and engagement.[65]

The new rules loosened restrictions on investors in three ways. First, those investing in a given company were now allowed to communicate freely with one another if each held less than 5 percent of its shares and had no special relationship to that company. In other words, they were permitted to form investor cartels within the 5-percent limit. But then, as now, this limit did not really constrain investors, especially when they were holding shares in large public companies. Institutional investors have generally held less than 5 percent of the shares outstanding, with only a few amassing more than a 5-percent share. To cite a recent example, as of November 20, 2018, there were only two institutional investors, Vanguard Group (7.2 percent) and Blackrock (6.4 percent), that held 5 percent or more shares of Apple Inc.[66]

Second, investors were now allowed to "engage" freely with management without worrying about potential breaches of accessing insider information. This freer engagement was expected to provide investors with more and better information about corporations and perhaps lead to "relationship investing."[67] Third, investors were in addition given the freedom not only to make public statements on proxy-voting issues but even to announce their voting intentions without violating the proxy-filing requirements.

The SEC made it clear that it was removing itself from the job of proxy censorship because it believed that contestants in proxy voting "should be free to reply to [an opponent's] statement in a timely and cost-effective manner,

---

[63] SEC (1992); Sharara and Hoke-Witherspoon (1993); Bainbridge (2005).
[64] See Section 5.1 of this chapter.   [65] Calio and Zahralddin (1994: 466).
[66] http://www.nasdaq.com/symbol/aapl/ownership-summary.
[67] On definition and pros and cons of "relationship investing," see Blair (1995: ch. 5).

challenging the basis for the claims and countering with their own views on the subject matter through the dissemination of additional soliciting material."[68] Some institutional activists argued for the proxy-rule changes even in the name of removing restrictions on the constitutional right of free speech, and the SEC eventually concurred with this argument.

In 1999, the SEC added new elements to the proxy rules (Rule 14a-12) that fully liberalized communication.[69] Investors were now allowed to conduct unlimited solicitation, not only among themselves but also with the public, including in the form of press releases, even if they abandoned proxy filing in the end. Additionally, oral communications were freely permitted with no need "to be reduced to writing and filed." This rule change allowed investors to engage more freely with corporate management and the public without incurring any obligation to state their intentions in a document that is legally binding.[70] In particular, this rule allowed activist shareholders "to gauge the level of support from other shareholders" before filing a proxy statement and thereby to "mitigate the risk of losing a costly proxy contest."[71]

5.4 Why has Institutional Activism Gone Astray?

In 2013, toward the end of his long career as a corporate-governance activist, Monks admitted in an interview, "It's broke," adding: "Ownership is a fiction, governance a mirage."[72] In a speech prepared in 2015, he also acknowledged, "The fundamental dynamics of Corporate Governance have been diluted into virtual meaninglessness."[73] He attributed this state of corporate governance mainly to the power of "manager-kings" and the passivity of institutional investors: "These trustees likely hold more than 50% of the voting shares of each of the Fortune 500, yet their influence is negligible *by choice*. So we have a controlling percentage of public companies in the hands of trustees who act powerlessly in the arena of the manager-kings."[74]

However, we should examine more carefully why institutional activism has gone astray, as Monks concedes. It is not constructive to blame individual actors, whether they are powerful CEOs or passive institutional investors, for its failures. We should investigate systemic reasons for the failures. In our view, institutional activism has fundamental flaws in its understanding of the actual relation between institutional investors and corporations. In particular, institutional activism fails

---

[68] Quoted in Briggs (2007: 687).   [69] Rule 14a-12.   [70] Briggs (2007: 689–90).
[71] Lu (2016).   [72] Monks (2013).   [73] Monks (2015).
[74] Monks (2013). Our emphasis. He even contends that "Capitalism has become a kleptocracy, run by and for the enrichment of CEOs, or what I term 'manager-kings.' So powerful have these manager-kings become, they now bend the will of governments, effectively capturing the power of state democratic institutions."

to distinguish between value creation and value extraction, and hence how they can be in balance or imbalance.

5.4.1 Ignorance of the Distinction between Value Creation and Value Extraction

An important supposition of institutional activism is that institutional investors have the capability, interest, and legitimacy to fix corporate problems. But this assumption is seriously flawed. The problems that corporations are perceived to have are associated with one of two phenomena: the way they create value or the way in which value is extracted from them; i.e., their operational performance and distribution of the income generated. As we discussed in Chapter 3, the stock market is a value-extracting institution and institutional investors are involved in the stock market mostly as value extractors, not as value creators. By their nature, they are hardly competent or dedicated fixers of corporate difficulties.

Even in the domain of pure value extraction, institutional investors have difficulty in agreeing on what to do because they are diverse in their perceptions of the problems' gravity and in their willingness and competence to tackle them. For instance, in the case of the executive-pay issue, managers of large mutual funds, who are often paid far more than corporate executives, tend to be more lenient, whereas pension-fund administrators and retail investors, who are paid much less than corporate executives, tend to be more critical.[75] Similarly, institutional investors with longer-term outlooks have a different view of what levels of dividend payouts are adequate from those with short-term outlooks. It is not easy for heterogeneous institutional investors to form a common perception and a common prescription.

Moreover, value extraction is not a matter confined to shareholders alone. It encompasses a broader spectrum of stakeholders including managers, workers, subcontractors, customers, taxpayers, and financial institutions that have claims on the companies concerned. Simply giving more power to shareholders does not guarantee an equitable distribution of income. Instead, it is more likely to result in "shareholder dictatorship" or "shareholder opportunism" by allowing shareholders to exercise their heightened influence to increase their portion of total value extracted. In fact, the strengthening of institutional activism over the last

---

[75] This tendency is already well-reported in proxy voting results. For instance, BlackRock, whose CEO Larry Fink was paid $26 million in 2015, voted to support pay practices at companies 96.2 percent of the time during the period from July 1, 2014, to June 30, 2015. Other big mutual funds also showed a very high percentage of yes votes on pay: 96 percent for Fidelity Funds, 95 percent for Vanguard, and 93 percent for Putnam Investments. By contrast, public pension funds tend to reject pay policies. Since 2011, the State Universities Retirement System of Illinois has voted no 63 percent of the time, while the city of Philadelphia rejected 52 percent of pay policies it voted on. See Morgenson (2016).

three decades has been coupled with a sharp rise in stock buybacks and dividend payouts, which have largely benefited shareholders and corporate executives at the expense of other stakeholders. In the case of stock buybacks, moreover, in addition to senior executives as "value-extracting insiders," much if not most of the gains from buybacks have gone to those stock-market traders—the "value-extracting outsiders" to be discussed in Chapter 6—who are in the business of timing, hedge funds in particular.

In the domain of value creation, most institutional investors lack the capability, interest, and legitimacy to intervene. Their professional capability primarily lies in portfolio management, which includes stock picking, market timing, and tracking stock-price movements. These stock-trading capabilities are very different from the managerial capabilities required for value creation, which is rooted in a combination of strategic control, organizational integration, and financial commitment. Most institutional investors also lack interest in monitoring their portfolio companies sufficiently closely to enable them to contribute to the value-creation process, as such monitoring would require not only substantial costs but also the acquisition of capabilities to comprehend the social conditions of innovative enterprise that, by their training, institutional investors simply do not have.

Intervention in the value-creation process by institutional investors in their attempts to increase their portion of value extracted can, and often does, have adverse impacts on value creation. Shareholder-value ideology and the agency theory that underpins it are based on the erroneous assumption that the purpose of the corporation is to maximize value extraction for shareholders and that, if corporate managers focus their efforts on this purpose, the corporation's performance—that is, its value creation—will be maximized, as discussed in Chapter 3. If institutional investors want to improve corporate performance through value creation, however, they should invest in developing capabilities to understand the value-creation process as it takes place in individual companies and how value extraction in the name of maximizing shareholder value can, and generally does, undermine the value-creation process.

Accepting MSV ideology, the SEC similarly erred in confusing value extraction with value creation. In its Final Rule on compulsory voting of mutual funds in 2003, the SEC referred to "capital formation" as follows: "The rule and rule amendments will likely increase investor confidence in investment advisers by making proxy voting more transparent and encouraging increased emphasis on proxy voting by advisers. Because capital formation is influenced by investor confidence in the markets, we believe that the rule could have a positive effect on capital markets." "Investor confidence," which is essentially institutional investors' confidence in value extraction, is treated here as a panacea, including "capital formation," which is value creation at the economy level. Given that value creation and value extraction are two fundamentally different processes, it is not surprising that empirical studies on institutional activism fail to establish clear, positive relations between institutional activism and corporate performance, as elaborated in Chapter 7.

5.4.2 Misguided Compulsory Voting: Shareholder Democracy Gone Awry

Monks invoked the concept of "citizenship" from political democracy when he pushed for compulsory voting of institutional investors. Like him, most advocates of shareholder democracy have tended to employ analogies taken from political democracy.[76] But Monks critically erred in using this analogy because compulsory voting is not a norm of political elections in most countries. He did not examine why voting is not compulsory in most political democracies or what the implications of compulsory voting would be for shareholder democracy. More important, he avoided assessing the real effects that imposing compulsory voting as a fiduciary duty would have on the behavior of institutional investors.

5.4.2.1 Incorrect and arbitrary analogy with political voting

In a political election, compulsory voting certainly has its pros and cons. It can have the positive effect of augmenting the power of representation by increasing the turnout of voters at the ballot box. However, it can have negative effects on an election outcome because it increases blank, randomly marked, and spoilt ballots from voters who are not interested in the election and do not know about the candidates. These uninterested voters are also prone to cast their votes in response to hot-button issues of the day or to political scandals, rather than trying to align their voting with ideological or policy preferences.[77]

The political reality around the world is that, whatever the balance of these pros and cons, there are only a few countries that have adopted a compulsory voting system. In 2015, in the entire world, there were ten countries, including Australia, Brazil, and Singapore, and two local governments that had made voting compulsory.[78] Most countries consider voting as a right, not as a duty that they should enforce on their citizens. Many countries also take the position that to abstain from voting is also an expression of political preference that should be allowed in accordance with the constitutional right of freedom of speech. The fact that most countries do not adopt compulsory voting in political elections tells us that they are much more concerned with its cons than with its pros.

---

[76] On the development and entrenchment of "shareholder democracy," see Ott (2011).
[77] See Birch (2009); Brennan and Hill (2014); Singh (2015).
[78] Wikipedia, https://en.wikipedia.org/wiki/Compulsory_voting#Current_use_by_countries.

Yet advocates of compulsory voting for institutional investors—including Monks and other corporate-governance activists, as well as regulatory authorities such as the SEC and the DOL—in adopting this position, presented only its potential advantages, without considering or presenting either its disadvantages or what the net effect of those advantages and disadvantages would be. If one looks into the nature and process of proxy voting by institutional investors, it is not hard to find that the disadvantages of compulsory proxy voting are a lot more pronounced than those of compulsory political voting.

In a political election, the secret ballot is the norm: Voters are guaranteed secrecy of their ballots and are not compelled to explain their voting decisions. In this situation, the negative effects of voting at random can be mitigated by the law of large numbers. In proxy voting, however, institutional investors are required not only to declare how they voted but also to provide justification for their voting decisions. This means that uninterested institutional investors are obligated to create justifications for their voting decisions, to purchase those justifications from third parties, or both. Even those who are interested in voting may decide to vote against their own preferences if a strong public backlash against their voting decisions appears likely.

Moreover, voting by institutional investors is proxy voting or surrogate voting where institutional investors vote on behalf of their customers. In exercising proxy voting, however, the room for conflict of interest has been wide open and the legitimacy of proxy voters is questionable. This contrasts with political voting, where there is no room for a conflict of interest (unless one can divide a person). In fact, the phenomenal growth of both the financial markets and institutional investment has greatly lengthened and complicated the chain of intermediaries involved in institutional investing. In pension-fund investments, for instance, the chain extends from pensioners to pension administrators, pension investment advisers, funds of funds, external asset managers, and others. These hired professionals may be experts in determining when it is best to buy, sell, or hold stocks, but they are not experts in corporate decision-making. The relation among those intermediaries has also become very complex because, even within one mutual fund, there are numerous sub-funds. Considering the length and complexity of this chain, it is questionable whether those at the end of the chain would really exercise voting rights over corporations on behalf of the customers who had put money into their custody. Far detached from the original customers, institutional investors have the opportunity to cast their votes in their own interest rather than in the interest of those whose proxies they hold. This possibility becomes greater if the original customers have little power to replace their intermediaries, as is typically the case with public pension funds. Putting it in the terminology of agency theorists, institutional investors are prone to their own agency problems when they cast their votes ostensibly in an attempt to resolve agency problems of corporate managers.

Nonetheless, the SEC expressed naïve expectations about the benefits of the transparency of compulsory proxy voting in the Final Rule in 2003 and this stance has not changed thus far:

> Although we recognize that compliance programs, including proxy voting programs, may require advisers to expend resources that they could otherwise use in their primary business, we expect that the rules and rule amendments may indirectly increase efficiency in a number of ways. Advisers would be required to carry out their proxy voting in an organized and systematic manner, which may be more efficient than their current approach. Requiring all advisers with voting authority to adopt proxy voting policies and procedures, and meet recordkeeping requirements, may enhance efficiency further by encouraging third parties to create new resources and guidance to which industry participants can refer in establishing, improving, and implementing their proxy voting procedures.[79]

The SEC position spelt out in the quote above was based on the optimistic expectation of institutional investors' developing analytic capabilities that would enable them to make voting decisions "in an organized and systematic manner," and that "third parties" would be competent and objective in providing advice. Reality has shown this optimism to have been unfounded. Far from taking compliance seriously, the largest institutional investors, especially index funds, have limited their efforts to setting up skeletal research units that have barely paid lip service to the new rule. Nor have the "third parties," the proxy-advisory firms, equipped themselves adequately for their task; still, they exert undue power over the voting decisions of institutional investors, and thereby over corporations. In addition, they have a serious potential for conflicts of interest. Let us first examine the true state of the "systematic" voting capabilities of large institutional investors.

5.4.2.2 "Corporate-governance teams" in large index funds: Lip-service voting organizations

Most large mutual funds had rarely taken part in corporate voting before it became compulsory in 2003. That was a natural and, in our view, appropriate position, considering the fact that the larger portion of their assets was held in index funds. Simply to track index movements rather than to research individual companies constitutes the critical competitive edge that has enabled mutual funds to charge very low management fees and, consequently, to rapidly increase assets under management (AUM).

When the SEC ruled proxy voting to be among their fiduciary duties, the mutual funds initially relied heavily on recommendations from proxy-advisory

---

[79] SEC (2003).

firms; in other words, they "purchased" proxy-voting decisions and related justi-fications. However, criticisms soon emerged of both this practice and the proxy-advisory firms. Large mutual funds were therefore under pressure to demonstrate to policy-makers, their own customers, and the public that they were dutifully fulfilling this new fiduciary obligation. Many of them then adopted the two-pronged approach of separating the voting decisions of the active funds and passive funds under their management and of setting up a corporate-governance team or stewardship team for the latter.

BlackRock provides the most illuminating case in this regard. It is currently the largest institutional investor as well as the largest index-fund manager in the world. Its total AUM stood at $6.3 trillion in 2017 and index-related funds amounted to $4.1 trillion, constituting about 65 percent of the total AUM.[80] BlackRock divides its voting decisions between active-management funds and passive-management funds. The proxy decisions of the former are made primarily by the fund managers in charge of the portfolio firms concerned. In contrast, the proxy decisions of the latter are under the control of its Stewardship Team (previously, Corporate Governance Team).[81] That is, voting decisions for all the portfolio companies under BlackRock's index-related funds are made centrally by the team.

To outsiders, this team is portrayed as being equipped to make informed voting decisions and to engage professionally with portfolio companies. The reality, however, lies far from this rosy picture. With BlackRock's corporate-governance team consisting of only twenty people, in the 2012 proxy season it voted on 129,814 proposals at 14,872 shareholder meetings worldwide.[82] BlackRock had increased the number of its team members to thirty-six by the end of 2017. But this increase was only in tandem with the increase in its AUM, which had nearly doubled from $3.39 trillion in 2012 to $6.28 trillion in 2017.[83] The only feasible way to deal with so many voting decisions with such limited personnel is to apply some general corporate-governance metrics rather than to examine the concrete contexts of individual companies' voting issues.

The *New York Times* thus described the team's decision-making as "the cor-porate governance equivalent of speed dating" and reported as follows: "These analysts have a language of their own, casually throwing around terms like 'over-boarding,' for when directors serve on multiple boards, possibly spreading them-selves too thin; 'engagement,' when a problem reaches a critical stage and merits a visit from a BlackRock analyst; and 'refreshment,' when engagement doesn't work

[80] BlackRock (2018).
[81] Others among the largest institutional investors maintain a similar structure of dividing voting decisions between passive funds and active funds.
[82] Loomis (2014).
[83] "BlackRock Investment Stewardship: 2018 Annual Report" (https://www.blackrock.com/corpo rate/literature/publication/blk-annual-stewardship-report-2018.pdf).

and a director needs a heaveho."[84] A glance at the internal operation of the corporate-governance team only strengthens the suspicion that keeping this team as small as possible is a cheap, and probably the only, option for the largest index funds to demonstrate to the public that they are carrying out their fiduciary duty of proxy voting sincerely. In this sense, one may say that corporate governance teams are "lip-service" units that have resulted from the imposition of compulsory voting on institutional investors.

This kind of "lip-service" proxy voting, nonetheless, exerts great impact on the actual outcome. Above all, some institutional investors are very powerful individually and have already become the largest shareholders in numerous companies, as mentioned in Section 5.2. Moreover, the voting decisions are implicitly coordinated among institutional investors even if there may not be explicitly collusive behaviors. This is because corporate-governance teams at those institutional investors tend to employ a similar set of corporate-governance metrics. Institutional investors are also increasingly under public pressure to make their "voting policies" explicit, and they tend to make public their policy statements on voting and engagement. It is then highly probable that institutional investors take account of others' policy statements and previous voting decisions on similar cases in making their voting decisions. "No explicit collusion is required to send highly aligned signals about what they want to each other and to management of portfolio companies," as John Coates points out.[85]

5.4.2.3 ISS, the proxy-voting monster: Its inadequacy, bias, and illegitimate power

Nor have the abilities of proxy-advisory firms turned out to be much more impressive than those of the internal corporate-governance teams of the largest institutional investors. The SEC counted on proxy-advisory firms "to create new resources and guidance" for institutional investors subject to the proxy-voting requirement it had imposed upon them. ISS currently controls 61 percent of the proxy-advisory market, while Glass Lewis. controls 35 percent, making the market a virtual duopoly. In its influence over large institutional investors, however, ISS is unmatched, having claimed at one point to be advising "24 out of the top 25" mutual funds and "17 out of the top 25" pension funds.[86] Considering the dominance it has enjoyed in the proxy-advisory market, focusing exclusively on the case of ISS will suffice for our purposes here.

Although ISS currently recommends yes-or-no decisions on more than 10.2 million ballots representing 4.2 trillion shares a year in 115 countries, it has only 1,800 employees, its administrative staff included.[87] How can it have developed the capacity and expertise to make so many informed voting decisions on such

---

[84] Craig (2013).   [85] Coates (2018: 15).   [86] Rose (2007).
[87] ISS website https://www.issgovernance.com/about/about-iss/.

diverse issues in so many companies around the world? Company managements and shareholders bring to shareholder meetings the proposals that they do mainly because those proposals are controversial; were they not controversial, research would not need to be done on them nor advice sought from proxy firms. It is not difficult to draft a reasoned report just by comparing the pros and cons of such controversial issues. But it is very difficult to write a report that determines a clear "yes" or a clear "no" on such issues. It strains credulity to think that ISS, with so few employees, has been able to assemble the complex, high-level expertise capable of making authoritative recommendations on so many issues. In reality, ISS tends to apply general and mechanical corporate-governance metrics to its voting recommendations, just as the largest index funds' corporate-governance teams tend to do. Institutional investors, in fact, did not care about or rely upon ISS before the SEC required them to vote. ISS, the only proxy-advisory firm at the time, was therefore struggling to stay in business. But compulsory voting brought great power and voluminous business to ISS because institutional investors needed its service simply to justify their voting decisions. The Avon letter of 1988 provided ISS with the big break that established its influence and business hegemony,[88] both of which got a second boost with the SEC proxy rule of 2003, even though that brought Glass Lewis. into its market in hopes of riding the new wave of demand for proxy-advisory services.

For the majority of index funds, just following the recommendations of proxy-advisory firms is the most convenient way to fulfill their fiduciary duty "because they can't justify to shareholders why they invest in their own analysis."[89] Only the largest index funds, such as BlackRock and Vanguard, set up in-house corporate-governance teams. Lesser index funds have no alternative but to rely heavily on proxy firms' advice. Even many active funds tend to follow the recommendations of proxy-advisory firms; combing through proxy firms' analyses and voting recommendations is a normal first step for fund managers. In addition, an internal convention at big institutional-investment firms dictates that, if fund managers want to go against proxy firms' recommendations, they provide a lengthy report to their superiors to justify their decisions—something they don't need to do if they simply go along with the recommendations. Going against proxy firms' recommendations thus requires courage and effort on the part of fund managers who are busy attempting to make profitable trades for the portfolios they manage. In this respect, the root of the power and influence of ISS is not the quality of its work, but rather the convenience it provides to institutional investors by lightening the burden of performing the unwanted regulatory obligation of voting proxies.

[88] Rosenberg (1999: 164–78).
[89] Bew and Fields (2012: 15). In this context, Winter (2011: 10) argues that voting by institutional investors following proxy advisory firms' recommendations "is essentially a form of empty voting" because "[t]he exercise of the voting right is determined largely by proxy advisors who do not have a shareholding interest themselves."

Moreover, proxy firms are wide open to conflicts of interest because, as unregulated private business entities, they are responsible to nobody except their own businesses. They normally combine proxy-voting advisory services with consulting services. When there is a proxy contest between one of their customers and a non-customer, it is hardly difficult for them to side with their customer, packaging their support as an "objective" assessment. As they are private and unregulated entities, there is no way for outsiders to determine whether the voting recommendations of the proxy firms were made objectively or shaped to serve their own business interests.

There is also a tendency for proxy firms to provide voting advice that reflects the investment philosophy of their owners. Set up by corporate-governance activist Robert Monks, ISS would be likely to side with an activist fund in a controversy pitting such a fund against company management. The ownership of ISS was later transferred to Vestar Capital, a private-equity fund that was founded by corporate raiders from First Boston's leveraged-buyout team, and then in 2017 to Genstar Capital, another private-equity fund. It would be only natural for ISS to support activist hedge funds, which are owned and run by today's equivalent of the corporate raiders of the 1980s and 1990s, when they have proxy battles with industrial companies.

In effect, compulsory voting for institutional investors has given ISS illegitimate power. Officially, it is only an "advisory" firm lacking any legitimate basis what-soever for exerting influence on corporate decisions of the kind that must be approved in shareholder meetings. Its influence cannot be ignored, however: A negative recommendation by ISS on a management proposal has been found to reduce the support of institutional investors by at least 13.6 percent and, at most, by 20.6 percent.[90] Corporate executives have to take a two-digit percentage difference very seriously, as it is often the case that the eventual voting outcome is decided by a difference of less than 10 percent in shareholder voting. Peter Iliev and Michelle Lowry report that over 25 percent of mutual funds "almost entirely" rely on ISS recommendations when they cast votes.[91] A Business Roundtable survey found that 40 percent of its member firms' shares were held by institutions that basically followed ISS's voting recommendations.[92] Its influence is so strong not simply because it recommends voting decisions to institutional investors but also because it coordinates with them in making those recommendations. As John C. Coffee, Jr. and Darius Palia remark, "[ISS and Glass Lewis] ... determine their voting policies based on interactions with (and polling of) institutional investors, so that proxy advisors and their clients reciprocally influence each other."[93] It is therefore not an exaggeration to say, as Leo Strine, Chief Justice of the Delaware

---

[90] Bethel and Gillan (2002: 30).   [91] Iliev and Lowry (2015).
[92] Briggs (2007: 692).   [93] Coffee and Palia (2016: 558).

Supreme Court has put it, that "[powerful] CEOs come on bended knees to ISS to persuade the managers of ISS of the merits of their views."[94]

The illegitimate power of proxy-advisory firms arose because the proxy-advisory market is a duopoly while, between its two members, ISS is easily the dominant one. If there were a number of proxy-advisory firms with similar reputations and if institutional investors could choose from among their diverse recommendations, their service might be defined as—and confined to—"advice." However, when the imposition of compulsory voting made it necessary to fill the vacuum of institutional votes that had previously existed, the larger part of this job fell to ISS, upon which nobody had conferred legitimate power to influence voting decisions in the corporate arena. ISS is a monster created by compulsory voting. No corporation anywhere in the world sends ISS a formal invitation to take part in its shareholders' meeting. But it effectively attends these meetings and casts votes, and nobody dares to expel ISS for exercising illegitimate influence on the voting outcomes of the meeting. Monks may not have been successful in achieving his activist agenda, as he has admitted, but there is no doubt that he is a successful entrepreneur who created a voting monster no one could ever have imagined.

5.4.3 Consequences of Free Communication and Engagement— Formation of De Facto Investor Cartels and Abuses of Communication and Engagement

In bringing about the 1992 proxy-rule amendments, shareholder activists also employed an analogy from political democracy. They portrayed corporate management as autocrats who ignored popular demands for freedom of speech and freedom of assembly while installing strict censorship in the form of proxy-filing procedures that, they charged, unfairly favored management. In contrast, they portrayed themselves as endeavoring to realize a "true shareholder democracy" by abolishing the censorship and thus obtaining the right of free communication and engagement. They then justified the proxy-rule changes by arguing that they would right the imbalance between shareholders and management and bring about a more efficient market outcome.

However, such expectations are based on the critical assumption that freer and easier exchange of information has an efficiency-enhancing effect in the market, an assumption that follows from conventional economic models of competitive markets, which are in turn based on the assumption that interaction among

---

[94] Strine (2005). For detailed accounts about how ISS and other proxy-advisory firms actually influenced voting outcomes and how they interacted with hedge-fund activists in major proxy battles, see Walker (2016).

players who have equal capability and equal access to information is the key to ensuring an efficient outcome. But markets in general, and the stock market in particular, do not function according to this neoclassical model, as discussed in previous chapters. Markets may be unduly influenced by strong "movers and shakers," and the stock market in particular is prone to manipulation. As it turned out, the very practices that the traditional regulations were meant to deter by preventing free communication and engagement, "fraud or deceit" and "manipulative or deceptive devices or contrivances," became more widespread because of the proxy-rule changes and compulsory proxy voting.

5.4.3.1 Allowing de facto investor cartels, facilitating market manipulation

Since the 1992 proxy-rule changes, the "wolf pack phenomenon"—sudden concerted campaigns of hedge funds against their target companies—has become a new normal.[95] Wolf packs can only be seen as de facto investor cartels—but in conventional economics cartels are considered prime obstacles to realizing the efficient allocation of resources, and they are therefore regulated heavily in most countries with capitalist economies. As the SEC employed the "market efficiency" argument in opening the door to investor cartels, one must draw one of two conclusions: Either it sincerely subscribed to the argument but was ignorant of market reality, or it exploited market-efficiency rhetoric to justify rule changes it was making for other reasons.

In the former case, the SEC might have thought that freely allowing investor cartels made up of shareholders, none of which held less than 5 percent of the target company's stock, would not undermine "market efficiency." However, in light of the broad dispersion of shareholding in big public companies, those with a 5-percent stake can easily become the largest shareholders and exert a strong influence on management.[96] Moreover, the 5-percent rule is easily circumvented through the formation of wolf packs. It is now a common practice for hedge funds to collaborate among themselves or with other investors around a target company and coordinate their strategies and tactics. Even if each of those collaborating may hold less than 5 percent of the target company's outstanding shares, their combined stake can easily elevate them to the status of controlling shareholders. It is also possible for one lead wolf to take a share exceeding 5 percent, make public its intention to campaign, and then recruit other, unidentified wolves, each holding less than a 5-percent share, to support its attack. In the fight over control of Barnes & Noble, for example, the lead activist investor held an 18.7 percent stake in the company, but it turned out that the actual wolf pack controlled a 36.14 percent

---

[95] For further details, see Chapter 6.

[96] At GE, Trian Partners called the shots with less than 1 percent of the shares. At DuPont, it had 2 percent of the shares. It is not the percentage of shareholding that matters, but rather the wealth, visibility, hype, influence, and insider information of hedge-fund activists that give them power (see Lazonick et al., 2016b; Lazonick 2018e).

stake.[97] In the campaign that forced the sale of Knight Ridder, "[w]hat started out as a 19% stake effectively grew to 37% in just 48 hours. The campaign succeeded almost instantly."[98]

Moreover, making it easier to form wolf packs made it easier to manipulate the market through the "wolf-pack effect," a phenomenon similar to the "Icahn lift," to be discussed in Chapter 6. Upon the announcement or leaking of information about the formation of a wolf pack, the stock market generally reacts positively. For instance, an international study on the wolf-pack effect reports "abnormal announcement returns of 7% for the U.S. during a $(-20, 20)$ day window" and of "6.4% and 4.8%, respectively," for Europe and Asia.[99] Those in the pack can easily develop trading strategies in advance because they exclusively know when they will trigger the wolf-pack effect. The market will also react to the way in which the wolves are moving together after the formation of the pack becomes public knowledge. Those in the pack again have advance knowledge of how they will act and can profit from front-running the market movements they create. The development of the derivatives market has made it a lot easier for them to profit from front-running without being detected in market manipulation by regulators.

If both the anti-cartel spirit of the 5-percent rule and the anti-manipulation spirit are so easily compromised, this leaves the SEC with two options: either to give up its regulation of collusive behavior in the market altogether or to tighten up the proxy rule so that wolf packs are difficult to form. But the SEC has so far done neither. This inaction points to our second explanation of the SEC's invocation of the "market efficiency" argument in explaining the proxy-rule changes: that it was misrepresenting the reason for its decision in order to disguise its actual motives. It only strengthens suspicion that the SEC as a regulatory body is in effect functioning as a promoter of financial interests, having been captured by shareholder activists who simply clamor for more power and freedom for themselves.

5.4.3.2 Abuses of free communication and engagement for profits

Allowing free communication and engagement with management has similarly failed to bring about "market efficient" outcomes, mainly because shareholders do not all have equal access to management despite the liberalizing measures adopted in 1992. While corporate executives can ill afford not to be serious in communicating and engaging with big institutional investors, they can simply ignore or offer perfunctory replies to the demands of small shareholders, who lack the larger players' resources. A critical question here is whether big institutional investors and other influential activists engage with management as impartial representatives of the general interests of shareholders or exploit their access to management mainly for their own gain. Common sense, as well as broad anecdotal evidence of

---

[97] Lu (2016: 778).   [98] Briggs (2007: 698).   [99] Becht et al. (2015).

institutions' self-serving utilization of communication and engagement with management, favors the latter answer.[100]

In this context, Joseph Calio and Rafael Zahralddin's research has pointed out that free communication and engagement with management provides institutional investors with a "tactical edge over the management and small shareholders because it occurs behind-the-scenes without media scrutiny or individual investor awareness."[101] John Cioffi has similarly concluded: "The 1992 proxy rule changes appear to have encouraged greater governance by institutional investors, but at the expense of transparency. Institutional investors, with some notable exceptions, preferred to voice their concerns and criticisms to management in private communications that would not become public. These communications thus became occasions for managers to disclose significant information to the representatives of institutional investors and analysts associated with investment banks and brokerages."[102]

In addition, allowing free communication between shareholders and the public, far from leveling the aforementioned imbalance between shareholders and management, intensified the imbalance, skewing it further to shareholders. Shareholders are now free to criticize the company's management "as long as the statements [they make] are not fraudulent."[103] In contentious issues, management makes its decisions by weighing their advantages and disadvantages. But shareholders can just focus on their perceived disadvantages and criticize management within the boundary of "not being fraudulent." It is even possible to criticize management for not achieving better performance in the name of maximizing shareholder value when the company concerned has been performing well. On the other hand, it is not often easy for management to criticize the company's shareholders unless it finds something seriously wrong with their statements or their behavior.

Owing to the free-communication rule, it has now become a convention among hedge-fund activists to criticize management, not only by sending letters but also by publishing "white papers" and even convening press conferences. This kind of public criticism puts enormous pressure on management and, rather than

---

[100] For instance, some public pension fund administrators exploited the occasion of engagements for their own career development. Romano (1993: 822) relates that many public pension fund managers desire elective office and therefore enhance their political reputations by becoming crusaders against the interests of large corporations. "For instance, Elizabeth Holtzman, New York City comptroller and a trustee for the city's pension funds, publicized her active approach to corporate governance while campaigning for the Democratic party's nomination for U.S. Senator." Union pension funds are also found to use their engagement and proposals as "bargaining chips to provide the union with a private benefit" (Matsusaka et al. 2018).

[101] Calio and Zahralddin (1994: 522–3). Immediately after the proxy-rule amendments, engagement became a more favored method than proxy contest. For instance, "TIAA-CREF reported in 1994 that it had submitted eighteen proposals during the proxy seasons but had 'successfully negotiated away fourteen of them' before voting" and, without waging a proxy contest, "From November 1992 through December 1993, IIs helped force turnover in top management at American Express, Borden, GM, IBM, Kodak and Westinghouse" (Blair 1995: 171–2).

[102] Cioffi (2005: 17, fn. 12).   [103] Calio and Zahralddin (1994: 522–3).

continuing the public warfare, company executives tend to prefer making compromises with activists by yielding to some of their demands. Daniel Loeb's (Third Point) attack on Dow Chemical is a case in point. Loeb opened a website specifically designed to criticize Dow management and their alleged "broken promises." Dow management gave in and accepted two directors nominated by Loeb in return for a one-year truce including the closure of the website. These two directors were under Loeb's "golden leashes" and soon played a central role in pushing Dow Chemical to conclude the merge-and-split deal with DuPont, which took place in December 2015.[104]

In Chapter 4, we showed that from the 1980s senior corporate executives, as insiders, embraced MSV ideology and became focused on increasing the company's stock price, incentivized by their stock-based pay. As we have shown in this chapter, by the end of the 1980s large public pension funds began criticizing corporate management both for lining their own pockets with excessive executive pay and for succumbing to "greenmail": quelling threats to their control from activist corporate outsiders by having the company pay premium prices for blocks of shares the outsiders had acquired, in hopes of inducing these "greenmailers" to go away. Spurred on by corporate-governance reformers, of whom Robert Monks was the most prominent, institutional investors lobbied the U.S. government to change the proxy-voting and shareholder-engagement rules to enable them to form voting blocs that could put more pressure on corporate executives to run companies in the interest of all shareholders—a throwback to the 1920s notion of "shareholder democracy." Ironically, in convincing the SEC to permit investor cartels through liberalizing proxy voting regulations and direct communication of public shareholders with corporate management, institutional investors gave corporate predators enormous power to extract value from companies for themselves, but not necessarily for shareholders in general.

The result, as we shall see in Chapter 6, has been the intensified looting of the U.S. business corporation, with corporate executives as insiders effectively aligning with corporate raiders as outsiders in the most massive frenzy of value extraction that the world has ever seen. The losers in this process have been U.S. households in their different capacities: households as savers who put their money into corporate shares, whether directly or indirectly; and households as workers and taxpayers, who contribute to the process of value creation only to see gains that should go to them sucked up by the new value-extracting class, from which the most numerous—and, in many cases, the wealthiest—members of the top 0.1 percent now come. In the next chapter, on the value-extracting outsiders, we will trace the history of extreme corporate predation from the corporate raiders of the 1980s to the "hedge-fund activists" of the 2000s and 2010s. We will also

---

[104] See Benoit and Lublin (2014); La Roche (2014); Mani (2014).

critique the work of the most prominent academic proponents of hedge-fund activism, emanating mainly from Harvard Law School. Lacking a theory of value creation—that is, a theory of innovative enterprise—these academics have no way of distinguishing between value creation and value extraction. To put it bluntly, these academic legitimizers of hedge-fund activism appear to be oblivious to the ways in which the operation of a business corporation can result in superior economic performance—that is, in stable and equitable economic growth—or to how predatory value extraction can result in employment instability, income inequity, and the decline of innovative capability.

6

The Value-Extracting Outsiders

Predatory value extraction in the United States accelerated from the middle of the 1990s, as Figure 4.3 and Table 4.2 have shown. The timing coincided with the rise of "hedge-fund activists," a new species of value-extracting outsiders descended from the corporate raiders of the 1980s. Taking advantage of regulatory changes in the late 1980s and the early 1990s aimed at strengthening shareholder activism, especially those introducing compulsory voting and allowing "free communication" as discussed in Chapter 5, corporate raiders recreated themselves as "activists" and targeted industrial companies for predatory value extraction in alliance with corporate executives as value-extracting insiders and institutional investors as value-extracting enablers.

In this chapter, we examine the evolution and current state of hedge-fund activism and critically evaluate its impact on value creation and extraction. After explaining the origin and expansion of hedge-fund activism, we separately investigate Carl Icahn's transformation from the most conspicuous corporate raider to the most prominent hedge-fund activist to delineate vividly the characteristics and methods of the new value-extracting outsiders. In Chapter 7, we critically assess works by Lucian Bebchuk and his colleagues, who function as the main academic advocates of hedge-fund activism.

6.1 Origins and Expansion of Hedge-Fund Activism

Labels are often inaccurate, and sometimes they are totally misleading. Hedge-fund activists, as well as hedge funds in general, provide a case in point. "Activist" is most familiar as a label placed on those who are dedicated to social causes, and who may even sacrifice themselves in pursuit of those causes. But hedge-fund activists are dedicated to their own self-interest and frequently achieve their goals by sacrificing others, even if they tend to package their activities as being carried out for the sake of the common good. Similarly, the term "hedge fund" refers to the management of a financial portfolio by "hedging" risks, a trading strategy originally adopted by Alfred Winslow Jones when he set up the first-ever hedge fund, A.W. Jones & Co, in 1949. However, the term has now been appropriated by

Predatory Value Extraction: How the Looting of the Business Corporation Became the U.S. Norm and How Sustainable Prosperity Can Be Restored. William Lazonick and Jang-Sup Shin, Oxford University Press (2020).
© William Lazonick and Jang-Sup Shin.
DOI: 10.1093/oso/9780198846772.001.0001

speculators and manipulators who ply global financial markets in pursuit of "absolute returns" for themselves.[1]

For nearly half a century after the launch of the first hedge fund, the hedge-fund industry grew anemically overall, experiencing periods of both expansion and retraction.[2] From the 1990s, however, hedge funds exploded in size and number. The number of funds grew from around 610 in 1990 to about 11,000 in 2015. Assets under management (AUM) grew from about $39 billion in 1990 to over $3 trillion in 2016.[3] There were both pull and push factors in this explosive growth of the industry.

In the early 1990s, some spectacular hedge-fund success stories came to be known to the public. One sensational story was that of the estimated $1 billion gain George Soros reaped on Black Wednesday in 1992 by "breaking the Bank of England" through shorting the British pound. And not only that: His Soros Fund was reported to have generated an average annual return of more than 30 percent since its inception. Julian Robertson received the sobriquet "Wizard of Wall Street" by running the largest hedge fund of its period, Tiger Management, which reportedly turned an $8 million investment in 1980 into $7.2 billion in 1996, an annual return of over 30 percent.[4] Hedge funds were beginning to be accepted as special investment vehicles that could create a persistent "alpha"— extra yield above the benchmark yield. Whether hedge funds are actually generating "alpha" for their clients is currently a matter of controversy, and many pension funds are pulling out of their existing investments in hedge funds.[5] In the 1990s,

---

[1] Loomis (1966). The term "hedge fund" was coined by journalist Carol Loomis in 1966. As late as 2003 there was still no agreed-upon definition of a hedge fund, though professional commentators would point to several characteristics of the funds: restricted access, performance fees, the ability to short, and the ability to leverage investments (Vaughn 2003). Section 404 of the 2010 Dodd–Frank Act created a provision to collect "systemic-risk" data for the financial system of the United States, modifying the Investment Advisers Act of 1940 such that the SEC, through form PF (private fund), has collected statistics on private funds (including hedge funds) in the United States since 2012. Hedge funds that must file form PF are described as private funds with one or more of the characteristics of charging "performance fees," using leverage to multiply investment scale, and engaging in short selling. Dodd–Frank Act (2011).

[2] A period of rapid growth had swelled hedge funds' ranks to an estimated number of 200 and their total assets to about $1.5 billion by the late 1960s; in subsequent years, however, fund failures or investor withdrawals ensued. See SEC (1969); Machan and Atlas (1994); Loomis (1970).

[3] See Figure 6.1; Ahuja (2012); Dayen (2016). These estimates cannot necessarily be considered definitive, as in many cases they are based on voluntary disclosure by hedge funds and do not necessarily capture the entire universe of funds. The SEC suggests that in the second quarter of 2016 some 1,700 hedge-fund managers oversaw gross assets of $6.3 trillion (with net assets of $3.4 trillion) and 8,900 distinct funds (SEC 2016a). Even here, not necessarily all hedge funds would be tracked, as the SEC is focused mainly on advisers of funds that have $150 million or more in AUM. In any case, the "average" fund manager might oversee as much as $3.7 billion. The 9,000 funds reported to the SEC would average as much as $654 million in gross AUM.

[4] Reiff (2017).

[5] For instance, the first comprehensive study of U.S. pension funds' investment in hedge funds, "All That Glitters Is Not Gold" conducted by the Roosevelt Institute, examined hedge-fund performance for eleven large public pensions in the United States over 88 fiscal years (eight fiscal years for each pension fund) and concluded that hedge-fund investment actually resulted in "high costs with low returns"

however, the allocation of a portion of their portfolios to hedge-fund investing emerged as a promising "alternative investment" for institutional investors, endowments, and rich individuals in their continued search for higher yields. For institutional investors in particular, which were under heavy regulation in the use of short sales, swaps, and leverage, hedge-fund investing served as a proxy for employing those investment tools.

6.1.1 The 1996 NSMIA: Allowing Unlimited "Alternative Investment" in Hedge Funds

The 1996 National Securities Markets Improvement Act (NSMIA), which was part of financial-market deregulation during the Clinton administration, also provided hedge funds with an impetus for growth. To be exempt from regulation under the Investment Company Act of 1940 as a private fund, a hedge fund had to serve fewer than 100 "high-net-worth" investors, who were persons with a net worth of at least $1 million or who had generated income of at least $200,000 annually for the previous two years.[6] However, Section 209 of the NSMIA modified the Investment Company Act of 1940 to remove the long-existing regulation on the number of clients, creating an exemption for an unlimited number of "qualified purchasers" that could include any individual investor with a net worth of $5 million or more or any institutional investor with financial assets of $25 million or more.[7] The 1996 NSMIA therefore continued to treat hedge funds as private entities while granting them the ability to draw their assets under management from the financial resources of a substantially larger pool of investors, especially from institutional investors. This change, "largely unnoticed at the time" and "advanced with broad Wall Street support and almost no

(Parisian and Bhatti 2016). From 2001, CalPERS was in the vanguard among U.S. pension funds in allocating a portion of its portfolio to hedge-fund investment, but it announced in 2014 that it could no longer justify investing in hedge funds because of "its high costs and complexity." In earlier empirical research on hedge-fund performance, Stulz (2007) concluded that the persistent existence and size of alpha in hedge-fund investment was at best "controversial."

---

[6] Hedge funds are notable (and definable) largely by their strategy of organizing *outside* existing financial regulations applicable to larger institutional funds. As they are organized in this way, hedge funds today have no real restriction on their size. Their major benefits include the ability to utilize performance pay schemes such as "2 and 20" (2% annual fee and 20% performance fee) as well as trading strategies considered too speculative and risky for institutional investors. Hedge funds and other private funds are structured specifically to avoid thresholds that would trigger certain disclosure rules and other regulations. For example, under the Securities Act of 1933 a hedge fund seeking to be a private (i.e., unregistered) fund cannot publicly solicit prospective clients, the rationale being that "private placement" attracts informed, experienced investors.

[7] Existing regulations under the 1934 Securities Exchange Act would force registration with the SEC when and if the total number of investors reached 500 or if total assets exceeded $10 billion. In practice, then, the post-NSMIA environment created a "threshold" for hedge funds and an incentive to limit their population of investors to no more than 499 institutions or very wealthy individuals.

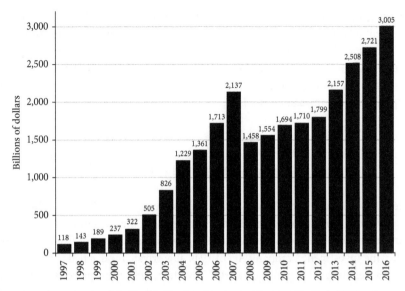

Fig. 6.1. The growth of the hedge-fund industry, 1997–2016 (AUM, $billions)
Source: BarclayHedge.

resistance in Congress," effectively allowed hedge funds to pool financial resources from institutional investors without regulations that would have required disclosure of the structure of their firms or prohibited overly speculative investments.[8]

As Figure 6.1 shows, it took only seven years after the enactment of NSMIA for hedge funds' AUM to increase more than tenfold, from $118 billion in 1997 to over $1.2 trillion in 2004. Since that time it has more than doubled, to over $3 trillion in 2016. While A.W. Jones' hedge fund managed approximately $70 million in 1966 (over $500 million in 2016 dollars), today there are several hedge funds managing in excess of $1 billion. The largest hedge fund in the world is probably Ray Dalio's Bridgewater Associates, with about $150 billion under management. A main contributor to this explosive growth and massive scale has been investment by institutional investors following the 1996 NSMIA. According to Preqin Global Hedge Fund Report published in 2016, about 5,073 institutional investors currently allocate funding to roughly 60 percent of hedge funds.[9] The leading sources of institutional funds are public and private pension funds and endowments, representing around 53 percent of the total assets of hedge funds. One of every five university endowment dollars is now invested in hedge funds.[10]

---

[8] Dayen (2016).   [9] Preqin (2016).
[10] The National Association of College and University Business Officers (http://www.nacubo.org/Research/Research_News/2013_Endowment_Study_Final_Report_Released.html).

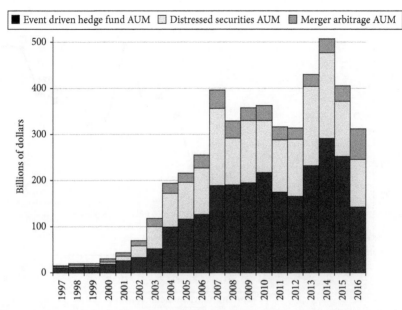

Fig. 6.2. The expansion of activist hedge funds, 1997–2016 (AUM, $billions; % share of AUM)

Source: BarclayHedge.

The rise of hedge-fund activism was a phenomenon that reflected the explosive growth of the overall hedge-fund industry that began in the 1990s. We estimate that the combined AUM of activist hedge funds increased almost eightfold in six years, from $15 billion in 1997 to $117 billion in 2003, and then more than quadrupled in the next 11 years, to reach $507 billion in 2014, as Figure 6.2 shows. The overall trend in the growth of hedge-fund activists' AUM is more or less the same in other estimates.[11]

The incidence of activist campaigns and their success ratio have also increased sharply. Schedule 13D filings with the SEC are often used as a proxy for activist campaigns because Schedule 13D must be filed when an investor accumulates a 5-percent-or-greater share of a corporation's outstanding stock, which also triggers a requirement that the investor disclose the purpose of its accumulation.[12]

---

[11] Following the SEC (2017) convention of including "distressed/restructuring" assets and "risk arbitrage/merger arbitrage" assets in "event-driven" assets, we estimated the AUM of activist hedge funds by combining "event-driven" assets, "distressed" assets, and "merger arbitrage" assets in BarclayHedge data above. The numbers then become similar to those of the SEC, where the overall size of "event-driven" assets is $430 billion. Marriage (2013), Foley and Johnson (2014), Chandler (2016), and Foley (2016) also equate activist assets with the overall assets devoted to an event-driven strategy.

[12] For instance, an investor should disclose whether it demands a change in management, stock buybacks or special dividends, a seat on the board, etc. In contrast, investors file schedule 13G when assuming a *passive* stake of 5 percent or more in a publicly traded corporation.

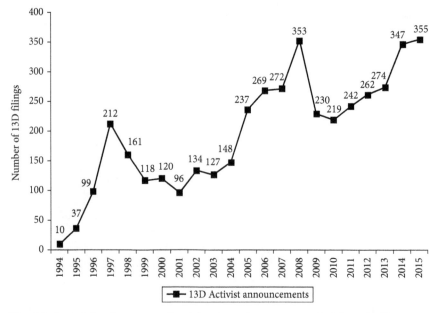

Fig. 6.3. Increasing frequency of activist campaigns as announced by 13D filings, 1994–2015

Note: The number of 13D filings may not be exhaustive; we have selected sources that find a greater number of campaigns than other, similar studies.

Sources: For the years 2008–16, *sharkrepellent.net* (August 31, 2016), accessed January 8, 2017 at https://www.sharkrepellent.net/. For the years 1994–2007, Bebchuk et al. (2015).

As Figure 6.3 shows, the incidence of 13D filings for activist purposes increased from 10 in 1994 to 212 in 1997.[13] It then increased to 353 in 2008. After a sharp reduction during the global financial crisis of 2008–09, the incidence recovered to 355 in 2015. In 2003, 39 percent of proxy fights for board seats resulted in settlements or victories for activists. This success rate soared to 60 percent in 2013.[14]

The quantum jump in the size of the hedge-fund industry that began in the mid-1990s was an important factor in the rise of hedge-fund activism. As the overall size of the hedge-fund industry was expanding, more specialized hedge funds that attacked publicly listed companies sprang up and activist hedge funds, broadly categorized as event-driven hedge funds, established themselves as a specialized asset class in the industry. The SEC currently classifies hedge funds by their strategies as follows: Equity ($1,528 billion, 35.3 percent), Relative Value ($722 billion, 16.7 percent), Macro ($546 billion, 12.6 percent), Event Driven

---

[13] The SEC requires purchasers of corporate stock to file form 13D within 10 days of the date on which their ownership stake crosses the 5-percent threshold. The form requires disclosure of the intent of the acquisition of stock.

[14] Laide (2014).

(Activist) ($377 billion, 8.7 percent), Credit ($279 billion, 6.4 percent), Managed Futures/CTA ($98 billion, 2.3 percent), Investment in Other Funds ($45 billion, 1.0 percent), and Other ($735 billion, 17.0 percent).[15] There is no doubt that hedge funds often mix these strategies in their actual operations. Nonetheless, the growth of the hedge-fund industry was accompanied by specialization within the industry.

6.1.2 The Transformation from Corporate Raiders to Hedge-Fund Activists

Another important factor in the rise of hedge-fund activism was regulatory change that strengthened shareholder activism by allowing "free communication and engagement" and introducing "compulsory voting" by institutional investors. In Chapter 5, we pointed out that the United Shareholders Association (USA), a lobbying organization set up by a leading corporate raider, T. Boone Pickens, declared "mission accomplished" and disbanded itself as soon as the 1992 proxy-rule amendments were passed.[16] With these regulatory changes, corporate raiders were able to evolve into hedge-fund activists.

In the late 1980s, the ability of corporate raiders to profit from their traditional takeover activities and greenmailing was reduced substantially. Their abusive behavior toward corporations and workers was increasingly coming under public scrutiny, prompting anti-greenmail as well as anti-takeover legislation.[17] Corporations strengthened their defenses against hostile takeovers by introducing devices such as "poison pills." Individual states also passed regulations such as "the freeze-out law," which made hostile takeovers more difficult. The junk-bond market, a major source of financial resources for corporate raiding, collapsed when Ivan Boesky, Michael Milken, and Dennis Levine were indicted and imprisoned.

The USA's lobbying for the proxy-rule change can be understood as an attempt to create a regulatory space for takeover activities in the face of adverse conditions.[18] The most critical part of the 1992 proxy-rule amendments was that they made it possible for "insurgents" or "dissidents" (as commonly called) to stage attacks on corporate management even when they held a minority of the company's shares. In the hostile-takeover movement of the 1980s, insurgents launched their campaigns by securing a significant shareholding in the company they were targeting in order to pose a credible threat to management that they had the potential to bring about changes in the power structure of the boardroom. For instance, when

---

[15] Securities and Exchange Commission (2017). Figure for 4Q 2015. CTA stands for commodity-trading advisors.
[16] See discussion in Section 5.3.   [17] Bruck (1989); Noked (2014).
[18] See Section 5.3 for details.

Carl Icahn was raiding TWA in 1985, he started by acquiring 25 percent of the airline's common stock and eventually, by increasing his share further, took control of the management of the company. He then took TWA private and managed it into bankruptcy in 1992.[19]

When, in 2013–15, the same Icahn demanded that Apple buy back $150 billion of its outstanding shares and undertake other "shareholder friendly" measures, his stake in the company was never greater than 0.9 percent.[20] During the "deal decade" of the 1980s, nobody holding such a small percentage of its shares would have dreamed of "threatening" the management of a major company. However, it has by now become common practice for hedge-fund activists to stage their interventions while holding a tiny minority of total shares outstanding.

Hedge-fund activists currently exert enormous power over corporations. As law professor and *New York Times* columnist Steven Davidoff Solomon points out, after the announcement of the hedge-fund-engineered merger between Dow Chemical and Du Pont in December 2015, "companies, frankly, are scared" and now "the mantra in corporate America is to settle with hedge funds before it gets to a fight over the control of a company." He even argued, "When historians look back at this era, they will see this [Dow–DuPont] deal as a turning point when corporate leaders threw up their hands and surrendered to activist shareholders."[21]

The power these hedge-fund activists can wield while holding only a small percentage of a corporation's stock derives mainly from the fact that the 1992 proxy-rule changes allowed the formation of de facto investor cartels. Activists are now free to communicate with each other and to form a common front against their target company until the shareholding of one among them reaches the 5-percent threshold. In contrast, management is left in the dark, not knowing what the actual or potential size of the "wolf pack" is. "Free engagement" has also strengthened the position of minority insurgents. After acquiring a small share-holding in the company, activists can freely engage with management and gauge its potential responses while expressing their "concerns." "Free speech" has also bolstered activists: They are now free to criticize management through press conferences, websites, advertisements, and other means of public expression.

As a result of the 1992 proxy-rule change, maneuvers by activists have become more "political." Previously corporate raiders only needed to persuade other shareholders to sell them their shares, and then, armed with a significant share-holding and a willingness to take over the target company eventually, they could determine its destiny. Hedge-fund activists, in contrast, need only to form a broad, united front by recruiting enough other shareholders to reach the level of voting

---

[19] Williams (1986); Stevens (1993); Chandler (1994); Grant (2006).
[20] Lazonick et al. (2016a).   [21] Solomon (2015).

power at which they can exert influence on the board. This process is analogous to recruiting voters for political causes by establishing a common front to win an election. It should also be noted that there is a political advantage in taking action against corporations as minority shareholders. Differentiating themselves from greedy corporate raiders who took over the whole company and stripped its assets to increase their wealth, hedge-fund activists can portray themselves as weak "minority shareholders" victimized by management and promising justice for all shareholders. In this way, hedge-fund activists position themselves as proponents of shareholder democracy rather than as corporate raiders.

6.1.3 "Co-Investments" between Hedge-Fund Activists and Institutional Investors

The most important component of the de facto investor cartels is actual and potential "co-investment" by hedge-fund activists and institutional investors. As we discussed in Chapter 5, institutional investors became more active through the 1980s and the 1990s. Compulsory voting imposed on them by the Avon letter in 1988 and the final rule of proxy voting in 2003 provided a further impetus to strengthening their overall activism. Moreover, corporate shareholding became concentrated among an extremely small number of "King Kong" institutional investors. Under these circumstances, it is easier for hedge-fund activists to exert power over corporations, provided they can secure support from large institutional investors. And the potential for co-investment has increased significantly, with institutional investors currently supplying about 60 percent of hedge funds' AUM. Of course, institutional investors claim that they vote independently of hedge-fund activists, which is what they are supposed to do. However, it is highly likely that, if an institutional investor holds shares both in a company targeted by an activist hedge fund and in the hedge fund itself, it will know the hedge fund's intended actions in advance and will have an incentive to cooperate with it in order to raise its yield from the hedge-fund investment. Anecdotal evidence of co-investment abounds.

For instance, it was revealed during the proxy battle between DuPont and Trian Partners that the California Teachers Retirement System (CalSTRS)—a leader amongst pension-fund activists and currently the third-largest pension fund in the United States, with AUM of $198.7 billion as of January 2017—had cooperated with Trian's campaign from the beginning. DuPont's management had never thought of this possibility because CalSTRS was a long-term shareholder and the company "generally had a congenial working relationship with the pension fund." But CalSTRS co-signed an early letter supporting Trian when the latter attacked DuPont in 2015 and turned out later to be one of the hedge fund's major investors. In detailing how DuPont went to war with Trian, *Fortune* magazine reported that "[t]ies like that have made it harder for companies like DuPont to argue that siding with activists isn't in the interest of shareholders."[22]

The most detailed incidence of co-investment revealed publicly so far has probably been that between CalSTRS and Relational Investors LLC, an activist hedge fund set up by Ralph V. Whitworth and David H. Batchelder, who used to work with T. Boone Pickens as fellow corporate raiders. CalSTRS committed $1 billion to Relational, $300 million to Trian, and $100 million to Starboard in 2013. Working in tandem from the beginning, Relational and CalSTRS increased their participation in Timken, a fifth-generation family business producing high-quality steel and bearings, until the holding of each reached the 5-percent thresh-old for a 13D filing. As part of their attempt to push the Timken family into breaking the company into two separate entities and increasing stock buybacks, Relational and CalSTRS set up a website, "unlocktimken.com," that criticized Timken management publicly. An investment officer from CalSTRS joined a roadshow organized by Relational, flying to New York to meet fellow pension-fund managers. A seat on the Timken board was filled by a CalSTRS representa-tive, and "the pension fund, long a champion of better corporate governance, made the case that Timken's board was dominated by family members who paid themselves liberally and put their own interests ahead of shareholders' interests."[23] In April 2012, three weeks before the proxy vote, Relational and CalSTRS put out a news release calling Tim Timken's $9 million pay package in 2011 "grossly out-of-line with other executive chairmen in Timken's peer group."[24] Their proposal to split the company into Timken and TimkenSteel eventually garnered 53 percent of shareholder votes.[25] The Timken case remains one of the most prominent cases of "how finance gutted manufacturing."[26]

A number of factors beyond the regulatory changes that opened the door to co-investment account for the practice's having become widespread. First, finan-cial investors, hedge funds and pension funds share a similar worldview that is focused on "shareholder value," which is different from corporate executives' responsibility to create corporate value by producing high-quality, low-cost goods and services. Second, as the dominance of the MSV view has grown among financiers and managers, it has become easier for hedge-fund activists and institutional investors to collaborate with each other under the common banner of that ideology. Third, even if an institutional investor should pursue long-term gains, its fund managers tend nonetheless to seek short-term gains because their compensation is based on short-term performance evaluations and therefore tend to ally with hedge-fund activists. A *Fortune* report following

---

[22] Gandel (2015).　　[23] Schwartz (2014).
[24] Relational Investors and CalSTRS (2013).
[25] Denning (2014); Orol (2014); Schwartz (2014).　　[26] Berger (2014).

the release of a letter to CEOs from BlackRock head Laurence Fink urging a long-term approach offers a vivid illustration: "[T]aking a very small survey of companies in the S&P 500, [we] immediately ran into two that said the BlackRock analysts covering them had their own short-term demands—for good quarterly results. 'My guy's a fanatic,' reported the CEO of one of those companies. So it cannot be said that Fink's letter has even influenced the whole of BlackRock."[27]

6.2 Hedge-Fund Activists' Methods of Predatory Value Extraction

Over the past decade, the extent and power of hedge-fund activism have increased to the point that no corporation in the United States is immune to attack. Indeed, hedge-fund activism has gone global, taking aim at, among others, Nokia in Finland,[28] Alcatel-Lucent in France,[29] Samsung in Korea,[30] 7-Eleven in Japan,[31] Fanuc in Japan,[32] Unilever in the UK and the Netherlands,[33] Akzo Nobel in the Netherlands,[34] BHP Billiton in Australia,[35] and ThyssenKrupp in Germany.[36] The modes of attack are various, and so too is the length of time that it takes for a hedge-fund activist to reap the gains. A knowledge of the methods of value extraction by which this predation takes place is of utmost importance to understanding the gross imbalance between value creation and value extraction that exists in the U.S. economy.

By definition, activist shareholders do not sit on the sidelines, putting their shares in bank safe-deposit boxes, collecting the dividends that the company chooses to pay, and ignoring opportunities to time the sale of their shares. Rather, they take actions to influence the company's distribution policies, whether it be through the implied threat of a proxy fight over demands for activist-friendly seats on the board of directors or, if it goes so far, an actual proxy fight. In many cases, these value-extracting outsiders are coming up against senior executives who have already been incentivized to act as value-extracting insiders, and together they engage harmoniously in looting the corporation. Should the outsiders need to put pressure on the insiders to take actions designed to boost the company's stock price, they can turn for proxy support to institutional investors, who are generally ready and willing to play the role of value-extracting enablers.

In attempting to influence corporate decision-making, the goal of the hedge-fund activist is, despite frequent claims to the contrary, *not* to improve a target company's operations or its financial stability. Nor is it to contribute expertise to formulating an innovative investment strategy with the potential to generate the

---

[27] Loomis (2014).   [28] Foley and Thomas (2013).   [29] Owusu (2015).
[30] Mundy (2016).   [31] Fujikawa and Narioka (2016).   [32] Ando (2015).
[33] Quinn (2017).   [34] Sterling (2017).   [35] Stewart (2017).   [36] McGee (2018).

next round of high-quality, low-cost products. Hedge-fund activists have neither the abilities nor the incentives to engage in the allocation of corporate resources to innovative strategies, which require massive financial commitments in pursuit of inherently uncertain outcomes combined with an intimate understanding of the company's productive capabilities and competitive possibilities. Taking their activist campaigns from one industry to the next, they never attain the deep knowledge of technologies, markets, and competitors needed to operate successfully in any of them. More important, they have no incentive to acquire, run, and maintain value-creating capability: Their goal is to extract value that was created in the past, not to engage in the innovative strategies that may create value in the future.

As we have seen in Chapter 3, the value-creating process depends on the efficacy of the collective and cumulative learning in which the company invests. But, through their methods of value extraction, hedge-fund activists tend to destroy those organizational processes through which learning takes place. As a general principle, activists' methods aim, first, to increase the cash flow over which the company has control, and, second, to distribute as much of this enhanced cash flow as they can to themselves.

Methods for increasing the volume of company cash that activist hedge funds can tap include mass layoffs of employees, avoidance of corporate taxes, price gouging of customers, sale of corporate assets, and acquisition of other cash-rich companies. Siphoning the cash off to the value extractors can be accomplished via cash dividends—including in many cases large, one-time special dividends—and stock repurchases. Dividends, an important mode of value extraction when the hedge-fund activists hold shares for an extended period of time, enrich hedge-fund activists, along with other shareholders, by providing a stream of income while shareholders actually *hold* their shares. Buybacks, however, yield gains for shareholders only when they decide to *sell* the shares. To gain an extra advantage from buybacks, the sales must be timed to take place when the buybacks are giving the company's stock price a temporary manipulative boost.

As discussed in Chapter 4, under SEC Rule 10b-18, U.S.-listed companies are not required to disclose, either at the time or after the fact, on which particular days they buy back their own shares. Senior executives have this information, of course, and since the SEC does not monitor when buybacks are done, they have every opportunity to trade on this insider information without fear of detection. As outsiders, hedge-fund activists should not have access to this non-disclosed information. Given that they are in the business of making gains from the buying and selling of shares, however, it may be fair to assume that hedge-fund activists can find out when buybacks are taking place, by gaining access to insider information (having a representative on the company's board can be very valuable in this regard); by observing the activities of the company's brokers, since Rule 10b-18 stipulates that all open-market repurchases on any given day must be done through one broker only; or by detecting trading patterns related to Rule 10b-18's "zero plus tick requirement."[37] Given the centrality of stock-price increases to the value that hedge-funds are able to extract from companies, hedge-find activists are universally in favor of stock buybacks.

The parties whom we call "predatory value extractors" are often accused of being "short-termists." But particularly in the case of a company that is generating substantial revenues, it may be worthwhile for the hedge-fund activist to hold its shares for years, during which the dual processes of enhancing and extracting cash flow can take place. Moreover, its methods may fail to yield the enhanced cash flows or higher stock prices expected, and the activist may have to wait years until a good opportunity for value extraction actually occurs. And, of course, methods meant to enhance cash flow for the sake of value extraction may fail, leaving the hedge-fund activist with a loss that, depending on the circumstances, may be huge. A recent case in point is the play of William Ackman's Pershing Capital for the drug company Valeant, which extended from March 2015 to March 2017, ending in a loss to Ackman of $4 billion.[38] After Valeant had failed in its attempt to acquire Allergan, possessed of a high cash flow emanating from its line of Botox products, Valeant's extreme price-gouging strategy evoked negative public attention.[39] Valeant's stock price, which had reached almost $207 in March 2015, averaged less than $12 in March 2017, when Ackman bailed out.

The biggest hedge-fund activists at any given time have obviously won far more than they have lost. Table 6.1 provides a list of the top ten hedge-fund activists in early 2016. Combined, these top ten had $130 billion in assets under management. The leader by far is Icahn Enterprises, run by Carl Icahn. His career as a corporate predator goes back to the 1970s, and in his early 80s he showed no signs of letting up. Indeed, for the first eight months of his friend Donald Trump's tenure in the White House, Icahn held a position as presidential adviser on corporate affairs— the official title being "Special Adviser to the President on Regulatory Reform"— charged with identifying for eradication any government regulations that

---

[37] For evidence on how professional traders can use Rule 10b-18's "zero plus tick requirement" to determine the days on which buybacks are being done, see Ramsay (2018). In this letter to the SEC regarding "A Petition for Rulemaking to Amend Rule 10b-18," Jack Ramsay, Chief Market Policy Officer of Investors Exchange LLC, argues that the "zero plus tick requirement" makes "corporate buyback orders predictable, easy to detect, and easy to exploit, thus opening the door for short-term traders to take advantage of these orders for short-term profit." Ramsay continues: "This problem is well-known in the industry and undermines the ability of a corporate issuer or broker acting on its behalf to properly construct a trading strategy to effectively purchase shares with minimal detection at the best prevailing prices. As the global head of trading at a large asset manager put it: 'When it comes to handling the corporate buyback, what's painfully obvious to us is that the corporate buyback is probably the most gameable order in the marketplace. If you pursue liquidity in a corporate buyback algorithm, other participants can easily sense how the algorithm is going to react and try to trade in front of it.'" See also McCrank (2018).
[38] Israel (2017).   [39] Eisinger (2014a); Pollack and Tavernise (2015).

Table 6.1. Top ten hedge-fund activists by assets under management (AUM), 2016

Rank	Company name	Key manager	AUM, $ billion
1	Icahn Enterprises	Carl Icahn	32.3
2	Third Point	Daniel Loeb	22.6
3	ValueAct	Jeff Ubben	19.4
4	Pershing Square	William Ackman	14.8
5	Cevian Capital	Christer Gardell	11.7
6	Trian	Nelson Peltz	11.3
7	Sachem Head	Scott Ferguson	4.7
8	Starboard Value	Jeffrey Smith	4.7
9	MHR	Mark Rachesky	4.6
10	Blue Harbor Group	Clifton Robbins	3.8

Source: Rachel Butt, "Here are the 10 biggest activist money managers and some of their most impressive bets," *Business Insider*, June 17, 2016.

stood as obstacles to the brand of value extraction Icahn himself has long practiced.[40] After just over three months as a Presidential policy adviser, however, Icahn caught the attention of a number of U.S. Democratic senators, who accused him of using his political influence for his own personal gain.[41] Rather than continue to face public scrutiny, in August 2017 Icahn quit his special-adviser post.[42]

A survey of the methods of predatory value extraction that Icahn has used over the course of his career provides a clear window into how hedge-fund activists can build their "war chests"—a term that Icahn has long used to describe his AUM— to be more powerfully positioned to prey on business corporations while even affording to make a substantially bad bet here and there. In what follows, we look at Icahn's emergence in the 1980s as a highly visible and successful corporate raider whose career foundered, albeit temporarily, with his calamitous takeover of TWA. Then, using data from the Forbes 400 annual lists of the wealthiest people in the United States, we note that during the last half of the 1990s and into the 2000s, Icahn was able to reverse his fortune, which had been in decline during and just subsequent to his stint at TWA, to expand his net worth dramatically, to the point that he consistently appeared among the thirty richest Americans from 2002 on. It would require an entire book to provide a complete analysis of the sources that have fueled Icahn's vast wealth over the last two decades; in what follows we document the types of activities in which Icahn has been involved. It was only in 2004 that he set up his first hedge fund, which he closed down in 2011 so that he could apply his talents for value extraction using only his recently replenished personal resources in order to avoid being beholden to or constrained by outside investors.

[40] Benoit (2016).   [41] Stevenson (2017).   [42] Goldstein and Stevenson (2017).

6.3 Carl Icahn as a Corporate Raider

Born in New York in 1936, Icahn went to work on Wall Street in 1961, having earned an undergraduate degree in philosophy from Princeton University and spent two years of medical school at New York University. In 1968, he set up his own firm, Icahn & Company, which engaged in risk arbitrage and options trading. In 1976, Icahn, along with his stock picker, Alfred Kingsley, sent a memo to prospective investors promoting a fund designed to go after companies with what they deemed to be undervalued shares, with a view to gaining from selling the stock once its value had been boosted. This document, dubbed "The Icahn Manifesto" by Icahn's biographer, Mark Stevens, laid out both the objective and the basic methods of the proposed endeavor:

> It is our contention that *sizeable profits can be earned by taking large positions in "undervalued" stocks and then attempting to control the destinies of corporations in question by*:
> a) trying to convince management to liquidate or sell the company to a "white knight";
> b) waging a proxy contest;
> c) making a tender offer, and/or;
> d) selling back our position to the company.[43]

Icahn's actual career as a corporate raider commenced in 1977, when he began buying up shares in Ohio-based Tappan, a kitchen-appliance company.[44] To Icahn, what the company produced was irrelevant. All that mattered was that he could make money by using one or more of the methods in his Manifesto. He amassed 10 percent of Tappan's shares and, in April 1979, won a seat on Tappan's board. From that position, he pushed Tappan to put itself up for acquisition with the expectation that competitive bidding for the company would lift its stock price.[45] When Tappan was sold to the Swedish company Electrolux in December 1979 at a 50-percent stock-price premium, Icahn took home $2.7 million.[46]

With his growing visibility, by the early 1980s Icahn did not necessarily have to gain a seat on the board of a company and help engineer its sale in order to extract a price premium for his shares. Icahn developed a reputation for being extraordinarily aggressive, untrustworthy, and persistent in his corporate raids, an approach that he used to increase the possibility that, when challenged, incumbent management would in effect pay him to go away. That is indeed what happened at two companies, Anchor Hocking and Owens-Illinois, that Icahn attacked in

---

[43] Stevens (1993); Carlisle (2014).   [44] Stevens (1993: 44).
[45] Business Week 1979.   [46] Stevens (1993: 57).

1982.[47] This practice became known as "greenmail"; the term appeared in print in a July 1983 report of the SEC's Advisory Committee on Tender Offers, which drew upon a conference the agency had hosted the previous month at which Icahn had been a participant. A "glossary of terms" in this report defined greenmail as "the purchase of a substantial block of the subject company's securities by an unfriendly suitor with the primary purpose of coercing the subject into repurchasing the block at a premium over the amount paid by the suitor."[48]

In an interview with *Business Week* in 1979, Icahn said: "I feel strongly about corporate democracy, about shareholders having more say in what they want from their investments. . . . When a company's performance is poor, something should happen to that management to ensure a return for the shareholders."[49] But the willingness of Icahn to engage in greenmail makes it clear that his "activism" had nothing to do with "shareholder democracy."

Icahn told his biographer, Mark Stevens: "If two sides to a negotiation sit down to work something out, say how to split $100 million, conventional wisdom holds that a fair approach is always best: ideally 50/50. But I want 100 percent. Why should I be satisfied with anything less?"[50] It was not simply a matter of greed, although, like Gordon Gekko of the Oliver Stone film *Wall Street*, Icahn undoubtedly believes that "greed is good." Icahn saw himself as a "lone wolf" who, to gain the power to extract value from companies, needed to build up a "war chest" of financial resources under his control. This fund would have the capacity to strike fear in the hearts of his targets and, if need be, to enable him to outlast them until he could sell his shares at much higher prices than he had originally paid for them. With every use of his war chest, he would be able to add yet more to it.

In 1978, Icahn had begun accumulating shares in Baird & Warner Mortgage & Realty Investors, a longstanding real estate investment trust (REIT) in Chicago. In this case, Icahn was after more than greenmail: He wanted a seat on the board so that he could push for the company's liquidation, the proceeds of which would further build his war chest. Each success in extracting value would allow him to accumulate more money of his own to work with, which he leveraged with money from investors in his fund as well as borrowed money, including shares bought on margin.[51] Stevens recounts how in 1982 Icahn built what was his "biggest war chest" to date to go after retailer Marshall Field. The Icahn group accumulated a 29 percent stake in the company in the winter of 1982, prompting Marshall Field

---

[47] Wall Street Journal (1982a; 1982b). For how Icahn's attack on Anchor Hocking set in motion the financialization of the company, wreaking havoc on Lancaster, Ohio, where the company had been based since 1905, see Alexander (2017: ch. 3); Lazonick (2017a).

[48] Securities and Exchange Commission (1983). The first use of the term "greenmail" in the press that we have located is Cook (1983), which referred to the SEC "Report on Recommendations." See also Christian Science Monitor (1983), which reproduces a portion of the glossary of terms in the "Report on Recommendations." In the wake of the "deal decade" of the 1980s, a number of states made greenmail illegal. See Noked (2014).

[49] Stevens (1993: 59).   [50] Stevens (1993: xi).

[51] Stevens (1993: 41). There are eight references to Icahn's "war chest" in the Stevens book.

to seek to sell itself to a "white knight," British American Tobacco (BAT), which twice raised its bid price before Icahn, as Marshall Field's largest shareholder, would agree to the sale.

Also in 1982, just after greenmail successes with Anchor Hocking and Owens-Illinois, Icahn acquired almost 7 percent of Dan River, a long-established and sizable textile manufacturer headquartered in Danville, Virginia, a company town. He eventually increased his stake to 22 percent of the voting shares to make Dan River,[52] only 2 percent of whose stock was closely held by others, vulnerable to a takeover.[53] Dan River's management mobilized the whole town of Danville against the corporate raider and, after having attempted a number of legal maneuvers to block Icahn's bid for control and sought out a "white knight," persuaded the company's employees to trade in their pensions for an Employee Stock Ownership Plan (ESOP). The ESOP purchased Icahn's shares, netting him $8 million.[54]

Icahn would need a war chest vastly larger than any he had commanded previously when, in 1986, he accumulated 40 percent of the shares outstanding of a then-leading U.S. airline, TWA. According to TWA CEO Ed Meyer, Icahn was "mesmerized by the $400–$500 million cash flow he saw in TWA." Meyer recounts how, with reference to this cash flow, he told the corporate raider: "Carl, that won't even cover the airplanes that you will have to buy."[55] Icahn would learn the truth of this statement: When TWA's share price fell, he had to assume control of the airline himself.

In accumulating his shares and, ultimately, assuming control, Icahn had out-competed Frank Lorenzo, owner of Texas International Airlines, a vehicle for taking over other airlines, including Continental in 1981. Since Lorenzo was known as a union-buster, TWA's unions saw Icahn as the lesser of two evils and made deals with him concerning wage and benefit concessions to go into effect should he take control of the company. These union agreements, and the opportunity for value extraction that they promised, induced Icahn to buy more TWA shares.[56]

Now Icahn actually had to run the airline to extricate himself from his huge investment in its shares. As the business journalist Carol Loomis put it in her *Fortune* cover story, "The Comeuppance of Carl Icahn," which appeared in February 1986, "the stock for which Icahn paid about $300 million is worth $227 million. He bought the stock on margin, has had margin calls, and is stuck with large carrying costs on the debt."[57]

Loomis continued: "Though Icahn has control of TWA, he cannot siphon out its cash. Agreements with lenders and unions (two of which have granted him large wage concessions) hamper his ability to pay dividends to himself and other shareholders or to distribute corporate cash to shareholders by repurchasing

[52] Wall Street Journal (1982c).   [53] Stevens (1993: 98).   [54] Stevens (1993: 108).
[55] Stevens (1993).   [56] Stevens (1993).   [57] Loomis (2013).

TWA stock. To prevent Icahn from profiting at the expense of other shareholders, a special watchdog committee of former TWA directors must approve transactions between TWA and other Icahn entities for two years."

In 1992, after Icahn had run TWA for six years, the company declared bankruptcy. The TWA phase of Icahn's career was not his finest hour—or, more precisely, his finest six years. Another deal that took up a lot of Icahn's attention in the late 1980s—with minimal gain, but without losses on the scale of the TWA fiasco—was his raid on USX, the conglomerate that had been built out of US Steel. Of that episode, which commenced in 1986 and concluded in 1991, Icahn's biographer wrote: "[H]is gross profit on the trade was only about $183 million. From this he had to take deductions for his costly proxy battles and interest on his margin purchases over the term of the investment. Even when the USX dividends are factored in, he would have fared better by investing his money in T-bills over the same period of time."[58]

Meanwhile, the "deal decade" of the 1980s had melted down as two of its biggest operators, Michael Milken and Ivan Boesky, went to jail for insider trading. In 1985, Icahn had had the backing of Milken's "junk bond" network in a bid to take over Phillips Petroleum.[59] But Icahn mistrusted Boesky, who functioned as the "arbitrageur" in the Milken coordinated raids, buying up blocks of shares that were then delivered to the actual raider—which was Icahn in the case of Phillips. Icahn had only indirect contact with Milken, and he was too independent to become part of the junk-bond king's inner circle. In February 1985, with Phillips in play, the company adopted a "poison pill" that would have turned shareholder equity into substantial debt should a raider accumulate 30 percent of outstanding shares. By the beginning of March, Icahn had dropped his takeover bid, but Phillips then made a tender offer to shareholders that yielded the corporate raider $50 million, plus $25 million for his bid expenses.[60]

If the Phillips raid netted Icahn $50 million in gains over a period of three months, he did even better in his subsequent attack from 1987 to 1989 on Texaco, one of the world's biggest petroleum companies. In this case, exploiting his position of strategic control over TWA, Icahn used TWA funds to accumulate Texaco shares to support his takeover bid. Icahn did not win the subsequent proxy fight, in part because Texaco's management appealed to the company's shareholders with a $2.4 billion special dividend in 1989.[61] Nevertheless, when Icahn sold his Texaco shares in June 1989, he booked a gain of over $500 million for a 19-month engagement.[62]

Icahn was the most visible corporate raider to emerge from the hostile-takeover movement of the 1980s. Icahn entered the list of the Forbes 400 list of wealthiest Americans in 1987 with a net worth of $525 million, placing him at number 120

---

[58] Stevens (1993).　　[59] Stevens (1993).　　[60] Potts (1985).
[61] Quint (1989).　　[62] Stevens (1993).

Table 6.2. Carl Icahn's estimated net worth and rank among wealthiest Americans, 1986–2018

Year	Icahn's net worth, $m	Rank in Forbes 400	Year	Icahn's net worth, $m	Rank in Forbes 400	Year	Icahn's net worth, $m	Rank in Forbes 400
1986	175	near miss	1997	2,000	70	2008	12,000	20
1987	525	120	1998	2,600	62	2009	10,500	22
1988	940	55	1999	4,200	41	2010	11,000	24
1989	1,200	63	2000	4,500	53	2011	13,000	25
1990	1,000	65	2001	5,000	31	2012	14,800	21
1991	660	138	2002	5,800	27	2013	20,300	18
1992	650	83	2003	7,300	26	2014	26,000	16
1993	575	164	2004	7,600	21	2015	20,500	22
1994	400	306	2005	8,500	24	2016	15,700	26
1995	500	264	2006	9,700	24	2017	16,700	27
1996	950	164	2007	14,500	18	2018	16,300	31

Source: Forbes 400 lists, various editions, *Forbes* magazine.

(see Table 6.2); his wealth that year was three times greater than in 1986, when he had just missed making the *Forbes* list. By 1989 his estimated wealth had more than doubled, to $1.2 billion, giving him a rank of number 63; as he absorbed his losses from TWA, it declined, its lowest point being $400 million in 1994. Then Icahn started to climb the *Forbes* list, reaching 31st in 2001, and then ranking higher than that through 2017. In 2018, *Forbes* put his net worth at $16.3 billion, making him the 31st richest person in the United States.[63]

A *New York Times* article published in June 1996 asked: "Where, oh where, have all the corporate raiders gone?"[64] Looking back, it observed: "They were the much-feared and often reviled commanders of the takeover wars of the 1980's. Fueled by junk bonds, they raided corporate America seemingly at will, and made vast fortunes. In their heyday, they hobnobbed with the junk-bond king Michael R. Milken at his annual 'Predators' Ball'." The article then provided updates on the whereabouts and activities of the most prominent value-extractors of the 1980s, including Carl C. Icahn:

> Mr. Icahn is perhaps the busiest of the bunch. He is now trying to wrest control of RJR Nabisco Holdings to force a spinoff of the food business from the tobacco operations, a move that he contends would produce a bonanza for stockholders. Mr. Icahn failed to win control of the board of the RJR Nabisco Holdings Corporation with his ally, Bennett S. LeBow, in April, but earlier this month he severed his agreement with Mr. LeBow, an increasingly unpopular figure with Wall Street. Mr. Icahn has also changed with the times, seeking out stakes in

---

[63] Kroll and Dolan (2018).   [64] Isa (1996).

distressed companies that he can turn into good investments. In 1995, he bought up debt of Rockefeller Center Properties Inc., the trust that holds the $1.3 billion mortgage on Rockefeller Center. Mr. Icahn has also gone into the consolidator business in a deal he made with Trans World Airlines Inc., a company he once owned. As part of its bankruptcy restructuring, T.W.A. gave Mr. Icahn the right to buy tickets with a face value of $610 million at a discount and then resell them. The airline plans to use the money it gets from selling him the tickets to pay him back the $190 million it owes him."

In 1997 Andrew Serwer, who frequently reported on Icahn in *Fortune*, wrote:

Carl Icahn is the one raider who never went away. True, he doesn't make runs at the likes of Phillips Petroleum anymore—and Lord knows, he doesn't try to actually run companies anymore, as he did during his disastrous stint at the helm of TWA some years ago. But he pops up a lot, usually on the periphery of a deal gone sour. He's constantly on the prowl for situations he can exploit profitably. His chief m.o. is to scoop up bonds of companies that are either bankrupt or close to it. Then he may use his clout as a major bondholder to extract terms that will ensure that he makes money.[65]

6.4 Carl Icahn as a Hedge-Fund Activist

As can be seen from the Forbes 400 data in Table 6.2, from the last half of the 1990s, Icahn was able to increase his net worth far beyond anything that he had achieved as a corporate raider: In nominal dollars, his net worth as estimated by *Forbes* grew every year from 1994 through 2007, when it reached $14.5 billion to place him 18th on the Forbes 400 list. His estimated fortune declined somewhat in the financial crisis of 2008–09, but Icahn turned that around, increasing his net worth to $26 billion in 2014, an accumulation that lifted him to a personal best of 16th on the *Forbes* list. Since 2014 Icahn's wealth, as estimated by *Forbes*, has declined substantially, but he remains among the richest people in the United States.

While we cannot vouch for the accuracy of the *Forbes* estimates of Icahn's wealth and its evolution over time, we have gathered together data, displayed in Table 6.3, on a selection of Icahn's activities since 1996 and the reported gains or losses from these deals. We do not seek to be comprehensive in Table 6.3. Rather, our purpose is to show the range of Icahn's undertakings over the past two decades and the magnitudes of their gains and losses. The information in Table 6.3 should be seen as the basis for a research agenda on how, in the age of hedge-fund activism, the most experienced among this new breed of corporate raider has extracted tens of billions of dollars from the U.S corporate economy.

---

[65] Serwer and Woods (1997).

Table 6.3. Carl Icahn's selected value-extracting activities and reported financial results, 1995–2017

Dates	Company Name	Description of Icahn's value-extracting activity	Reported financial results
1995–2000	RJR Nabisco	Proxy contests, demands spin-off, buys and sells the stock more than once	$893 million
2004–2005	Mylan Labs and King Pharma	Blocks merger with King, "long/short" position generates value on the news	$40–$70 million
2004–2006	Kerr-McGee	Stock Buybacks, argues for sale of company, spin off of chemical business	$470 million minimum
2006–2008	ImClone	Credited with engineering acquisition by Eli Lilly, leading to buyout of shareholders at 50% premium	$418 million
2004–2010	Blockbuster	Bankruptcy following activism that includes CEO removal, board member replacement	−$180 million
2007–2011	Motorola	Spin off, IP sale, stock buybacks	$1,340 million
2009–2011	Genzyme	Proxy contest, stock buybacks, helped to bid up sale of company to Sanofi	$300 million
2008–2012	Amylin	Proxy contest, stock buybacks, sale of company to Bristol-Myers Squibb	$115 million
2010–2014	Forest Labs	Acquisition by Actavis	$600 million
2012–2015	Netflix	Acquires 10% of Netflix to begin agitating for a sale of the company, but ends up riding stock's meteoric rise, sells holdings one year later for $800 million, retains 4.5% stake sold in 2015 for over $1 billion	$1,900 million
2010–2016	Chesapeake Oil	Takes loss "for tax purposes"	−$500 million
2013–2016	TransOcean	Special dividend, loses money, files capital loss "for tax purposes"	−$1,100 million
2013–2016	Apple	Demands massive stock buybacks, Apple complies with largest buybacks in history	$2,000 million

Source: Data collected for this report by Matt Hopkins, The Academic-Industry Research Network, from a variety of published sources.

Icahn's most lucrative single gambit over these two decades has been the transformation of $3.6 billion in Apple shares held over slightly more than two and a half years on the public market into $5.6 billion in cash, for a $2.0 billion gain by March 31, 2016, at which time Icahn had sold all of his Apple shares.[66] In August 2013 Icahn announced that he had purchased 27,125,441 shares of the publicly traded stock of Apple Inc.[67] By the end of January 2014, Icahn had

---

[66] Lazonick et al. (2016a).
[67] All stock prices and share counts have been adjusted to reflect Apple's 7:1 stock split for share-holders of record on June 2, 2014.

increased his stake in Apple to 52,760,848 shares, equal to 0.9 percent of the company's outstanding shares, at the $3.6 billion total purchase price. We analyze Icahn's method of value extraction as a hedge-fund activist by focusing on this most prominent case.[68]

When on August 13, 2013, Icahn announced his first purchase of Apple shares, he said in an interview that it was a "no brainer" because "even without earnings growth, we think [an Apple share] ought to be worth $625 [$89 stock-split adjusted]," on a day that the stock closed at $463 [$66 adjusted].[69] What made Apple shares a "no brainer"—a term that Icahn would repeat in a letter to Apple shareholders in January 2014, as well as in a few tweets—was that Apple had the cash and borrowing capacity to do massive stock buybacks that could jack up the price of its shares.

On April 28, 2016—four weeks after Icahn had sold his last share and two days after Apple had disclosed its first year-on-year quarterly sales decline in 13 years—Icahn told CNBC that he had unloaded his Apple holdings because he was "worried about China," where unsteady business conditions meant Apple stock was "not the no-brainer it was" when he had bought it.[70] It was then that he revealed that his 32-month foray into Apple shares had netted him $2 billion.

How, with ostensibly little mental effort, did Icahn reap a gain of some $2 billion in 32 months? The answer to this question is undoubtedly of interest to activist shareholders who would like to emulate King Icahn.[71] But it should be of even more interest to legislators, regulators, and informed citizens who would like to put an end to the extreme concentration of income at the top that has come to be a defining characteristic of the U.S. economy.

In actuality, Icahn's "no brainer" entailed a well-thought-out strategy, honed by decades of experience, for buying, holding, and selling a company's shares—in this case those of Apple, one of the most successful companies in history before Icahn had anything to do with it. The implementation of this strategy depended on at least four factors: (1) wealth, (2) visibility, (3) hype, and (4) influence. And there is circumstantial evidence that it may have also been based on a fifth factor: trading on material insider information.

6.4.1 Icahn's Wealth

Very few Americans have $3.6 billion to put into the stock market, let alone into the shares of one company. Table 6.2 on Icahn's *Forbes* rankings shows that, by

---

[68] The following account is adapted from Lazonick et al. (2016a). As background on Apple, see Lazonick et al. (2013).
[69] Sherr and Benoit (2013).   [70] Wapner (2016).
[71] For Icahn's career to the beginning of the 1990s, see Stevens (1993).

2013, Icahn had that kind of wealth. Indeed, as mentioned earlier, in 2011 Icahn had closed to outside investors the hedge fund that he had launched in 2004, so he was accountable to no one but himself for the deployment of his war chest. At 75 years of age, he had been playing financial markets for about half a century.

Icahn undoubtedly watched as Apple shares fell from a daily-average high of $90 in September 2012 to $57 in June 2013, even as the company's sales rose to $135.4 billion over the first three-quarters of its fiscal year (FY) 2013 (ending June 29, 2013) from $120.4 billion over the same nine months in 2012. Apple's profits for this nine-month period dropped from $33.5 billion 2012 to $29.5 billion in 2013, but even so, on June 29, 2013, the company showed $146.6 billion in cash, cash equivalents, and marketable securities on its books. Seeing little debt on Apple's balance sheet, Icahn envisioned a massive transformation of these liquid assets into stock buybacks that, with appropriate timing of the sale of his shares, he could translate into "no brainer" profits for himself, and in August 2013 he decided to put $1.6 billion of his cash into Apple shares.

6.4.2 Icahn's Visibility

The preeminent corporate raider of the 1980s, Icahn had remained highly visible among Wall Street traders and institutional investors. He did not win all the time, but, given the ways in which he became a multibillionaire, he had a track record that other stock-market players found hard to ignore. Besides 37 Apple-related tweets (with 283,000 followers),[72] between October 2013 and May 2015 Icahn wrote six open letters dedicated to the proposition that Apple could and should "increase shareholder value" by doing massive stock buybacks.[73] On October 1, 2013, he sent out the following tweet: "Had a cordial dinner with Tim last night. We pushed hard for a 150 billion buyback. We decided to continue dialogue in about three weeks." Icahn's dinner guest had been Apple CEO Tim Cook.

On October 23, Icahn posted on his website an open letter to CEO Cook in which he wrote: "With such an enormous valuation gap and such a massive amount of cash on the balance sheet, we find it difficult to imagine why the board would not move more aggressively to buy back stock by immediately announcing a $150 Billion tender offer (financed with debt or a mix of debt and cash on the balance sheet)."[74] Icahn wanted a tender offer because its announcement would attract lemming-like institutional investors to buy Apple stock in anticipation of the massive buyback, thus pushing up the stock price at which Apple would repurchase shares. Moreover, SEC Rule 10b-18 governs only open-market repurchases, which it does in part by limiting the volume of daily buybacks

---

[72] See Icahn's Twitter account at https://twitter.com/Carl_C_Icahn.
[73] See Icahn's letters at http://carlicahn.com/letters/page/2/.   [74] Icahn (2013).

that can be done without risking manipulation charges, constraining Apple's daily purchases to a mere $1.4 billion. Icahn wanted buybacks that would be much bigger and faster than that. And just in case anyone assumed that Icahn was out solely for himself, he concluded the open letter by saying: "I hereby agree to withhold my shares from the proposed $150 Billion tender offer. There is nothing short term about my intentions here."

6.4.3 Icahn's Hype

Of course, given a buyback pump, Icahn would then have been looking for a propitious time to dump his Apple shares. He did not mind collecting the dividends that Apple had started paying in 2012, but gains befitting a billionaire would only come with the sale of some or all of his holdings in Apple. When, however, Cook and the board ignored Icahn's call for the $150 billion tender offer, he was in for a longer haul, whether he liked it or not.

With Apple's stock price in the $65–$75 range, Icahn picked his times—first in October 2013, again in January 2014—to purchase additional blocks of shares, reaching what would be his maximum Apple shareholding on January 23, 2014. On that date, he wrote a letter to shareholders urging them to support his non-binding proxy proposal that would have instructed Apple to complete $50 billion in buybacks in FY2014, the amount by which the board had increased Apple's buyback program (from $10 billion to $60 billion) in April 2013.[75] His request for a $150 billion tender offer having been ignored, Icahn felt that Apple was being a bit slow in doing the price-boosting buybacks.

Then, on January 27, Apple released disappointing results for the first quarter of its fiscal year 2014 (October–December 2013).[76] The launch of the iPhone 5 in September 2012 had driven sales to a record $54.5 billion in 2013Q1. The launch of the iPhone 5c and 5s in September 2013 yielded $57.6 billion in sales in 2014Q1, again a record-breaking sum, but hardly the explosive growth to which Apple shareholders had become accustomed. Moreover, year-over-year first-quarter net income actually fell a tad, from $13.078 billion to $13.072 billion. These results pushed Apple's stock price down 8 percent from a close of $74.87 on January 27 to $68.88 on January 28.

On February 6 Cook did a *Wall Street Journal* interview in which he revealed that "Apple Inc. has bought $14 billion of its own shares in the two weeks since reporting financial results that disappointed Wall Street," saying that in doing these buybacks Apple was being "aggressive" and "opportunistic."[77] That move led ISS, the proxy-advisory firm, to come out against Icahn's $50 billion buyback

---

[75] Icahn (2014a).   [76] Apple Inc. (2014).   [77] Wakabayashi (2014).

proposal. Given the ISS position, in a letter to shareholders on February 10 Icahn withdrew the proposal, stating that "Tim and the board have exhibited the 'opportunistic' and 'aggressive' approach to share repurchases that we hoped to instill."[78] As it turned out, Apple did $45 billion in buybacks in FY2014—a record sum for any one company at the time[79]—and in April 2014 the board increased the buyback authorization to $90 billion from its previous $60 billion.

Higher earnings can also increase stock prices, and to get significantly higher earnings a company generally needs significantly higher sales. In his letter of February 10, Icahn informed Apple shareholders that "in light of Tim Cook's confirmed plan to launch new products in new categories this year (in addition to an exciting product roadmap with respect to new products in existing categories), we are extremely excited about Apple's future." Even though Apple's sales and profit growth continued to be modest over the remaining nine months of FY2014, Apple's stock price rose from $70.23 in January to $103.30 in September, surpassing the record stock price of $95.80 set in September 2012. Helping to push up the stock price were not only Apple's demonstrated commitment to buybacks and dividends, along with a 7:1 stock split in June 2014, but also, and probably of greater importance, expected sales growth from the long-awaited launches of the iPhone 6 and 6 Plus in September 2014.

About three weeks after the iPhone 6 debut, on October 9, 2014, Icahn posted another open letter to Cook, entitled "Sale: Apple Shares at Half Price."[80] Even though Apple's stock price of $98 was at a near-record level, Icahn insisted that it should be $203. He once again called for a tender offer, which in an interview he pegged at as much as $100 billion.[81] In addition, although lauding Cook as "the ideal CEO for Apple," Icahn provided his sales-and-earnings projections, which would, in his view, justify an immediate doubling of Apple's stock price. He repeated this exercise in a letter to his Twitter followers on February 11, 2015,[82] and in yet another open letter to Cook on May 18, 2015.[83] These projections predicted revenue growth of about 25 percent in FY2015 and 20 percent each in FY2016 and FY2017. In the February 2015 letter, Icahn said that Apple's share price should be $216 (it was $122) and, in the May letter, $240 (it was $128).

The problem is that Icahn's sales-and-earnings projections for 2016 and 2017 were based on dubious assumptions about the prospective drivers of Apple's growth. The big new product in Icahn's "exciting product roadmap" was the Apple Watch, launched on April 24, 2015. In his forecasts of October 2014 and February 2015, Icahn projected Apple Watch sales of $9 billion in 2015, rising to over $20 billion in 2016 and $33 billion in 2017. In the May 2015 forecast, with the

---

[78] Icahn (2014a).
[79] Apple would break its own record in 2018, with $72.7 billion in buybacks. See Lazonick (2018b).
[80] Icahn (2014b); see Lazonick (2014e)
[81] Lee (2014).   [82] Icahn (2015a).   [83] Icahn (2015b).

Apple Watch now on the market, he reduced its 2015 sales forecast to $6 billion but saw its sales rising to $22.5 billion in 2016 and $45 billion in 2017. In retrospect, it is clear that these sales projections were wild, and self-serving, guesses. Apple refuses to release sales figures for the Apple Watch, bundling them into the category "other products," which includes accessories and the iPod. Published numbers indicate, however, that sales of Apple Watch, which has dominated the smartwatch market, were about $5 billion in both 2015 and 2016.[84]

Apple's mainstay product is, of course, the iPhone. Icahn's October 2014 forecast had 2015 iPhone sales at $130 billion. In fact, its 2015 sales were $155 billion, including a huge year-over-year first-quarter leap from $32.5 billion to $51.2 billion. Icahn adjusted for this error in his May 2015 forecast, predicting $146 billion in iPhone sales in 2015. Assuming that Apple would maintain the iPhone's premium pricing in competition with other smartphone makers, Icahn forecast iPhone sales of $149 billion in 2016 and $159 billion in 2017. In 2016Q1 iPhone sales were $51.6 billion, a small increase over 2015Q1. But iPhone sales fell sharply, from $40.3 billion in 2015Q2 to $32.9 billion in 2016Q2, accounting for virtually all of the decline in Apple's year-over-year second-quarter sales.

Clearly, Icahn had ignored something in his iPhone sales forecasts, and that something was China. Notwithstanding his "worried about China" excuse for dumping his Apple shares in 2016Q2, Icahn had only two references to China in his letters to Cook and Apple shareholders, and no references to China in his Apple tweets. All three of his sales-and-earnings forecasts ignored geographic segments. In his January 2014 letter, Icahn opined: "The naysayers question whether Apple will be able to participate in this growth without sacrificing pricing and gross margins, especially with competition from Google, Samsung, Microsoft, Amazon and Chinese manufacturers." Well, the naysayers were right. In his October 2014 letter, Icahn said: "Now that Apple is offering larger phones with roughly the same size screen as competitors' offerings, and targeting mainland China at the time of its 4G rollout, we expect Apple to take significant market share."

Yes, from 2014 to 2015 Apple's sales in Greater China increased from $31.9 billion to $58.7 billion, accounting for 63 percent of Apple's total sales growth. And comparing 2015Q1 with 2016Q1, Greater China sales increased from $16.1 billion to $18.4 billion, representing 175 percent of Apple's year-over-year first-quarter sales growth. But comparing 2015Q2 with 2016Q2, Greater China sales declined from $16.8 billion to $12.5 billion, representing 58 percent of Apple's year-over-year second-quarter sales drop of $7.5 billion, the company's first year-over-year quarterly decline in 13 years. In April 2016 Icahn professed to have sold all his Apple shares—his 13F filing of May 16, 2016, shows that he held no Apple

---

[84] Lamkin (2016); Jones et al. (2017).

stock at the end of March 2016—because he was "worried about China." Maybe he should have worried more about China during the 20 months or so that he spent hyping Apple's stock. But, then, throwing China into the mix might have raised a red flag for institutional investors, whom he needed to buy into his hype.

It is easy, moreover, for Icahn to say he was worried about China in an interview two days after Apple's 2016Q2 report had been released—showing that, indeed, Apple did have something to worry about in China. But we know that Icahn had sold all of his Apple shares by March 31, 2016, almost four weeks before the release of the quarterly report. Yet our searches of news databases, including Factiva and Lexis Nexis, have uncovered no public information through the end of March 2016 on any problems that Apple was having in China. If knowledge of these problems led Icahn to sell all his Apple shares by the end of March 2016, where did he get that insider information? Maybe his influence with the people whom he refers to as "Tim and the board" had something to do with it.

6.4.4 Icahn's Influence

Central to Icahn's hyping of Apple's stock was his argument, stated in his February 2015 letter, that Apple's current price-earnings (P/E) ratio was "totally irrational" because "the market is somehow missing a very basic principle of valuation: when a company's future earnings are expected to grow at a much faster rate than that of the S&P 500, the market should value that company at a higher P/E multiple." Icahn's view, in keeping with share-holder-value ideology, is that all of a company's profits belong to shareholders; his argument to other shareholders in this open letter is that Apple's current stock price should reflect Carl Icahn's expectations of Apple's future earnings. If the "totally irrational" market cannot recognize his expectations, then the company—in this case Apple—should do massive stock buybacks to make the market price rational.

Of course, having captured all the gains for "expected" earnings, shareholders would then, quite rationally, sell their stock. That is the bill of goods that Icahn, with all his wealth, visibility, and hype, tried to sell to "Tim and the board," and in his letters and tweets he touted his ready access to the Apple CEO. Icahn's influence on Cook was not enough to secure him as an ally for a $150 billion tender offer. Nevertheless, his influence on Apple's resource-allocation decisions is unmistakable. From 2012, when Cook's Apple started paying dividends, through the second quarter of 2016, Apple did a record-breaking $116.6 billion in buybacks along with declaring $39.1 billion in dividends.

Apple calls these distributions to shareholders its "Capital Return" program. But our account of Icahn's involvement in Apple reveals an obvious and critical question: How can a company *return* capital to parties who never supplied it with capital? As Lazonick has shown, the only time Apple Inc. ever raised money from the stock market was in 1980, through its $90 million initial public offering.[85] Haven't these initial public shareholders long since sold their shares and taken their gains? Even founder Steve Jobs sold all his stock in Apple (except one share) when he was ousted from the company in 1985.[86]

From 1986 through 1996, in the name of maximizing shareholder value, Apple CEOs and their boards did buybacks and paid dividends to the point where, in 1996 and 1997, the company was on the brink of bankruptcy.[87] Jobs returned to Apple in 1997 and over the course of the next 14 years, until his death in 2011, eschewed distributions to shareholders, instead retaining and reinvesting the company's financial resources to build one of the most successful business enterprises that the world has ever seen.

Where was Icahn when the iPods, iPhones, and iPads were being developed? He was busy extracting value from other already-successful companies, adding to the billions that he then used, via his purchase of outstanding Apple shares, to extract value from Apple. It was because Apple had already become a successful company, *and* because, after being attacked by hedge-fund activist David Einhorn earlier in 2013,[88] Apple's board had already demonstrated its willingness to "return" capital to shareholders who had never given the company any capital, that Carl C. Icahn saw the buying of Apple shares as a "no brainer."

Icahn extracted $2 billion buying and selling Apple shares because he bought Apple shares when the stock price was low and sold them when it was higher—even though, as we have shown, he had little if any idea of what was driving the company's growth. If he had really been all-knowing at buying and selling shares, he would have sold his Apple shares on April 28, 2015, when the company's stock price peaked at $134.54, for a gain of $3.5 billion instead of the $2 billion he took home, bailing out as soon as Apple's sales growth stalled. Some part of Icahn's $2 billion "no brainer" came not from Apple's growth but from the company's record-breaking buybacks, which reduced the number of its shares outstanding by 16 percent from 2013Q2 to 2016Q2, in the process jacking up earnings per share and supporting higher stock prices.

That having been said, it may very well be the case that Apple's earnings from selling innovative products would be even stronger now if "Tim and the board" had spent less time dealing with the likes of Icahn and more time focusing on the development and marketing of innovative products. In his October 2013 letter to Cook, Icahn told the Apple CEO that "it is our belief that a company's board has a responsibility to recognize opportunities to increase shareholder value, which includes allocating capital to execute large and well-timed buybacks." Thus it

---

[85] Lazonick (2014a).   [86] Morrell (2016).   [87] Lazonick et al. (2013).
[88] Lazonick et al. (2013: 262–3).

was that the person who takes his living as a value extractor laid down the law to the person who is supposed to be making his living as a value creator[89]—and, clearly, when Carl Icahn speaks, Tim Cook listens.[90] Yet we wonder why, in the economy more generally, so much of the value that millions upon millions of workers create daily keeps ending up in the hands of the billionaire class.

[89] Foroohar (2016).
[90] Lazonick (2014b). Lazonick published his own open letter to Apple CEO Tim Cook on the *Harvard Business Review Blog*, but to date has received no response from Apple.

7

Innovative Enterprise Solves the Agency Problem

Over the past decade or so, Lucian Bebchuk, Harvard law professor and PhD in economics, and his colleagues have emerged as the most influential academics in support of hedge-fund activism as a means of confronting managerial power and improving corporate performance. Bebchuk propounds a particular version of (neoclassical) agency theory, which argues that public shareholders are "principals" and corporate executives are "agents" who manage corporate resources to maximize shareholder value (MSV) for their principals. Bebchuk's work builds on that of Michael Jensen, the foremost proponent of MSV in the 1980s and 1990s. But, in aiding and abetting hedge-fund activism in the twenty-first century, Bebchuk takes the legalized looting of the business corporation even further.

This chapter uses innovation theory to provide both a general theoretical critique and a selective empirical critique of agency theory by focusing on these academic apologies for hedge-fund activism. We argue that, for the sake of analyzing the operation and performance of the economy, innovation theory should replace agency theory. Agency theorists do not address, let alone explain, why, since the 1980s, the United States has experienced an extreme concentration of income among the richest households and the erosion of middle-class employment opportunities. At the same time, we find "short-termism" and "quarterly-capitalism" arguments lacking as explanations for the unproductive, unstable, and inequitable U.S. economy. Rather, we argue that the critical issue for understanding the role of corporate governance in supporting or undermining economic performance is the relation between value creation and value extraction for those "stakeholders" engaged in the development and utilization of productive capabilities. We contend that innovative enterprise solves the agency problem. By incentivizing and rewarding the real value creators, the innovative enterprise can mobilize the skill, effort, and finance required to generate the high-quality, low-cost products that can improve the performance of the economy—defined in terms of stable and equitable economic growth.

Predatory Value Extraction: How the Looting of the Business Corporation Became the U.S. Norm and How Sustainable Prosperity Can Be Restored. William Lazonick and Jang-Sup Shin, Oxford University Press (2020). © William Lazonick and Jang-Sup Shin. DOI: 10.1093/oso/9780198846772.001.0001

7.1 Agency Theory and the Persistence of Managerial Power

From the perspective of agency theory, one would have thought that coming into the twenty-first century the agency problem would have been solved. In the boom period 1997–2000, with profits soaring, 410 S&P 500 companies distributed 45 percent of net income as buybacks and another 34 percent as dividends. In 2000, the mean total remuneration of the 500 highest-paid U.S. executives was $32.3 million, of which about 80 percent was realized gains from exercising stock options and another 5 percent was from the estimated value of stock awards. The incentives of top executives were assumed to be aligned with shareholders, and these executives were distributing massive sums of cash flow to them. MSV ideology prevailed, virtually unchallenged, in corporate boardrooms and business schools.[1] During the Internet boom of 1997–2000, the application of agency theory and the prosperity of the U.S. economy seemed to go hand in hand.

But in 2001–02 the boom of the late 1990s turned to bust, and the Enron scandal, which broke in late 2001, followed by the Worldcom bankruptcy the following year, left self-dealing corporate executives open to blame. In the wake of the bursting of the Internet bubble, the excesses of the late 1990s brought a critique of overvalued equities even from Michael Jensen, the Harvard Business School professor who throughout the 1980s and 1990s had been the most prominent MSV academic arguing for the need to increase the stock-based pay of top executives to align their interests with those of shareholders.[2] Yet a 2002 article, "Just Say No to Wall Street: Putting a Stop to the Earnings Game," which Jensen co-authored with consultant executive Joseph Fuller, exhorted CEOs to resist the demands of Wall Street financial analysts for companies to report higher earnings to justify higher stock prices.[3] They blamed corporate executives for collaborating with Wall Street in the overvaluation of their companies' shares, with a resultant misallocation of resources. As one of their two examples (the other being Enron), Fuller and Jensen found fault with the telecommunications-equipment company Nortel Networks for spending over $32 billion in 1997–2001 on acquisitions, purchased mainly with overvalued stock instead of cash, that subsequently had to be written off or shut down. Encouraging Nortel's top management in this behavior, Fuller and Jensen recognized, was "the incentive to maintain the value of managerial and employee stock options."[4]

For agency theorists, therefore, the experience of the Internet boom and bust suggested that, notwithstanding supposedly shareholder-friendly stock-based pay, corporate executives retained too much power. Lucian Bebchuk and Jesse Fried put forward the "managerial power" thesis in a 2004 book, *Pay Without*

---

[1] See Section 3.4.   [2] Jensen and Murphy (1990).   [3] Fuller and Jensen (2002).
[4] Fuller and Jensen (2002: 44). For the case of Nortel, see Carpenter et al. (2003); Lazonick and March (2011).

Performance: The Unfulfilled Promise of Executive Compensation.[5] Their argument in the book is straightforward:

1. Senior corporate executives control the appointment of boards of directors, placing limits on the power of shareholders to exert influence on managers to ensure that these executives refrain from "empire building" (a phrase that they use repeatedly) rather than serving the interests of shareholders.
2. Senior executives use this power to get the board to approve high levels of senior-executive pay, generous benefits, and low- or no-interest loans, all at the expense of shareholders.
3. Of particular importance in "decoupling" executive pay from the interests of shareholders is stock-based compensation in the form of stock options, which gives executives windfall rewards for stock-market booms and is open to abuse through practices such as the repricing of stock options that are under water.

Bebchuk and Fried call for improvements in (i) executive compensation, through the indexing of stock options to the stock market so that the gains from them reflect actual managerial contributions to shareholder value rather than rewards from and reactions to more general stock-market volatility, and (ii) corporate governance, so that boards serve the interests of the corporation's shareholders rather than managers, who are assumed to be the shareholders' agents.

Bebchuk and Fried conclude with a call to arms:

> The power of the board, and its insulation from shareholders, is [sic] often viewed as an inevitable corollary of the modern corporation's widely dispersed ownership. But this power is partly due to the legal rules that insulate management from shareholder intervention. Changing these rules would reduce the extent to which boards can stray from shareholder interests and would much improve corporate performance.[6]

There is much truth in the Bebchuk and Fried arguments about managers' power and its translation into their excessively high levels of remuneration. There are, however, enormous gaps in their analysis. They provide no discussion of how the exercise of managerial power and "excessive" executive pay actually inflict losses on shareholders. They fail to explain why, if executives reap windfall gains from stock-market booms, shareholders do not gain from these booms as well. And they do not consider the powerful incentives created for executives who are given repriced stock options when the stock market is down to pursue strategies to boost the company's stock prices, thus benefiting shareholders.

---

[5] Bebchuk and Fried (2004).   [6] Bebchuk and Fried (2004: 216).

A particularly glaring omission in their analysis is the critical issue of distributions to shareholders in the form of dividends. They do not discuss dividend-payout policy at all—the term "dividend" is never mentioned in their book! Whether executives should be paying more in dividends and retaining less in profits in line with MSV is a fundamental question for assessing how managerial resource-allocation decisions affect shareholders' interests.

Corporations also distribute cash to shareholders in the form of stock buybacks. Bebchuk and Fried's only mention of stock repurchases is in an endnote. Citing previous research by Fried on insider trading around stock repurchases, they argue that managers may use "material" insider information, "without much fear of detection" by the SEC, when trading in company stock.[7] Some pages later, Bebchuk and Fried argue: "Executives who are free to unload shares or options may have incentives to jack up short-term stock prices by running the firm in a way that improves short-term results at the expense of long-term value."[8] They go on:

> A growing body of empirical work supports the view that managers' freedom to unload options and shares has provided them with undesirable incentives. Several studies find evidence that managers whose compensation is more directly tied to share prices are more likely to manipulate earnings. The empirical evidence also suggests that managers engage in earnings manipulation and fraud in order to unload shares at a higher price.

There is, however, no explicit mention of buybacks as one of the methods that executives might use to "jack up short-term stock prices." Hence Bebchuk and Fried fail to raise, let alone answer, the most salient questions concerning the role of stock buybacks in the exercise of managerial power. Should shareholders have an interest in open-market stock repurchases done under SEC Rule 10b-18, which gives executives and the board an expansive "safe harbor" against charges of stock-price manipulation? Given that only insiders know the specific days on which open-market repurchases are being done, would it not be expected that buybacks would be of most benefit to senior executives who have material insider information that can be used to time the exercise of their stock options to enhance the realized gains from their stock-based pay?[9]

A central critique of executive pay that Bebchuk and Fried put forward is that the stock-based pay of senior executives benefits from movements in stock prices unrelated to a firm's performance but, rather, reflecting general stock-price fluctuations. They observe that senior executives benefit from general stock-market volatility, and they argue for indexing executive stock options to eliminate this "pay without performance." But, given general stock-market volatility, what

---

[7] Bebchuk and Fried (2004: 179, 251). They cite Fried (1988, 2000, 2001).
[8] Bebchuk and Fried (2004: 184).   [9] See discussions in Chapter 4.

drives a company's stock price? As argued in Chapter 3, a company's stock price can be driven by innovation, speculation, and manipulation. If we want stock-based executive pay to be linked to a company's performance, we should structure it to reflect stock-price movements that result from innovation rather than movements that result from speculation or manipulation.

The formulation of policy to regulate executive pay would require a theory of innovation as a driver of stock prices, a perspective which is absent from the Bebchuk–Fried analysis, as from agency theory more generally. While Bebchuk and Fried contend that executives "jack up short-term stock prices by running the firm in a way that improves short-term results at the expense of long-term value," they put forward no theoretical perspective on what types of actions managers should take to generate "long-term value." Drawing on the Theory of Innovative Enterprise, we ask what roles strategic control, organizational integration, and financial commitment play in generating the high-quality, low-cost products that are the source of "long-term value." Bebchuk and Fried have absolutely nothing to say about organizational integration and financial commitment.

Their sole argument, which relates to strategic control, is that public share-holders should exert their power to rein in self-dealing managers. But they do not ask how shareholders have the ability, even if they have the incentive, to correct the problem of executives as value-extracting insiders. They do not explain how public shareholders, who merely buy and sell shares on the stock market, could and would make contributions to "long-term value" if they could exercise more power over managers. They look to activist shareholders to counter managerial power, but they provide no analysis of what these activist shareholders are able or willing to do as "long-term investors."

7.2 The Purported Efficiencies of Hedge-Fund Activism

This lack of an analysis of the sources of "long-term value" has not stopped Bebchuk from advocating the methods by which it should be achieved. In a paper "The Long-Term Effects of Hedge Fund Activism," co-authored with Alon Brav and Wei Jiang, Bebchuk uses a dataset that purports to provide evidence that, over the five-year period after a hedge-fund intervention in a company, operating profits and stock prices tended to increase.[10] Bebchuk et al. summarize their findings in a blog post on the website of the Harvard Law School Forum on Corporate Governance and Financial Regulation (hereafter "HLS Forum") as follows:

> Our study uses a dataset consisting of the full universe of approximately 2,000 interventions by activist hedge funds during the period 1994–2007. We identify

---

[10] Bebchuk et al. (2015).

for each activist effort the month (the intervention month) in which the activist initiative was first publicly disclosed (usually through the filing of a Schedule 13D). Using the data on operating performance and stock returns of public companies during the period 1991–2012, we track the operating performance and stock returns for companies during a long period—five years—following the intervention month. We also examine the three-year period that precedes activist interventions and that follows activists' departure.

Starting with operating performance, we find that operating performance improves following activist interventions and there is no evidence that the improved performance comes at the expense of performance later on. During the third, fourth, and fifth year following the start of an activist intervention, operating performance tends to be better, not worse, than during the pre-intervention period. Thus, during the long, five-year time window that we examine, the declines in operating performance asserted by supporters of the myopic activism claim are not found in the data. We also find that activists tend to target companies that are underperforming relative to industry peers at the time of the intervention, not well-performing ones.

We then turn to stock returns following the initial stock price spike that is well-known to accompany activist interventions. We first find that, consistent with the results obtained with respect to pre-intervention operating performance, targets of activists have negative abnormal returns during the three years preceding the intervention. We then proceed to examine whether, as supporters of the myopic activism claim to believe, the initial stock price reflects inefficient market pricing that fails to reflect the long-term costs of the activist intervention and is thus followed by stock return underperformance in the long term.[11]

The most vocal critic of Bebchuk et al. has been the lawyer Martin Lipton of the law firm Wachtell, Lipton, Rosen & Katz. Lipton has spent his career defending incumbent executives against corporate raiders. In the 1980s, as a managerial defense against takeover bids, Lipton designed the "poison pill," a legal arrangement that sets in motion stock issues that dilute the shareholding and voting power of the corporate raider. In February 2013, about six months before the initial release of the Bebchuk et al. paper, in an HLS Forum blog post, "Bite the Apple; Poison the Apple; Paralyze the Economy; Wreck the Economy," Lipton had criticized in no uncertain terms the attack on Apple led by hedge-fund activist David Einhorn that was taking place at the time.[12]

As Lipton led off the post: "The activist-hedge-fund attack on Apple—in which one of the most successful, long-term-visionary companies of all time is being told

[11] Bebchuk et al. (2015).

[12] Lipton (2013). On Apple's business model and the quest for "shareholder value," see Lazonick et al. (2013); Lazonick (2014b; 2018b); Lazonick et al. (2016b).

by a money manager that Apple is doing things all wrong and should focus on short-term return of cash—is a clarion call for effective action to deal with the misuse of shareholder power." Lipton took specific aim at Bebchuk as an agent of the hedge-fund activists:

> These self-seeking activists are aided and abetted by Harvard Law School Professor Lucian Bebchuk who leads a cohort of academics who have embraced the concept of "shareholder democracy" and close their eyes to the real-world effect of shareholder power, harnessed to activists seeking a quick profit, on a targeted company and the company's employees and other stakeholders.[13]

Given that Bebchuk had announced that he was conducting (in Lipton's words) "empirical studies to prove his thesis that shareholder demand for short-term performance enforced by activist hedge funds is good for the economy," Lipton countered that

> if Professor Bebchuk is truly interested in meaningful research to determine the impact of an activist attack (and the fear of an activist attack) on a company, he must first put forth a persuasive (or even just coherent) theory as to why the judgments as to corporate strategy and operations of short-term-focused professional money managers should take precedence over the judgments of directors and executives charged with maximizing the long-term success of business enterprises.[14]

Lipton is correct to demand that Bebchuk articulate a plausible theory about why the judgments of financial outsiders concerning business strategy should prevail over those of managerial insiders. The problem, however, is that since the 1980s senior executives of major U.S. corporations, with their stock-based pay, have become "value-extracting insiders,"[15] who, to their own benefit, have been participating in the legalized looting of the business corporation. We argue that, on an ever-increasing scale, senior executives have become predatory value extractors who secure gains from the corporation that are far in excess of their contributions to the value-creation process. Hence, we reject Lipton's assumption that, after a quarter-century of embracing MSV ideology, incumbent directors and executives of U.S. business corporations have the incentives, or even the abilities, to make resource-allocation decisions consonant with "the long-term success of the business enterprises" over which they exercise strategic control. One cannot begin to analyze the long-term success of the business enterprise unless one possesses a theory of the value-creating firm that, through the interactions of strategic control,

---

[13] Lipton (2013).   [14] Lipton (2013).   [15] See Chapter 4.

organizational integration, and financial commitment, generates high-quality, low-cost goods and services that are competitive on product markets.

As manifested in distributions to shareholders, buybacks in particular, and by the explosion of stock-based executive pay, the financialization of the U.S. business corporation took root in the late 1980s and 1990s, preceding the rise of the new corporate predators called "hedge-fund activists." Both senior executives as value-extracting insiders and activist shareholders as value-extracting outsiders place personal gain ahead of the investments in the value-creating capabilities of the business enterprise that are necessary for "long-term success." From this perspective, the distinction between "short term" and "long term" misses the point: The real problem is a growing imbalance of power between those who make contributions to value creation and those who reap income through value extraction.

At major business enterprises that, typically over decades, have accumulated value-creating capabilities, predatory value extraction can take place over many years, and in some cases over one or more decades, before those accumulated capabilities are run into the ground. For the largest companies that have been subjected to predatory value extraction—Exxon Mobil, IBM, Microsoft, Cisco, Hewlett-Packard, Pfizer, Merck, and many more—there is a middle stage between "retain-and-reinvest," during which value-creating capabilities are accumulated, and "downsize-and-distribute," during which the value generated by the previously-created productive capabilities is extracted. We can call this middle stage "dominate-and-distribute," a period that may stretch out over the "long term," during which a company continues to generate substantial revenues and profits from product segments that it came to dominate in its "retain-and-reinvest" stage.

For a major company, "dominate-and-distribute" can last for a decade or two, but eventually the domination of those product segments will decline. Without successful investments in innovative products on a scale that can sustain a large company into the future, it will enter into the "downsize-and-distribute" stage, with, under the MSV-oriented institutional framework that prevails in the United States, households as workers and taxpayers bearing the burden of "downsize" while predatory value extractors—senior executives, hedge-fund managers, and Wall Street bankers—reap the rewards of "distribute."

Missing from the Bebchuk–Lipton debate over whether it should be public shareholders or corporate managers exercising strategic control over the allocation of corporate resources is any acknowledgment of the role of households as workers and taxpayers as contributors to the process of value creation. At the same time, the short-termism and quarterly-capitalism arguments are lacking as explanations for the unproductive, unstable, and inequitable economy that has become characteristic of the United States. Rather, the extent to which the increasing financialization of the corporation comes at the expense of these stakeholders is the result of the processes of predatory value extraction. Lipton in effect argues that Bebchuk lacks a theory of who should control corporate resource allocation, i.e., a theory of strategic control. But what agency theory most conspicuously lacks is a theory of the value-creating enterprise, which includes not only strategic control but also organizational integration and financial commitment as social conditions that enable a company to generate high-quality, low-cost products.

In suffering from this theoretical weakness, Bebchuk is by no means unique. He was nurtured on the neoclassical theory that *the unproductive firm* is the foundation of the most efficient economy and propounds a particular version of agency theory. Jensenite agency theory exhorted corporate executives to increase the distribution of cash flow from companies to shareholders in order to allocate resources away from allegedly inefficient companies to purportedly efficient companies. Jensen argued that corporate executives should be incentivized by stock-based pay to "disgorge" the "free" cash flow. The use of the term "disgorge" implies that managers are seeking to obstruct the distribution of cash that rightfully belongs to shareholders. In fact, a major portion of the so-called "free" cash flow represents value created by the skills and efforts of employees with the support of tax dollars spent through government agencies to provide companies with infrastructure and knowledge. In *Pay Without Performance*, Bebchuk and Fried in effect argue— although, as we have seen, in an inchoate manner—that, from the perspective of the early 2000s, stock-based incentives for senior corporate executives have not worked to benefit the shareholders, for whom, in their view, the business enterprise should be run. In doing so, they set the stage for advocating that shareholder "activists" intervene directly in companies to "create value" for all shareholders.

Bebchuk, Brav, and Jiang adduce empirical evidence to respond to critics like Lipton, jurist Leo Strine, legal scholar William Bratton, economists Michael Wachter and (in the UK) John Kay, retired executive Bill George, journalist Justin Fox, and business academic Jay Lorsch,[16] who say that hedge-fund activists are reaping rewards in the "short term" at the expense of the long-term performance of the firm. Bebchuk et al. state:

> Even assuming that capital markets are informationally inefficient and activists have short investment horizons, the claim that activist interventions are detrimental to the long-term interests of shareholders and companies does not necessarily follow as a matter of theory. The claim is thus a factual proposition that can be empirically tested. However, those advancing the myopic-activists' claim have thus far failed to back their claims with large-sample empirical evidence, relying instead on their (or others') impressions and experience.[17]

---

[16] Bebchuk et al. (2015: 1094, note 22).
[17] Bebchuk et al. (2015: 1088–9). On the theory that shareholder activism creates long-term value, they cite Bebchuk (2013).

There are, however, fundamental flaws in the Bebchuk, Brav, and Jiang analysis of "large-sample empirical evidence" (as described by them, above). The first major problem is that, over the course of five years from the date of the 13D filings, almost half of the firms disappear from the Compustat database that Bebchuk et al. use to calculate Tobin's Q (the measure of the firm's market value to book value) and return on assets (ROA).[18] In the case of Q, the number of firms that remain in Compustat declines from 1,611 in the year of the 13D filing to 831 five years later, and in the case of ROA, the decline is from 1,584 to 815. These firms disappear because they are delisted from the stock market. It would require research on each case to know why the delisting occurred; disappearance from Compustat may have been caused by a firm's going out of business, its failure to maintain the minimum listing requirements of the stock market, or its having been acquired. Once these firms have disappeared, Bebchuk et al. cannot calculate Q or ROA for them.

Bebchuk et al. assert that most of the disappearances from Compustat result from acquisitions, but this conclusion seems to be based on surmise. They also state that "when we compare the target firms to peer companies matched by size and performance, we find that the matched firms also have a high attrition rate of 42% within five years; most of the disappearances from Compustat are again due to acquisitions."[19] Even if a firm disappeared through acquisition, *the key question is whether the acquirer's purpose for the acquisition was to build value-creating capabilities or, alternatively, to gain control over existing productive resources for the sake of value extraction.*

What we want to know, that is, is the extent to which *predatory value extraction* is the underlying cause of the delisting of firms, even if the proximate cause was firm liquidation, listing-requirement insufficiency, or acquisition. Furthermore, the fact that the firms in the Bebchuk et al. control group were not the subjects of a 13D filing does not, on that basis, necessarily mean they were immune to predatory value extraction. Given that predatory value extraction is perpetrated by both senior executives as insiders and activist shareholders as outsiders, excessive distributions to shareholders could have triggered any of these outcomes among the control group. Moreover, even without a 13D filing, value-extracting outsiders can pressure value-extracting insiders to intensify "downsize-and-distribute." The Bebchuk et al. analysis provides no information on why the firms disappeared from the database for either the 13D group or the control group.

As for the firms that remained in the dataset after the 13D filings, the Bebchuk et al. analysis tells us nothing about whether an increase in Tobin's Q, ROA, or stock prices, even one coming as long as five years after a 13D filing, *reflects*

---

[18] Bebchuk et al. (2015: 1104).

[19] Bebchuk et al. (2015). Again, it is not clear that the authors carried out research to document that acquisitions account for most of the disappearances, or whether this statement is merely an assertion.

investments in value creation or resource-allocation decisions for the sake of value extraction. As a rule, agency theorists view corporate investments in value-creating projects as wasteful "empire-building" expenditures *ex ante.* But they are only too ready to assume that the profits from successful value-creating projects belong to shareholders, including corporate raiders, *ex post.* There is virtually no evidence that hedge-fund activists intervene in companies to promote investments in innovative products that may, or may not, pay off in the future. There are mountains of evidence, if only by their own accounts, that hedge-fund activists intervene in companies to put a stop to the allocation of corporate resources to investments in value-creating projects. Instead, they insist that the target company sell off assets and slash "costs"—which often means layoffs and wage cuts inflicted on the very employees whose skills and efforts helped to create the value that shareholder outsiders, with the assistance of executive insiders, are determined to extract for their own personal benefit.[20]

In the process, these outsider interventions may very well undermine the value-creating investments that a firm has undertaken. Some three to five years after the announced intervention (the 13D filing), measures of performance such as Q, ROA, and stock price may show improvement, but that improvement may reflect the fact that the hedge-fund activists have targeted a company with an accumulation of revenue-generating capability that, from their MSV perspective, is ripe for being hollowed out. Indeed, these are precisely the types of targets over which predatory value extractors salivate as they use the power of purchased shareholdings to (as they put it) "create" value for themselves.

Increasingly since the 1980s, the real value creators—workers and taxpayers—have been paying the price for predatory value extraction run wild. Bebchuk et al. provide no explanation for the extreme concentration of income among the richest households and the erosion of middle-class employment opportunities in the United States over the past three decades. We have amassed considerable research that attributes these macroeconomic outcomes to the growing imbalance between value creation and value extraction in major U.S. business corporations, under the influence of MSV.[21] With the transformation of corporate resource allocation from a regime of retain-and-reinvest to one of downsize-and-distribute, senior corporate executives and powerful activist shareholders have gained at the expense of increasing proportions of the U.S. labor force, who find that middle-class employment opportunities have disappeared.

[20] See the discussion in Chapter 6.
[21] Much of this research can be found on the websites of the Institute for New Economic Thinking (https://www.ineteconomics.org/research/experts/wlazonick) and the Academic-Industry Research Network (www.theAIRnet.org).

7.3 Financial Flows and Innovative Enterprise

By the beginning of the 1990s, U.S. corporate executives had almost completely embraced MSV ideology. Since the 1980s, corporate raiders, now known as hedge-fund activists, have also become profoundly involved in this process of predatory value extraction. In the 1980s, one often heard the term "hostile" in discussions of the attacks on a corporation by a raider such as Carl Icahn. One rarely hears that term now because senior executives and activist shareholders have found common cause in predatory value extraction. The rise of the hedge-fund activists has made a bad situation—unstable employment, inequitable income, and sagging produc-tivity—far worse.

Lazonick has been a critic of agency theory since the late 1980s, when he witnessed first-hand its rise to dominance as the ideology of corporate governance at Harvard Business School (HBS). After an HBS seminar in 1992 in which he presented a paper, "Controlling the Market for Corporate Control," that critiqued agency theory from a historical perspective,[22] the paper's discussant, HBS Professor Michael C. Jensen, issued an informal but effective ban on his being invited back to HBS.[23] Beyond Jensen's activist intervention, however, agency theorists have been inclined to ignore both his research on the innovative enterprise and his critiques of their point of view.

Recently, however, Jesse Fried and Charles Wang published a working paper, "Short-Termism and Capital Flows,"[24] that critiques one of Lazonick's central propositions in "Profits Without Prosperity." We have already met Fried as the co-author with Bebchuk of the 2004 book *Pay Without Performance*. Like Bebchuk, Fried is a professor at Harvard Law School, while Wang, with a PhD in economics from Stanford University, is a junior faculty member at HBS. Fried and Wang contend that, contrary to Lazonick, the fact that distributions to shareholders in the form of dividends and buybacks absorb almost all of the net income of companies in the S&P 500 Index does not undermine companies' investment in innovation and provision of good wages to their workers. There are, however, glaring omissions, factual inaccuracies, and logical inconsistencies in their arguments.[25]

---

[22] Lazonick (1992).

[23] The story is told, with some minor inaccuracies, in McDonald (2017a, 2017b: 376–8).

[24] Fried and Wang (2017).

[25] The reader should note that Lazonick's critique of Jesse Fried and Charles Wang on "short-termism and capital flows" does not end with this chapter. A bit of publication history is in order. The Institute for New Economic Thinking (INET) published a previous version of this chapter, "Innovative Enterprise Solves the Agency Problem." as a working paper with the same title on its website (www.ineteconomics.org/research/research-papers/innovative-enterprise-solves-the-agency-problem) at the beginning of October 2017, and it received press coverage in Foroohar (2017). In December 2017 Lazonick's working paper was also posted on the Social Science Research Network website (papers.ssrn.com/sol3/papers.cfm?abstract_id=3081556). Lazonick's INET working paper critiques a working paper by Fried and Wang that first appeared as "Short-Termism and Shareholder Payouts: Getting Corporate

Fried and Wang agree that, among S&P 500 companies, buybacks and dividends absorb more than 90 percent of net income. But they argue that because S&P 500 companies issue debt and because they raise money from stock issues, they have plenty of capital to finance investment in innovation and to pay good wages. They also observe that money that companies spend on R&D counts as an expense and is deducted before arriving at net income—so that, even if the payout ratio is high, there exist R&D expenditures that can fund investment in innovation and result in good wages. Furthermore, they note, companies issue stock to provide income to employees via stock-based pay and use it as a currency to do acquisitions. In addition, they argue that distributions to shareholders may be used to fund venture-backed startups. These sources and uses of funds, they assert, result in innovation and good wages.

Yet, they say: "Academics, corporate lawyers, asset managers, and politicians point to such shareholder-payout figures as compelling evidence that 'short-termism' and 'quarterly capitalism' are impairing firms' ability to invest, innovate, and provide good wages."[26] At the beginning of their paper, they write: "Much of the focus on shareholder payouts is due to the work of economist William Lazonick, who has repeatedly and forcefully argued that these shareholder pay-outs—and buybacks in particular—impair firms' ability to invest, innovate, and provide good wages." They then quote a passage from the *HBR* article in which Lazonick says that high payout ratios leave "very little for investments in productive capabilities or higher incomes for employees."

Note that in their paper, Fried and Wang document aggregate "capital"—or, more correctly, financial—flows, but *they do not provide an iota of empirical*

Capital Flows Right," January 8, 2017, and was then revised as "Short-Termism and Capital Flows," February 9, 2017, with both versions designated as Harvard Business School Working Paper 17–062. Then, over a year later, on February 21, 2018, Fried and Wang published yet another revision of Harvard Business School Working Paper 17–062, again entitled "Short-Termism and Capital Flows," in which their critique of Lazonick's 2014 *Harvard Business Review* article, "Profits Without Prosperity," continues to hold center stage. In this 2018 revision, however, Fried and Wang make no reference to Lazonick's INET working paper, "Innovative Enterprise Solves the Agency Problem," even though it had been publicly available since October 2017. Yet the Fried–Wang 2018 revision omits some of their most egregious arguments in its 2017 versions that Lazonick had critiqued in his 2017 INET working paper. For example, in the 2017 versions of their working paper, Fried and Wang claim that companies can issue debt to fund innovation and higher wages, but they omitted this argument in the 2018 version, presumably because Lazonick's INET working paper, published in 2017, adduced evidence that U.S. companies were issuing debt to do buybacks. The third version of the Fried–Wang working paper apparently forms the basis for their article, "Are Buybacks Really Shortchanging Investment? What the Case Against Stock Repurchases Gets Wrong," *Harvard Business Review*, March–April 2018, pp. 2–9, again targeting Lazonick's 2014 *HBR* article, "Profits Without Prosperity." Since their 2018 revision of their working paper and their *HBR* article neither respond to Lazonick's 2017 INET working paper nor negate any of its arguments, we have decided to publish "Innovative Enterprise Solves the Agency Problem" as a chapter in this book, as originally planned. Meanwhile, in collaboration with Matt Hopkins and Mustafa Erdem Sakınç, Lazonick is writing a specific critique of the Fried–Wang 2018 *HBR* article and their underlying working paper in its latest incarnation.

[26] Fried and Wang (2017, Abstract).

evidence of the results they claim from these flows: innovation and good wages. The overriding reason for this omission is that, like agency theorists in general, they lack a theory of the value-creating enterprise, including a theory of the distribution of the gains from value-creation among participants in the value-creation process. Hence, Fried and Wang are unable to test the very hypotheses that they purport to refute. As for evidence that Lazonick and his colleagues have to offer on this subject, save for citing another article by him co-authored with Mary O'Sullivan,[27] Fried and Wang make no reference to the substantial body of theoretical and empirical research that underpins Lazonick's arguments.[28]

Drawing on this body of research, the critique of Fried and Wang centers on two broad points:

1. Cash flows that represent certain SOURCES of funds—Fried and Wang discuss debt issues and stock issues—tell us nothing about the USES of funds.
2. Cash flows that represent certain USES of funds—Fried and Wang discuss stock-based pay, R&D, acquisitions, and venture capital—tell us nothing about the PERFORMANCE of funds: that is, whether or not these uses of funds result in innovation and higher wages.

Fried and Wang assume that the particular source of funds—equity or debt—is immaterial to corporate investment in productive capabilities. In this, they echo the Modigliani–Miller theorem of the irrelevancy of corporate capital structure,[29] the dominant, yet naïve, view of corporate finance. The Modigliani–Miller theorem makes no sense from the perspective of *strategic control* over the allocation of resources and the need for *financial commitment* to implement an innovative investment strategy, two social conditions that are central to the Theory of Innovative Enterprise.

The use of debt exposes the firm to financial fragility and even bankruptcy, while the use of equity does not. Those who exercise strategic control over the allocation of corporate resources need to pay close attention to the company's capital structure and its relation to corporate cash flow.[30] In an innovative enterprise, committed finance is critical to fund not solely, or even primarily, physical capital expenditures, but also organizational learning, which is an uncertain, collective, and cumulative process. Financial commitment is required to sustain this learning process from the time at which investments in productive

[27]   Lazonick and O'Sullivan (2000b).
[28]   See recent research posted at https://www.ineteconomics.org/research/experts/wlazonick.
[29]   Modigliani and Miller (1958).
[30]   This sensible view of corporate finance prevailed in U.S. business schools before the 1980s when, via agency theory, the absurdities of neoclassical economic theory invaded that academic territory. See, for example, Donaldson (1961).

capabilities are made until the time that the generation of high-quality, low-cost products that can compete on markets provide profits to the firm.

Innovation secures financial commitment from equity finance, of which retained earnings are a critical foundation, *leveraged* if need be by debt. The use of debt as a *replacement* for equity to fund the innovation process would require that a company take on high levels of debt without the flow of revenues or the accumulated equity being available to service that debt. It is a recipe for financial disaster that any value-creating enterprise would seek to avoid.

More generally, the Fried and Wang arguments reflect the neoclassical notion that all that matters to economic performance is the uninhibited movement of finance through the economic system to its most efficient uses. But lacking a theory of innovative enterprise, the neoclassical economist is bereft of an explanation of the value-creating processes that permit those most efficient uses to come into existence. Indeed, it is the free-market economist's notion that financial mobility trumps financial commitment in the determination of economic outcomes that often gives rise to the charges of "short-termism" and "quarterly capitalism" that Fried and Wang seek to dismiss.[31]

That having been said, as already indicated, the short-termism and quarterly-capitalism arguments are lacking as explanations for an unproductive, unstable, and inequitable economy. Rather, the critical issue for understanding the role of corporate governance in supporting or undermining the achievement of stable and equitable economic growth is the relation between value creation and value extraction for those "stakeholders" engaged in the development and utilization of the company's productive capabilities.

One needs a theory of innovative enterprise to analyze whether cash flows result in innovation—that is to say, value creation—and higher wages—that is to say, value extraction that accurately reflects the contributions of a company's workers to value creation. Armed with the Theory of Innovative Enterprise, we can focus on the social conditions—strategic control, organizational integration, and financial commitment—that result in innovation and higher wages. And we can then see the logic, consistent with the facts, of why massive stock buybacks tend to undermine the social conditions of innovative enterprise. Agency theory is rooted in an ideology that justifies value extraction—an inequitable form of which is designated by the term "maximizing shareholder value"—while lacking a theory of value creation, and as such serves to legitimize growing income inequality and the erosion of middle-class employment opportunities. Both have been widely recognized "performance" outcomes of the U.S. economy since the 1980s—albeit not the outcomes that most of us want. The allocation of corporate resources to stock buybacks has been central to the generation of these outcomes, with damaging impacts on innovation and income distribution.

---

[31] In the same vein, see Kaplan (2017).

This critique of Fried and Wang summarizes the factual problems and logical inconsistencies with their arguments concerning (a) debt issues, (b) stock issues, (c) stock-based pay, (d) R&D, (e) acquisitions, and (f) venture capital. One cannot assume that the sources of funds (debt issues and stock issues) and uses of funds (stock-based pay, R&D, acquisitions, and venture capital) that Fried and Wang identify as resulting in "investment, innovation, and good wages" have in fact had those results. And, we repeat, Fried and Wang provide no empirical evidence that the sources and uses of funds that they identify result in innovation and higher wages. Our research adduces empirical evidence that just the opposite is often the case.

7.3.1 Debt Issues by S&P 500 Companies as a Source of Funds

Fried and Wang argue that companies *recapitalize* by repurchasing stock and taking on debt, and that the debt enables the companies to invest in innovation and provide good wages. The debt that they take on offsets to some extent distributions to shareholders. Therefore, by Fried and Wang's account, finance equal to much more than the 7 percent of net income that S&P 500 companies retained after distributions of dividends and repurchases in the decade 2005–14 was allegedly available for investment that could result in innovation and good wages.

But why do companies issue debt? What uses do their executives have in mind? Conventionally, when companies issue debt for the sake of investment in productive capabilities, that debt leverages retained earnings. Debt that is used for investment in productive capabilities does not replace earnings that have been depleted through buybacks. Innovation entails the development and utilization of productive capabilities in the face of technological, market, and competitive uncertainties. Given that it takes time to develop and utilize these investments in productive capabilities and that there is no guarantee of returns, a company has to be prudent in taking on debt if it wants to avoid cash-flow problems and, possibly, bankruptcy. Hence the need to leverage the debt on a foundation of retained earnings that the company controls.

But a financialized company may take on debt to do stock buybacks for the sake of boosting its stock price. There is considerable evidence that, especially in the low-interest-rate environment that has prevailed since the financial crisis of 2008–09, U.S. companies have done just that.[32] Companies may also be issuing debt at low interest rates with a view to building up cash balances so that they can do stock buybacks in the future. We know that as the stock market booms, stock

---

[32] Johnson and Ablan (2013); Rodrigues (2014); Lahart (2016); Mackenzie and Platt (2016); Melvin (2016); Linnane (2017).

buybacks escalate as companies compete with one another by giving manipulative boosts to their stock prices. They may want to do large open-market repurchases to hit quarterly earnings-per-share (EPS) targets; we do not know to what extent companies engage in this practice because, under Rule 10b-18, the SEC does not require them to disclose the particular days on which they do open-market repurchases. Keeping a readily available pool of cash on hand, even if borrowed, can be very useful to senior executives who want to intervene opportunistically in the workings of the stock market to elevate their company's stock price.

For many corporations, a considerable portion of cash or near-cash reserves is not available for buybacks. Especially under the tax rules that prevailed prior to the Tax Cuts and Jobs Act of 2017, many U.S. corporations borrowed to do buybacks in order to avoid repatriating foreign profits on which they would have to pay U.S. corporate taxes. In 1960, at the end of the Eisenhower administration, a change in the tax code whose ostensible purpose was to encourage U.S. multinational corporations to invest in poor countries permitted U.S. companies to defer taxes on corporate profits made abroad until those earnings were repatriated.[33] The 25 U.S. corporations with the highest accumulated unrepatriated profits at the end of fiscal 2015, as identified in a report by Citizens for Tax Justice,[34] included sixteen of the top twenty-five repurchasers for the period 2006–15. Combined, these twenty-five corporations had an accumulated $1.488 trillion in untaxed profits abroad, while at home they did a combined $1.368 trillion in buybacks and dispensed $911 billion in dividends in the decade 2006–15.

Cisco Systems, which is high up on the lists of both unrepatriated profits and stock buybacks, is a prime example of a company that has kept its foreign profits offshore while borrowing to do buybacks at home. From 2002 through 2016, Cisco did $97.5 billion in buybacks, equal to 95 percent of its net income. It also paid $18.1 billion in dividends. At the end of 2016, Cisco's cash and near-cash assets (cash, cash equivalents, and available-for-sale securities holdings) held abroad amounted to $59.8 billion, but the company stated that if it were to repatriate these funds, it would have to pay additional U.S. taxes.[35] The amount of cash and near-cash assets that Cisco held in the United States at the end of 2016 was only $5.9 billion.

Therefore, Cisco has had to borrow to sustain its buyback habit. Cisco did the first debt issue in its history in 2006 when it borrowed $6.5 billion to acquire Scientific-Atlanta.[36] Subsequently, through 2016, Cisco issued another $33.0 billion in long-term bonds for unstated purposes, while paying back $11.2 billion. At the end of 2016, the company had long-term debt of $28.6 billion on its books,

---

[33] Lazonick (2011a).   [34] Citizens for Tax Justice (2016).   [35] SEC (2016b: 58).
[36] As a company that in the late 1990s had become known for a growth-through-acquisition strategy, Cisco had done nearly all of its acquisitions from 1993 to 2004 using its stock as the combination currency, before turning to the use of cash for its acquisitions. See Carpenter et al. (2003); Bell et al. (2014).

which, with most of its liquid assets sitting abroad, we can assume had been incurred primarily, and probably entirely, to fund distributions to shareholders. Except for the Scientific-Atlanta acquisition, Cisco did not make use of debt to finance investments in productive capabilities in the United States.

7.3.2 Public Stock Issues by S&P 500 Companies as a Source of Funds

Fried and Wang posit that, even as S&P 500 companies do stock buybacks, they have been using stock issues to invest in innovation and provide good wages to their employees. It is, however, unusual for established U.S. companies that are already listed on the stock market to do public stock issues, and when they do, it is rarely to fund investment in innovation. As stated in Chapter 3 of this book, in the late 1920s many established publicly listed companies did large-scale stock issues on the New York Stock Exchange even as they were channeling large sums of surplus cash to speculators, who were buying corporate shares on margin with funds borrowed on the call-loan market at interest rates of 10 to 15 percent. Indeed, the very same corporations that were cashing in by selling shares at highly speculative prices were the main sources of these funds for call loans to speculators. The purpose of these corporate share issues, however, was not to raise funds for new investment in productive capabilities, but rather to take advantage of soaring stock-prices driven by stock-market speculation to secure an influx of cash to pay off corporate debt or bolster the corporate treasury.[37]

This type of financial engineering would stand these companies in good stead at the beginning of the 1930s after the economy had moved from boom to bust. In retrospect, this financial behavior contrasts dramatically with the practice of major U.S. corporations over the past two decades of doing large-scale stock repurchases when the stock market is booming for the purpose of pushing up their stock prices—and, with them, executives' stock-based pay. If anything, when boom has turned to bust, some desperate S&P 500 companies have sought to stay afloat by doing secondary share issues after their stock price had fallen in value. For example, with the bursting of the Internet bubble in 2001–02, Lucent Technologies, then one of the world's leading telecommunication-equipment companies, found itself with a junk-bond rating and a stock price that had plunged to as low as 1 percent of its Internet-boom peak. Even as Lucent sold off assets and laid off tens of thousands of employees to avert bankruptcy, it was forced to issue convertible bonds at rock-bottom prices that reflected that of its almost-worthless stock.[38]

---

[37] Smiley and Keehn (1988).   [38] Carpenter et al. (2003); Lazonick and March (2011).

As we also know, some corporations are "too big to fail." Included in the Fried and Wang data on stock issues are Wall Street banks that, in need of financial support, issued stock to foreign entities, including sovereign-wealth funds, in the run-up to what turned out to be the Great Financial Crisis. Then, once the crisis hit, many of the same banks, in even more desperate need of cash, issued stock to the U.S. government for the purpose of recapitalization. In neither case were the stock issues done to invest in innovation or pay higher wages to workers. Rather, the stock issues were done because of the previous profligate behavior of these financial institutions, including massive stock buybacks to boost their stock prices.

Indeed, in September 2008, just after the collapse of Lehman Brothers, which would precipitate the U.S government's Troubled Asset Relief Program (TARP), Lazonick wrote about this relation between stock buybacks and stock issues by major U.S. financial institutions in a *Financial Times* comment, "Everyone is paying the price for share buy-backs."[39] Lazonick documented how, in the two years prior to Lehman's collapse, once-powerful Wall Street banks had issued stock to foreign sovereign-wealth funds to recover from their reckless behavior in the previous boom years:

> In November 2007, the $7.5bn equity investment that Citigroup secured from the Abu Dhabi Investment Authority was almost as much as it spent on buy-backs in 2006 and 2007. Merrill Lynch did more than $14bn in repurchases in those two years, but by January 2008 had given up a 12.7 per cent equity stake to raise $9bn from foreign investors. Morgan Stanley, which did over $7bn in buy-backs in 2006–07, traded a 9.9 per cent equity stake with China's sovereign wealth fund for $5bn. It has now agreed to a takeover. Lehman Brothers, which repurchased more than $5bn in 2006–07, is now bankrupt.[40]

And when foreign finance could not right these sinking ships, the U.S. government had to step in as the lender of last resort:

> The taxpayer is also paying the price of buy-backs. When the US government bailed out Bear Stearns, by assuming the risk of $29bn of its subprime mortgage assets, there was almost $6bn less cash on Bear's balance sheet because of buy-backs during 2003–07. So too with the government takeover of Fannie Mae and Freddie Mac, the government sponsored housing entities. They have spent $10bn on repurchases since 2003, including $4bn in 2006–07.[41]

Lazonick concluded with a critique of agency theory:

> The crisis in the US financial sector demonstrates that the so-called "free cash flow" distributed as buy-backs was not really free. Wall Street banks could use

---

[39] Lazonick (2008).   [40] Lazonick (2008).   [41] Lazonick (2008).

that cash now to avert financial crisis rather than turn to foreign governments and the US taxpayer for a bail-out.[42]

A significant portion of the stock sales that are included in the Fried and Wang data were, therefore, desperation issues as these financial institutions got caught up in the financial maelstrom that they helped to create. And that *Financial Times* comment pre-dates the TARP bailout. As it turned out, the initial infusions of foreign and U.S.-government cash were insufficient to mitigate the threat of bankruptcy for these financial institutions, and the U.S. Congress had to step in with TARP—resulting in more desperation stock issues that were integrally related to the companies' previous financial behavior, including massive distributions to shareholders. These stock issues had nothing to do with investment in innovation and providing higher wages for employees.

On October 13, 2008, Neel Kashkari, the Treasury official who oversaw the implementation of TARP, outlined its features, including "a standardized program to purchase equity in a broad array of financial institutions. As with the other programs, the equity purchase program will be voluntary and designed with attractive terms to encourage participation from healthy institutions. It will also encourage firms to raise new private capital to complement public capital."[43] Under TARP, the U.S. government purchased $266 billion in equity in 18 corporations. Included among them were six major Wall Street banks, with the U.S. government investing $45 billion each in Citibank and Bank of America, $25 billion each in JPMorgan Chase and Wells Fargo, and $10 billion each in Goldman Sachs and Morgan Stanley, for a total of $160 billion.[44] Yet in the decade before the crisis, from 1998 through 2007, these six banks spent a combined $211 billion on buybacks, equal to 45 percent of net income, along with $182 billion on dividends, another 39 percent of net income. These banks did buybacks to manipulate their stock prices, and then had to turn to U.S. taxpayers, who absorbed massive stock issues to bail them out.

Another company that did stock issues induced by the financial crisis was General Electric (GE). In the decade 1998–2007, GE, long one of the biggest repurchasers, recorded buybacks totaling $74.6 billion (49 percent of net income) while paying $62.2 billion in dividends (another 41 percent of net income). GE's buyback activity continued during the first three-quarters of 2008, as the company repurchased $3.1 billion in shares at an average price per share of $31.25. Then, as the company suffered large losses from its financial arm, GE Capital, it had in October 2008 to issue $12.0 billion in common shares at only $22.25 per share to

---

[42] Lazonick (2008).   [43] Kashkari (2008).   [44] Wikipedia (n.d.).

retain its bond rating.[45] During 2008, therefore, GE bought high and sold low. Its stock issue helped GE recover from the financial fiasco of which it was a part. It was not done to invest in innovation or to provide GE employees with higher wages.

The financial crisis also had a severe impact in the U.S. automobile industry, forcing General Motors and Chrysler to turn to the U.S. government for some TARP funding to bail them out. General Motors was a major stock issuer in November 2010, when the "New GM," which had gone bankrupt in 2009, did one of the largest initial public offerings in history, worth $23.1 billion.[46] One should also accord this case close scrutiny before assuming, simplistically and without mustering the facts, that stock issues fund investment in innovation and payment of higher wages.

In June and July 2009, the U.S. government had taken the lead in the bailout, which enabled GM to emerge from bankruptcy in just forty days. U.S. taxpayers put up $49.5 billion in rescue funding,[47] and Canadian taxpayers pitched in another $10.9 billion.[48] The United Auto Workers (UAW) agreed to layoffs and pay cuts worth $11 billion. The union-run Voluntary Employee Beneficiary Association (VEBA) was forced to assume GM's pension liabilities in exchange for shares in the New GM, a step that saved the company $3 billion per year.[49] From 2008 to 2010, GM's employment was chopped from 243,000 to 202,000.

After taking losses of $82.1 billion from 2005 through 2008, GM showed net income of $6.1 billion in 2010 and total profits of $50.0 billion from 2010 through 2016. Business interests played no role in the equity financing that enabled GM to emerge from bankruptcy and relist on the stock market. In the New GM's 2010 IPO, the U.S. and Canadian governments and the VEBA sold common shares to the public for $18.1 billion. GM used the $4.9 billion that it netted from a preferred stock issue (with a 4.75 percent dividend) to repurchase $2.1 billion in outstanding preferred shares held by the U.S. Treasury, with the remaining $2.8 billion making up part of a $4.0 billion cash contribution to GM's pensions plans for salaried and hourly U.S. workers.[50] In other words, GM allocated the proceeds from this preferred stock issue to restore some of the funds contributed by two of the parties—U.S. taxpayers and U.S. workers—that had enabled GM to do its IPO.

The longer-run historical context is also important for understanding how a company such as GM got into financial distress to the point that taxpayers and workers found themselves in the position of having to keep the company from liquidating. Many factors were involved, but buybacks played a role. As Lazonick wrote in a *BusinessWeek* article in the immediate aftermath of GM's emergence from bankruptcy in 2009: "If bailed-out General Motors (GM) had banked the $20.4 billion distributed to shareholders as buybacks from 1986 through 2002

[45] SEC (2008, p. 45).   [46] Lazonick and Hopkins (2015).   [47] Woodyard (2013).
[48] Morrow and Keenan (2015).   [49] Lazonick and Hopkins (2015).   [50] SEC (2011).

(with a 2.5% after-tax annual return), it would have had $35 billion in 2009 to stave off bankruptcy and respond to global competition."[51]

Or as Bob Lutz, the veteran auto executive, put it when new pressure was placed on GM to repurchase its stock in 2015, stock buybacks are "always a harbinger of the next downturn... in almost all cases, you regret it later."[52] Since 2015, on the insistence of a group of hedge funds and their front man—Harry J. Wilson—the now-profitable GM has been doing buybacks again, to the tune of $6.0 billion in 2015–16. In 2009 Wilson had been a central figure in the Obama bailout task force, from which position he insisted, over objections from labor and taxpayer interests, that the bailout should be done with equity, not debt.[53]

If the bailout had been done with debt, the U.S. government would have been GM's senior creditor, and the U.S. taxpayer would have had to be made whole on this debt or the company could have been forced into bankruptcy again. As it was, after GM went public in 2010,[54] the U.S. government was the company's biggest shareholder (even after an initial sale of a portion of its shares in the IPO), and Wall Street began calling the reemerged company "Government Motors," insisting that the U.S. Treasury sell its stake as soon as possible. The U.S. government sold the last of its shares in December 2013, at a loss to U.S. taxpayers of $11.2 billion.[55] It has been estimated that GM workers gave up multiples of that amount in layoffs, wage cuts, and reduced benefits to help finance the rebirth of the company.[56]

Meanwhile, with the aid of taxpayer subsidies and union concessions, as well as the growth of the China market and a bankruptcy-induced focus on innovation, GM was profitable from 2010—and, in January 2015, Harry J. Wilson—the very same man who had designed the Obama administration's 2009 bailout of GM—showed up in GM CEO Mary Barra's office representing hedge funds that had purchased shares outstanding on the stock market. On their behalf, and with a handsome cut for himself, Wilson demanded that GM do $8 billion in buybacks and put him on the GM board. Unlike the U.S. and Canadian governments and the UAW, the hedge funds that Wilson represented had not invested any money in GM in bringing the company out of bankruptcy in 2009 or in putting the company in position to do its 2010 IPO. Yet now, through their duplicitous mouthpiece, these hedge funds were asserting their right to financial "returns" through buybacks, as well as participation in strategic control by occupying a seat on the board. In the event, GM and Wilson agreed to a $5-billion buyback but no board seat.

If GM's 2010 stock issue, therefore, provided the New GM with funds for investment in productive capabilities, it was because taxpayers and workers, not public shareholders, had made the New GM possible. And if the bailout had been

[51] Lazonick (2009a).   [52] Spector and Lublin (2015).
[53] Lazonick and Hopkins (2015).   [54] Baldwin and Kim (2010).
[55] Beech (2014); Higgins et al. (2013).   [56] Lazonick and Hopkins (2015).

done with debt rather than equity, taxpayers and workers would have benefited far more from GM's return to profitability, if only because they could have then insisted on recouping their own investments in the restructuring before parasitical shareholder activists could get their greedy hands on corporate profits that they had played absolutely no role in generating.

Nor, as in most cases in which predatory value extractors have used distributions to shareholders to line their own pockets with returns to investment in productive capabilities that should have gone to taxpayers and workers, were the gains to the value extractors the result of "market forces." Rather, the predators used their power to influence the corporate allocation of resources and returns. Agency theorists such as Fried and Wang assume that these resource-allocation decisions result in superior economic outcomes, i.e., innovation and higher wages. Neither facts nor logic are on their side.

7.3.3 Internal Stock Issues for Stock-Based Pay as a Use of Funds

If some of the largest and best-known cases of public stock issues over the past decade fail to support the Fried and Wang argument, the fact is that the vast majority of the cash from stock issues in the data for S&P 500 companies that they present did not come from stock-market sales to the public. They came, rather, from sales of shares to employees exercising their stock options or taking advantage of an employee stock-purchase program. In the case of a stock option, the amount of cash raised depends on the option exercise price, which is the market price of the stock on the grant date. In the case of an employee stock purchase, the amount of cash raised is customarily at 85 percent of the market value of shares on the date that the stock is purchased.[57] For example, in fiscal 2016 Cisco, a company that is well known for using a broad-based stock-option plan, secured $1.1 billion from the sale of shares to its employees, of which $615 million (32 million shares) came from stock options and the remainder (25 million shares) from the employee stock-purchase plan at 85 percent of the market price.

Recognizing the importance of stock issues to employees as a source of equity funds, Fried and Wang argue that stock-based pay is one way in which a company uses stock buybacks to provide "good wages" to employees. As they state:

> Recall that one of the main concerns raised about buybacks is that they give shareholders capital while leaving "very little for ... higher incomes for employees" (Lazonick, 2014). However, one of the most important reasons firms repurchase stock is to acquire shares to pay employees (Kahle, 2002; Bens et al., 2003). For such compensation-driven repurchases, the cash that flows out to public

---

[57] Burton (2003).

shareholders in the repurchase leg of the transaction finds its way to employees when they get the repurchased shares and sell them back to public shareholders.[58]

Fried and Wang are correct to point to the link between stock-based pay for a broad base of employees and the buyback activities of the companies that employ them. But the relation between buybacks and employee incomes is much more complicated than the simple "flow-of-funds" model that Fried and Wang lay out. Especially when the stock market is volatile, the use of stock options as a component of pay for a broad base of workers is fraught with problems for an innovative enterprise.[59]

First, historically the use of stock options for a broad base of employees by "New Economy" startups came at the cost of the high-tech personnel eschewing the "Old Economy" norm of employment security with one company over the course of a career. The use of broad-based stock-option plans spread rapidly in the 1980s and 1990s as a mode of pay with which, in venture-backed high-tech industries—in particular, information and communications technology (ICT) and biotechnology—New Economy startups could lure professional, technical, and administrative employees away from established Old Economy firms, at which a "career-with-one-company" was the norm. By the 2000s, the career-with-one-company norm was largely gone not only in these high-tech industries but across U.S. business, exposing even college-educated workers to high levels of employment insecurity and, often, truncated careers when the companies for which they worked turned from retain-and-reinvest to downsize-and-distribute.[60]

Second, at certain high-tech companies during the Internet boom of 1996–2000, employees' gains from exercising stock options were *so high* that they fostered a hypermobility of labor that undermined the commitment of these employees to engage in the collective and cumulative learning processes that are central to innovation. In Chapter 3, in discussing the "compensation" function of the stock market, we gave the case of Microsoft, where the average gains from exercising stock options per employee exploded to $369,700 across 29,200 employees in 1999 and $449,100 across 35,200 employees in 2000, precipitating a hypermobility of labor that undermined Microsoft's innovation processes.[61]

Third, major differences in earnings from stock options, both across employees in a particular company and over time, may be caused by stock-market volatility

---

[58] Fried and Wang (2017, note 16) add a footnote: "Repurchases are not necessary to provide shares for employee stock compensation arrangements. In principle, a firm could use only newly issued shares to pay employees and, when it reaches the share-authorization limit in its corporate charter, seek shareholder approval to increase that limit (Fried, 2005). However, for a variety of reasons, firms will generally use repurchases to acquire at least some of the shares given to employees."

[59] See Lazonick et al. (2014: 34). Of course, in making their "good wages" argument, Fried and Wang could have consulted the research cited in the previous notes, but from their treatment of the question, there is no evidence that they did.

[60] Lazonick (2009a).   [61] See this book, Chapter 3, and Lazonick (2009a: ch. 2).

and have nothing to do with differences in productive contributions. In the Microsoft example, since options take at least one year to vest, an employee with years of career experience who joined the company in 2000 would miss out on the stock-option-gains bonanza reaped by many employees with less career experience who had joined the company in earlier years. An advantage of stock-based pay for the company is that the funding of employee gains comes not from its internal cash flow but rather from the pockets of stock-market traders who have bid up the company's stock price. This "outsourcing" of pay determination to the volatile stock market, which is driven by a combination of innovation, speculation, and manipulation, is bound to generate substantial pay inequities because of the timing and circumstances under which employees join a company, receive their options, and have opportunities to exercise them.

Fourth, high-tech companies often say that they are doing buybacks to offset dilution of shareholding caused by their broad-based stock-option plans. But the number of shares repurchased is generally a multiple of the number of shares issued when employees exercise stock options. Moreover, companies typically repurchase shares when stock prices are high, making this mode of employee pay very expensive.[62] In short, employee stock options may generate high pay for some non-executive workers at certain times and in certain places, but this mode of compensation is often part of the problem of the financialized corporation. Moreover, the use of broad-based stock-option plans has encouraged the tendency of U.S. high-tech companies to look to buybacks to manipulate their stock prices while often undermining the organizational integration and financial commitment that innovation requires.

Obviously, the gains from exercising stock options depend on the trajectory of a company's stock price. If the stock price were to reflect *only* the company's innovative success, one might argue that an employee's gains from exercising stock options represent a way in which he or she shares in that success. The problem is that, as well as by innovation, a company's stock price may be determined by speculation and manipulation. As a result, the gains from exercising stock options can become detached from the innovative performance of the firm.

7.3.4 R&D as a Use of Funds for Innovation

Fried and Wang argue:

> The focus on shareholder payouts as a percentage of net income is highly misleading; it wrongly implies that "net income" reflects the totality of a firm's resources that are generated from its business operations and are available for

---

[62] Lazonick (2015d).

investment. In fact, net income is calculated by subtracting the many costs associated with future-oriented activities that can be expensed (such as R&D). These amounts are substantial. Firm spending on R&D is, on average, equal to about 25–30% of net income. In other words, much of the resources generated by a firm's business operations have already been used for long-term investment before net income is calculated. Indeed, a firm that spends more on R&D will, everything else equal, have a lower net income and a higher shareholder-payout ratio. At most, net income indicates the additional resources generated by a firm's business operations that are available for (a) investment activities whose cost must be capitalized rather than expensed and (b) additional R&D and other activities whose costs are expensed.[63]

Some basic facts about R&D spending make it clear that there are a number of problems with the Fried and Wang argument. Investments in R&D are concentrated in a few sectors of the economy: ICT, pharma, and aerospace. The companies in the S&P 500 Index in January 2016 recorded a total of $250.4 billion in R&D expenditures for fiscal 2015. But 289 of the 500 companies recorded *zero R&D expenses*, with the R&D expenditures of the other 211 companies ranging from $16.0 million to $12.5 billion. Of the companies that recorded R&D expenditures, fifteen companies with $5 billion or more did 49 percent of the total R&D spending in 2015, while another forty companies with between $1 billion and $5 billion in R&D expenditures accounted for another 35 percent of total R&D spending.[64] The R&D leader was Amazon, which did not do any buybacks or pay dividends from 2013 through 2016 as it ramped up its R&D spending from $4.6 billion in 2012 to $16.1 billion in 2016.[65] In contrast, Microsoft, perennially among the largest repurchasers, was no. 4 in R&D spending ($12.0 billion) in 2015, a year in which it also did $14.4 billion in buybacks and $9.9 billion in dividends, which, combined, equalled 199 percent of its net income.

The argument that R&D spending funds innovation and higher wages is applicable, therefore, to a specific set of companies, among which—because of both business strategy and stages of development—there may be very different relations between R&D expenditures and distributions to shareholders. Understanding the relation between buybacks and R&D spending requires the accumulation of case-study research of companies in R&D-intensive sectors. For example, in 2005–07, following the success of its 2G Razr cellphone, Motorola did $7.8 in buybacks, equivalent to 94 percent of net income, along with $1.3 billion in dividends, and then failed to compete in 3G phones. Losing $4.3 billion in 2007–09, Motorola slashed R&D expenditures from $4.5 billion in 2007 to $2.5 billion

[63] Fried and Wang (2017: 4).
[64] For R&D spending in the U.S. economy more generally, see Hopkins and Lazonick (2014).
[65] See Lazonick (2018c).

in 2010. The company was divided the next year into Motorola Solutions and Motorola Mobility, with the latter becoming part of the Chinese computer company Lenovo in 2014. It is worth noting that in 2007 corporate predator Carl Icahn took a large position in Motorola stock, attracted by the fact that the company had made $8.2 billion in profits and done $4.7 billion in buybacks in 2005–06. Icahn did not originate the pattern of corporate resource allocation that resulted in Motorola's downfall, but he helped to ensure that it remained on its "downsize-and-distribute" path.

At the same time, it is at best naïve for Fried and Wang to assume, as they do, that R&D expenditures will necessarily result in innovation and higher wages. Indeed, it is surprising to see them make this assumption because it is a basic tenet of agency theory—as espoused, for example, in the 2004 Bebchuk and Fried book—that R&D spending is one way in which corporate executives seek to "build empires" at the expense of "shareholder value." The fact is that innovation is a process that is uncertain, collective, and cumulative. If a high-tech company does not invest in R&D, it will certainly fail to be innovative. But if a company does invest in R&D, then it needs to ensure that the social conditions of innovative enterprise—strategic control, organizational integration, and financial commitment—support the uncertain, collective and cumulative processes that can transform R&D expenditures into higher-quality, lower-cost products than were previously available.

When, however, strategic control is in the hands of corporate executives and activist shareholders who have neither the incentive nor the ability to invest in innovation, we should expect that those investments in R&D will fail. Moreover, when these strategic decision-makers allocate resources in ways that undermine the collective and cumulative learning that is the essence of innovation, organizational integration as a condition of innovative enterprise weakens. Furthermore, even if the financialized company does show high levels of R&D spending—often to convince the stock market that, notwithstanding massive distributions to shareholders, it is still a high-tech company—these distributions to shareholders tend to undercut not only the efficacy of organizational learning but also the financial commitment to sustaining all of the non-R&D functions that an innovative enterprise requires to generate competitive products.

7.3.5 Acquisitions as a Use of Funds for Innovation

Fried and Wang argue:

> Even net shareholder payouts (adjusted for net debt issuances) tell us little about the effect of such capital flows on public firms' financial capacities—because firms can always choose to issue more stock. The amount of equity issued by any

given public firm in any given year does not represent a cap; the firm could have chosen to issue even more stock to raise cash, acquire assets, or pay employees. Thus, if that firm has a valuable investment opportunity, but little cash, the firm should generally be able to use equity financing to exploit the opportunity. As long as a firm can issue more shares, even firm-shrinking net shareholder payouts (those not offset by net debt issuances) cannot impair the firm's subsequent ability to invest, innovate, and grow.[66]

Here again, it is surprising to see agency theorists arguing that if a company uses its stock, with its price elevated by buybacks, as an acquisition currency, the result will be innovation and higher wages. I would expect agency theorists to assume that, in doing stock-based acquisitions, senior executives are engaged in diluting shareholding in order to build their personal empires. And again, from the perspective of the Theory of Innovative Enterprise, one would not assume that acquisitions, however they are financed, will result in innovation and higher wages *unless* the social conditions of innovative enterprise—strategic control, organizational integration, and financial commitment—are in place to support the transformation of the acquired capabilities into higher-quality, lower-cost products than had previously been available. As we have shown in our research on innovation and competition in the global communication-technology industry, a theory of innovative enterprise is required to perform the analysis of the social conditions under which some acquisitions succeed and others fail.[67]

Cisco Systems is a prime example of a company that effectively used stock as an acquisition currency, as it did in the period 1993–2000 when it came to dominate enterprise equipment, but then afterwards, as it did massive buybacks, failed to invest sufficiently in developing the productive capabilities of key service-provider-equipment acquisitions it had made in 1998–2000. As we have shown in an in-depth study of the company, Cisco's acquisitions from 2004 on were done mostly with cash because, with all its buybacks, it did not want to dilute shareholding. Moreover, many of the acquisitions that Cisco did in the 2000s to expand its product offerings generated nothing more than commodities, an outcome that we attribute to CEO John Chambers' obsessive focus on doing buybacks to manipulate the company's stock price.[68] We have also shown how the leading Old Economy communication-equipment companies Lucent Technologies and Nortel Networks sought to imitate the Cisco model of growth-through-acquisition-and-integration in the late 1990s, using stock as an acquisition currency, and destroyed themselves in the process.[69]

---

[66] Fried and Wang (2017: 4).   [67] Carpenter and Lazonick (2017).
[68] Bell et al. (2014) "Cisco's Evolving Business Model."
[69] Bell et al. (2014); Carpenter and Lazonick (2017).

There is no reason to assume, as Fried and Wang do, that any acquisition, however it is financed, will result in innovation and higher wages. Examples of disastrous deals by major technology companies are Hewlett-Packard's acquisition of the British software company Autonomy and Microsoft's acquisition of Nokia's cellphone business. HP's acquisition of Autonomy in August 2011 was done for $10.2 billion in cash from its offshore holdings, which were protected from U.S. corporate taxation as long as the profits were not repatriated.[70] In November 2012, HP announced that it was taking an $8.8 billion accounting charge because of the failure of the acquisition.[71] Microsoft's acquisition of Nokia's cellphone business followed a strikingly similar trajectory. The acquisition, which included 25,000 Nokia employees, was done in September 2013 for $7.2 billion in cash from Microsoft's offshore holdings.[72] By May 2016 the Nokia acquisition was deemed a failure, with Microsoft losing about $8 billion because of write-offs and restructuring (i.e., layoff) charges.[73]

Fried and Wang are correct: A company can use its stock as an acquisition currency. But they have no grounds for assuming that (a) the use of stock or cash is independent of a company's policy for distributing cash to shareholders, or (b) all acquisitions result in innovation and higher wages. Lacking a theory of the value-creating company, in this, as in other parts of their discussion of the sources and uses of funds, Fried and Wang make statements that defy both facts and logic.

7.3.6 Venture Capital as a Use of Funds for Innovation

Fried and Wang argue:

> The concern about the volume of shareholder payouts appears to be based, in part, on an implicit assumption that there is no economic benefit to putting cash in the hands of public shareholders. But net shareholder payouts from public companies do not disappear down the economic drain. Just as much of the net shareholder payouts from S&P 500 firms flow to smaller public firms outside the S&P 500, much of the net shareholder payouts from public companies in the aggregate are likely to be invested in firms raising capital through an IPO, or in non-public businesses backed by private equity or venture capital. Historically, these firms have been generators of tremendous innovation and job growth in the U.S. economy. Thus, even if net shareholder payouts were to reduce public firms' ability to invest, innovate, and provide higher wages, some of these funds will find their way to private firms and enable these firms to invest, innovate, and provide higher wages. In short, any economic costs borne by stakeholders of

---

[70] HP Press Release (2011).   [71] Armstrong and Kirk (2013).
[72] Microsoft Press Release (2013); Tellis (2013).   [73] Keizer (2015); Warren (2016).

public firms as a result of net shareholder payouts must be weighed against the economic benefits generated by the investment of at least some of these funds in private firms.[74]

Do the massive distributions to shareholders done by established companies such as those included in the S&P 500 Index provide funds to U.S. venture capitalists that enable them to back new firms? As funds flow through the economy, there is no doubt that some of the dividends that shareholders receive for holding shares and some of the stock-price gains that some shareholders reap when they sell shares whose prices have been boosted by buybacks end up in venture-capital funds. But Fried and Wang offer no solid evidence that U.S. venture capital relies on these massive distributions to shareholders as significant sources of funds.[75]

The limited-partnership business model that would come to dominate the U.S venture-capital industry was first set up in 1959 with the launch of the firm of Draper, Gaither, and Anderson in Palo Alto, CA, with funding of $6 million from the Rockefeller Brothers, Lazard Freres, and some wealthy individuals.[76] Even in the 1970s, when, centered in Silicon Valley, venture capital evolved into a distinct industry to fund new-firm creation, institutional-investor funding remained scarce.[77] That changed after July 1979 when the U.S. Department of Labor clarified that pension-fund managers could allocate a small fraction of a fund's assets to risky investments such as venture funds without transgressing the "prudent man" rule contained in the Employee Retirement Income Security Act (ERISA) of 1974. As a result, pension-fund money poured into venture-capital funds. Limited venture-capital partnerships of the type that prevailed in Silicon Valley increased their access to the capital of pension funds from (measured in 1997 dollars) $69 million in 1978, just 15 percent of all funds raised, to $1,808 million in 1983. As stated in Chapter 3 of this book, throughout the 1980s and 1990s, pension funds provided anywhere from 31 percent to 59 percent of the funds raised by limited partnerships, which in turn increased their share of all venture funds raised from 40 percent in 1980 to 80 percent a decade later.[78]

Especially after the Apple and Genentech IPOs of 1980, there was far more venture capital available than good projects in which to invest. One of the chapters of a well-known book, *The New Venturers*, written by *BusinessWeek* reporter John Wilson in 1985, is titled "Vulture Capital," signifying the extent to which the flooding of funds into the industry in the first half of the 1980s resulted in too much money chasing too few good startup opportunities. The same problem,

---

[74] Fried and Wang (2017: 4–5).
[75] Lazonick (2009b, 2009c); Lazonick and Tulum (2011); Chapter 2 of this book.
[76] Business Week (1960).
[77] Lazonick (2009a: ch. 2).
[78] See the discussion in Chapter 3 of this book; Gompers and Lerner (2002).

which appeared on a gigantic scale during the dot.com boom of the late 1990s,[79] exists today in the biomedical industry. In a phenomenon that Lazonick and co-authors Mustafa Erdem Sakınç and Öner Tulum call "product-less IPOs" or "PLIPOs," biomedical startups with no commercial product become listed on NASDAQ, which enables stock-market speculators and manipulators—including top executives, board members, venture capitalists, and hedge-fund managers—to make vast amounts of money even when no innovative product is forthcoming.[80]

The new ventures that do evolve into innovative going concerns achieve this outcome through a regime of "retain-and-reinvest" in which, in order to grow, they tend to pay no dividends and do few if any buybacks.[81] But given the critical role of the stock market—in such instances, almost invariably NASDAQ—in providing "exit" opportunities for both venture-capital investments and employee stock options, when New Economy companies such as Intel, Microsoft, Oracle, and Cisco become successful, concern with keeping down the volume of out-standing shares turns them into rabid stock repurchasers. Finally, there is no evidence that the "war chests" hedge-fund activists build up by buying and selling shares of companies that do massive distributions to shareholders represent a significant source of venture capital for building new companies. There is, on the contrary, abundant evidence that activists fill their war chests, and increase their own personal wealth, by tearing apart established companies, helping to create the enormous imbalance between value creation and value extraction that has become a characteristic feature of the unstable and inequitable U.S. economy.[82]

7.4 Replace Agency Theory with Innovation Theory

For about three decades after World War II, the United States consolidated its position as the world's leading economic power, driven by business enterprises that engaged in "retain-and-reinvest." During these decades, the distribution of income became somewhat more equal and a middle class of both high-school-educated blue-collar workers and college-educated white-collar workers thrived. Over the past four decades, in contrast, the United States has experienced extreme concentration of income among the richest households and the erosion of middle-class employment opportunities for the vast majority of the population.

These two economic problems are integrally related, as, under the influence of the mantra that companies should be run to "maximize shareholder value," the

---

[79] Cassidy (2002); Gimein (2002).

[80] Lazonick and Tulum (2011); Lazonick et al. (2017); Tulum and Lazonick (2019).

[81] See our study of what happened to Apple when, in the decade after Steve Jobs left the company in 1985, its senior executives became obsessed with MSV. Lazonick et al. (2013).

[82] See the discussion in Chapter 6 of this book.

resource-allocation regimes of business corporations have shifted from retain-and-reinvest to downsize-and-distribute. With the rise of ultra-aggressive hedge-fund activism, the current period of U.S. economic history can be called "The Era of Predatory Value Extraction." In this book, we have analyzed the perpetrators of this predation as a concatenation consisting of senior executives as value-extracting insiders, institutional investors as value-extracting enablers, and activist shareholders as value-extracting outsiders.

Academics have played an important role as agents of activist aggression. Since the 1970s, agency theory has aided and abetted predatory value extraction by providing an ostensible economic rationale for why the legalized looting of the business corporation should result in the more efficient allocation of society's economic resources. Fundamental to agency theory is the argument that shareholders as principals need to rely on managers as agents to make decisions concerning corporate-resource allocation. Agency theory contends that the efficient allocation of economic resources requires governance structures that maximize the economic value that accrues to shareholders. If, as a result, the distribution of income is highly unequal, so the agency story goes, that is because economic efficiency requires extreme inequality.

The agency-theory argument raises two critical and related questions: Why are public shareholders deemed to be the "principals" in whose interests the firm should be run? And what contributions do public shareholders make to the value-creation process? As already shown in Chapter 3, the answers to these questions expose agency theory's logical and factual flaws.

Agency theory's answer to the first question is that only shareholders invest in the firm, while all other participants in the firm provide marketable inputs for which they are paid market-determined prices. Its answer to the second question is that, having invested in the firm, public shareholders take the risks of whether those investments will yield profits or losses, and hence, for the sake of economic efficiency, only shareholders have a claim on the firm's profits if and when there is a positive "residual" of revenues over costs.

In this book, we have delineated the logical and factual flaws in these answers. In brief, public shareholders do not, as a rule, invest in the firm. They invest in shares outstanding by simply purchasing them on the stock market. And in purchasing shares on a liquid stock market such as the New York Stock Exchange or NASDAQ, public shareholders take little risk because they enjoy limited liability if they hold the shares while, at any instant and at a very low cost, they can sell the shares at the going market price.

Public shareholders are portfolio investors, not direct investors. The generation of innovative products, however, requires direct investment in productive capabilities. These investments in innovation are uncertain, collective, and cumulative. Innovative enterprise requires strategic control to confront uncertainty, organizational integration to engage in collective learning, and financial commitment to sustain cumulative learning. That is why, to understand the productivity of the firm, we need a theory of innovative enterprise.

When, as in the case of a startup, financiers make equity investments in the absence of a liquid market for the company's shares, they are direct investors who face the risk that the firm will not be able to generate a competitive product. The existence of a highly speculative and liquid stock market may enable them to reap financial returns—in some cases, even before a competitive product has been produced. It was to make such a speculative and liquid market available to private-equity investors, who were to become known as "venture capitalists," that in 1971 the National Association of Security Dealers Automated Quotation exchange was launched by electronically linking the previously fragmented, and hence relatively illiquid, Over-the-Counter markets. NASDAQ became an inducement to direct investment in startups precisely because it offered the prospect of a quick IPO: one that could take place within a few years after the founding of the firm.

It is for that reason that venture capitalists call a listing on NASDAQ an "exit strategy." In effect, they are exiting their illiquid, high-risk direct investments by turning them into liquid, low-risk portfolio investments. If, after an IPO, the former direct investors decide to hold onto their shares, they are in precisely the same low-risk portfolio-investor position as any other public shareholders: they can use the stock market to buy and sell shares whenever they so choose.

But venture capitalists are not the only economic actors who bear the risk of making direct investments in productive capabilities. Taxpayers through government agencies and workers through the firms that employ them make risky investments in productive capabilities on a regular basis. From this perspective, households as taxpayers and workers may have, by agency theory's own logic, "residual claimant" status: that is, an economic claim on the distribution of profits if and when they occur.

As risk bearers, therefore, taxpayers whose money supports business enterprises and workers whose efforts generate productivity improvements have claims on corporate profits if and when they occur. MSV ignores the risk–reward relation for these two types of economic actors in the operation and performance of business corporations. Instead, based on agency theory, it erroneously assumes that shareholders are the only residual claimants.

The irony of MSV is that, as has been noted above, the public shareholders whom agency theory holds up as the only risk bearers typically never invest in the value-creating capabilities of the company at all. Rather, they purchase outstanding corporate equities with the expectation that while they are holding the shares, dividend income will be forthcoming, and with the hope that when they decide to sell the shares, the stock-market price will have risen to yield a capital gain. Following the directives of MSV, a prime way in which the executives who control corporate resource allocation fuel this hope is by allocating corporate cash to stock buybacks to pump up their company's stock price.

Yet it is the senior executives themselves who are best positioned to gain from these manipulative price increases. Senior executives cause cash flow to be "disgorged" not for the sake of efficient resource allocation, but rather with the goal of increasing their own stock-based pay.[83] On an increasing scale since the early 2000s, hedge-fund activists have joined with senior executives and their boards in corporate predation, causing the looting of the U.S. business corporation to accelerate.

Why have agency theorists gotten it so wrong? Because they lack a theory of innovative enterprise: a theory of how business organizations transform technologies and access markets to generate products higher in quality and lower in cost than those previously available. Yet these innovative products are the basis of economic growth. Moreover, based on comparative-historical analysis, we contend that the ways in which innovative enterprises allocate resources and returns provide microfoundations not only for economic growth but also for the employment stability and income equity that are associated with a robust and expanding middle class.[84]

If agency theorists have a coherent theory of the firm, it is the notion that the small, unproductive firm that optimizes subject to given technological and market constraints provides the microeconomic foundation for the most efficient economy. Hypothetical firms of this description play the leading role in the absurd theory known as "perfect competition." From such a neoclassical perspective, it is markets, not organizations, that allocate resources to their most efficient uses. Thus, without specifying the value-creation process, Fried and Wang see financial flows of any type as somehow being allocated to more efficient uses. From this perspective, the large corporations that have dominated the U.S. economy for over 100 years are massive "market imperfections." In line with this reasoning, if we want a more efficient economy, corporate executives should be incentivized, as Michael Jensen and his acolytes have told us, to "disgorge the free cash flow."

It is not surprising, therefore, that Jensen's 1993 American Finance Association presidential address, "The Modern Industrial Revolution, Exit, and the Failure of Internal Control Systems,"[85] is, as the title states, all about *exiting* industrial investments, not about *entering* new ones. Jensen even interprets Joseph Schumpeter's notion of "creative destruction" as being about "efficient exit," i.e., "destruction,"[86] when in fact Schumpeter's entire theoretical orientation was toward the conditions for "entry" through entrepreneurship and innovation: that is, toward the "creative" part of the catchphrase, the part that called for making old ways of doing things obsolete (to which Schumpeter's "destruction" refers).[87] To understand

---

[83] See the discussion in Chapter 4 of this book.
[84] See Lazonick (1990, 1991, 1998, 2003, 2007b, 2009a, 2010, 2015e); Lippert et al. (2014).
[85] Jensen (1993).   [86] Jensen (1993: 833).   [87] Schumpeter (1942: 81–5).

entry, one needs a theory of innovative enterprise, which is precisely what agency theory lacks.

The Theory of Innovative Enterprise recognizes the roles of households acting as taxpayers, workers, consumers, savers, and investors in the value-creation process, and hence provides an economic rationale for their claims on the extraction of value from that process. Through government agencies, households as taxpayers make investments in physical infrastructure and human knowledge without which even, and perhaps especially, the largest business enterprises would not be able to generate competitive products. Hence, through the tax system, the body of taxpayers should get shares of corporate profits if and when they accrue. Through the employment relation, households as workers supply business enterprises with skill and effort that are central to the processes of generating competitive products. Hence, through job stability as well as higher pay and benefits, workers should also share in profits if and when they accrue. Through demand for goods and services, households valorize the products that businesses generate. Hence, households should gain from the innovative capabilities of companies through the production of higher-quality, lower-cost products, which is indeed the purpose of the business corporation.

Finally, the Theory of Innovative Enterprise permits the distinction between *investors*, who participate in the process of *value creation*, and *savers*, who derive incomes from the process of *value extraction*. Investors in value creation provide *financial commitment* to industrial enterprises to sustain the development and utilization of productive resources, and hence should receive an equitable share in profits from the generation of competitive products if and when they accrue. In contrast, savers who, as value extractors, use their money to purchase outstanding corporate shares without in any way contributing to the value-creation process, should get an income in the form of dividends *after all other valid claims of value creators have been paid*. In providing *financial liquidity*, the stock market permits this separation of ownership and control, making savers as passive shareholders able and willing to place their savings in securities in the hope that they will be able to obtain dividends or, if they choose to sell their shares, capital gains.

The theory of the firm that "well-trained" economists, including agency theorists, bring to the policy debate is the antithesis of a theory of innovative enterprise.[88] With its MSV ideology, agency theory is a theory of value extraction, posing as a theory of value creation. As amply demonstrated since the 1980s, the application of agency theory, with its focus on MSV, undermines the achievement of stable and equitable economic growth. Agency theory is part of the problem and is in need of a solution.

---

[88] See the discussion in Chapter 2 of this book.

Innovative enterprise solves the agency problem. By incentivizing and rewarding the real value creators, the innovative enterprise can mobilize the skill, effort, and finance that, by generating high-quality, low-cost products, can improve the performance of the economy—defined in terms of stable and equitable economic growth. The application of innovation theory to corporate governance solves the "agency problem" by setting up governance structures that induce individuals with varied hierarchical responsibilities and functional specialties to work together in business organizations toward the achievement of higher levels of productivity, embodied in higher-quality, lower-cost products. These value-creators share in the gains to innovative enterprise, and they collectively support tax payments as returns for governmental contributions to the value-creation process.

The United States can start the transition from the value-extracting economy to the value-creating economy by banning stock buybacks, compensating senior executives for their contributions to the value-creating enterprise, and placing representatives of households as workers and taxpayers on corporate boards.[89] No progress will be made, however, as long as agency theory with its MSV ideology holds sway. How can academics contribute to the process of putting the United States on a path to achieving stable and equitable growth? The Theory of Innovative Enterprise can help get economic analysis back on track.

---

[89] See the discussion in Chapter 4 of this book.

8

Reversing Predatory Value Extraction

In this book, we have emphasized the growing imbalance between value extraction and value creation, and its destructive consequences for the accumulation of productive capabilities, employment stability, and income distribution. Long viewed as the world's greatest value-creating economy, the United States has become the world's foremost example of the value-extracting economy. In the United States, economically and politically, predatory value extraction has trumped sustainable prosperity.

Driving the transformation of the U.S. economy from a paragon of middle-class strength to the woeful exemplar of the division between "the 1 percent" and "the 99 percent" has been an ideological insistence that business corporations should be run to maximize shareholder value (MSV). The emergence of MSV as an ideology of corporate governance dates back less than half a century, and its actual application in the business world took root only in the mid-1980s. Previously, during the post-World War II decades, the retain-and-reinvest mode of corporate resource allocation had been the accepted and dominant corporate-governance norm among corporate executives, corporate board members, shareholders, academics, policy-makers, and the public. Retain-and-reinvest was key to creating the upward socioeconomic mobility of the population that marked an optimistic age of American capitalism in the decades after World War II. Yet since the 1970s retain-and-reinvest has given way to downsize-and-distribute, with its deleterious impacts on employment opportunity, income distribution, and productivity growth. Needed now are dramatic and concrete policy changes to prevent the implementation of MSV ideology from inflicting even more severe damage on workers, taxpayers, companies, and the economy. There is a pressing need to bring value creation and value extraction back into balance, and, in the process, install the social institutions and build the business organizations that can provide foundations for sustainable prosperity.

This concluding chapter lays out a basic agenda for combatting predatory value extraction and restoring sustainable prosperity. There are five broad planks in the scaffolding on which a value-creating economy can build:

- Rescind SEC Rule 10b-18 and ban open-market stock repurchases.
- Redesign executive pay to incentivize and reward value creation, not value extraction.

Predatory Value Extraction: How the Looting of the Business Corporation Became the U.S. Norm and How Sustainable Prosperity Can Be Restored. William Lazonick and Jang-Sup Shin, Oxford University Press (2020). © William Lazonick and Jang-Sup Shin. DOI: 10.1093/oso/9780198846772.001.0001

- Reconstitute corporate boards of directors to include representatives of households as workers, as taxpayers, and as savers as well as households as founders—and exclude the predatory value extractors.
- Reform the corporate tax system so that it returns profits to taxpaying households and funds government spending on infrastructure and knowledge for the next generation of innovative products.
- Redeploy corporate profits and productive capabilities to support collective and cumulative careers, and thus enable widespread upward socioeconomic mobility.

8.1 Rescind SEC Rule 10b-18

In the New Deal of the 1930s, the United States Congress set up the Securities and Exchange Commission (SEC) to rid financial markets, including the stock markets, of manipulation and fraud. Dominated by lawyers who searched for legal and effective ways to implement this mandate, the fight against financial predation remained the objective of the SEC until January 1981, when Ronald Reagan was inaugurated as President of the United States. As the new chair of the SEC Reagan chose John Shad, a Wall Street banker who had been the head of Reagan's New York State presidential campaign. His thinking shaped by the neoclassical economics of the free-market Chicago School, Shad had a deep interest in derivatives as instruments for securing higher yields on financial portfolios.[1] More generally, Shad held to the view that more money moving around financial markets meant larger supplies of finance for capital formation (an agency theory perspective that we have thoroughly critiqued in Chapter 7). In line with this neoclassical belief that markets allocate resources to their most efficient uses, under Shad's leadership in November 1982 the SEC adopted Rule 10b-18, which, as we have seen, effectively legalized the use of stock buybacks by companies to manipulate their own stock prices.

With the adoption of Rule 10b-18, the SEC transitioned from being a *regulator* of the stock market for the purpose of eliminating manipulation and fraud to being a *promoter* of the stock market in ways that enable predatory value extraction—all in the name of MSV. The Reaganite reshaping of the mission of the SEC was integral to the rise of MSV as the dominant ideology of corporate governance over the course of the 1980s. SEC Chair Shad appointed to the position of SEC chief economist Charles C. Cox, who in 1975 had received his economics PhD from the University of Chicago on the subject of financial derivatives. In 1983 Cox became an SEC commissioner, replacing a Nixon-era Republican commissioner,

---

[1] Vise and Coll (1991); Jacobson and Lazonick (2019).

John Evans, who objected to Shad's dramatic reorientation of the SEC's mission and who in November 1982 had voiced his opposition to the adoption of Rule 10b-18.[2] Shad then chose as the new chief economist Gregg A. Jarrell, a 1977 University of Chicago economics PhD, who was a cheerleader for the hostile-takeover movement and the unfettered operation of the market for corporate control.[3]

With Chicago School economics redefining the mission of the SEC, this supposed regulatory agency was placed in the service of MSV. With Rule 10b-18, for the past thirty-seven years the SEC has permitted the legalized looting of the US business corporation, with, as we have documented in this book, the SEC's promotion of the financialized use of stock-based executive pay and the game-changing proxy-voting system aiding and abetting the looting process. The stated mission of the SEC is to "protect investors; maintain fair, orderly, and efficient markets; [and] facilitate capital formation."[4] The facts and logic that we have presented in this book support the argument that, partly because of the adoption and implementation of Rule 10b-18, *the SEC is failing in all three of these missions.*

When, under Rule 10b-18, the SEC permits massive manipulation of the stock market, it fails to protect "investors"—by which the SEC presumably means households as savers. Households that allocate a portion of their savings to purchase the shares of publicly listed companies want those shares to yield an income stream from dividends while they are holding the shares and capital gains from stock-price increases if and when they decide to sell the shares. It is only by generating innovative products that a company can provide these yields on a sustainable basis, with the payment of dividends to shareholders being determined after all of the needs of the company for reinvestment of profits to remain competitive in the future have been met. Stock buybacks done as open-market repurchases do not, except by accident, benefit households as savers. As we have emphasized, open-market repurchases carried out in accordance with Rule 10b-18 benefit those stock-market traders—including senior corporate executives, hedge-fund managers, and Wall Street bankers—who are in the business of timing the buying and selling of shares to reap gains from stock-price changes and who, as an essential business tool, have access to real-time information on buyback activity that households as savers do not possess. If the SEC wants to protect households that place some or all of their savings in outstanding corporate shares, it should rescind Rule 10b-18 and call for a ban on open-market repurchases by publicly listed corporations.

When, under Rule 10b-18, the SEC permits massive manipulation of the stock market, it fails in its mission of ensuring "fair, orderly, and efficient" markets. The stock market is not fair, when predatory value extractors are granted the right to

---

[2] Hudson (1982).   [3] Vise and Coll (1991); Jacobson and Lazonick (2019).
[4] The SEC website (https://www.investor.gov/introduction-investing/basics/role-sec).

manipulate stock prices for their own gain. The stock market is not orderly when, as was the case in the stock-market booms of 2003–07 and 2009–19, stock prices have been boosted by stock buybacks, funded by not only profits but also debt—as well as the massive Republican tax cuts of 2001/2003 and 2017.[5] In a competitive process to keep up with the market in stock-price performance, companies escalate buybacks when stock prices are high, helping to set up the manipulated stock market for a precipitous fall. By enabling manipulation of stock prices and fomenting speculation in a surging stock market, stock buybacks contribute to disorderly markets. And, obviously, there is nothing "efficient" about a stock market that is manipulated by stock buybacks. For households as savers, the stock market cannot be an efficient way of enhancing the value of their savings when a small number of predatory value extractors benefit from rules of the game that give insiders most of the stock-market gains. If the SEC wants to use its regulatory power to make U.S. stock markets fairer, more orderly, and more efficient, it should rescind Rule 10b-18 and call for a ban on open-market repurchases by publicly listed corporations.

Far from facilitating capital formation, as the SEC claims they do, stock buy-backs done under Rule 10b-18 undermine capital formation, including invest-ments in human capabilities as well as physical capital. Earnings retained out of profits are the foundation of corporate finance for investment in productive capabilities, and stock buybacks coming on top of ample dividends have been persistently depleting the retained earnings of U.S. business corporations. A significant portion of those distributions augment the war chests of hedge funds, giving them even more power to engage in predatory value extraction. If the SEC wants to use its regulatory power to encourage capital formation, it should rescind Rule 10b-18 and call for a ban on open-market repurchases by publicly listed corporations.

8.2 Redesign Executive Pay

As we detailed in Chapter 4 on the value-extracting insiders, U.S.-style executive compensation incentivizes and rewards value extraction, not value creation. As we have seen, the average total compensation of the 500 highest-paid executives in the United States in each year from 2008 through 2017 ranged from $15.8 million in 2009, of which, with the stock market depressed, stock-based pay was 60 percent of the total, to $34.1 million in 2015, of which, with the stock market booming, stock-based pay was 83 percent of the total. Stock-based pay takes the form of stock options and stock awards. Stock options were much more widely used than

---

[5] See, for example, Pearlstein (2018); Helmore (2018).

stock awards in the 1990s. But since the mid-2000s stock awards have become more popular. In 2007, with the average total compensation of the 500 highest-paid executives at $31.0 million, realized gains from stock options represented 57 percent of the total, while realized gains from stock awards represented 19 percent. In 2017, the average total compensation of the 500 highest-paid executives was $32.1 million, with realized gains from stock awards at 46 percent and realized gains from stock options 35 percent.

The design of both U.S.-style stock options and stock awards incentivizes value extraction rather than value creation. A stock option, which includes a certain number of shares, will typically vest over four years, with one-quarter of the shares in the option vesting at the end of each year (although, particularly for senior executives, many other arrangements are possible). The executive then has (provided that he or she stays with the company) a vast "window" of anywhere from six to nine years before the options expire, during which time he or she can choose *the particular day or days* on which to exercise the option. If the executive thinks that the company's stock price will be higher, say, six months from now, then he or she would wait to exercise the option with that expectation. By the same token, when executives exercise stock options, they usually sell the acquired shares immediately to lock in the realized gains—all the more so because the executives will pay taxes on these realized gains, regardless of whether the executive sells or holds the acquired shares.

Prior to 1991, under an SEC rule to prevent insiders from making short-swing profits, senior executives had to hold the shares obtained from exercising options for six months after the exercise date in order to realize the gains.[6] This rule impeded their ability to time the market. In May 1991, however, the SEC changed the rule so that the six-month waiting period starts when the option is awarded, not when it is exercised, thus permitting the executive to sell the acquired shares immediately upon exercising the option, locking in the realized gains. U.S.-style stock options, therefore, provide incentives to executives to take advantage of what they think may be short-term surges in the company's stock price. And stock buybacks, the timing of the exercise of which these executives control, are an ideal mode of making these surges happen. By design, U.S.-style executive stock options incentivize value extraction, not value creation.

So too with stock awards. Executives realize the gains from stock awards when they vest. The least complicated stock awards will simply vest after a stated period of time; say, three years from the award date. As in the case of stock options, the executive can then, if he or she chooses, sell the acquired shares to lock in the gains. Or the executive can continue to hold the shares to collect dividends and, possibly, reap a future capital gain. But the presence of a liquid stock market

---

[6] Lazonick (2013: 886–7).

makes it easy and inexpensive for the executive to sell the shares immediately upon acquiring them, and (again, as is the case with stock options) the fact that the company will immediately withhold personal taxes on the value of shares at the vesting-date stock price provides an incentive to sell the shares as soon as they vest. However, most stock awards to senior executives do not simply vest after a period of time but include financial performance targets, with vesting triggered by achieving a stock-based financial metric such as earnings-per-share or total-shareholder-yield. Many stock awards provide bonus shares when such a target is hit. As with stock options, stock awards reward executives for stock-price increases, however short-lived, making stock buybacks the tried and true companion of executive stock-based pay.

If we want to incentivize value creation rather than value extraction, we should get rid of U.S.-style stock-based pay. As currently structured in the United States, stock options and stock awards reward speculation and manipulation far more than innovation. Indeed, these forms of stock-based compensation tend to incentivize senior executives to make corporate resource-allocation decisions that foment speculation and machinate manipulation. Senior executives should be incentivized and rewarded by metrics related to the success of the innovative enterprise. They should be incentivized to invest in higher-quality products that build on the distinctive productive capabilities of the firms that they lead. They should be rewarded by indicators of innovative enterprise such as the new competitive products that the firm generates and the enhanced employment security and income gains of the employees whose skills and efforts brought those products into being. These executives should view retained earnings as a precious resource that provides the financial commitment necessary to support the innovation process. And they should view stock buybacks as a leading indicator of senior executives who are *not* doing their jobs.

8.3 Reconstitute Corporate Boards

It would be an immense help in the transformation of business corporations from value extraction to value creation if, in business schools, future executives were educated in innovation theory rather than agency theory. And then corporations would have to be governed in ways that would elevate the proponents of value creation rather than the proponents of value extraction to positions of strategic control. Such a corporate-governance outcome depends on the education, experience, outlooks, and interests of the people who sit as directors on corporate boards. In particular, boards should be populated by people who reject the mantra that companies should be run to maximize shareholder value, recognizing that it is a pernicious ideology of value extraction and not the virtuous prescription for value creation that its proponents make it out to be.

We have offered a fundamental critique of MSV ideology, attacking its basic premises concerning investment, risk-taking, and economic performance. MSV is an ideology that assumes that, of all participants in the activities of the business corporation, only shareholders take the risk of whether the company will generate profits from its productive activities, and hence only shareholders have a legitimate economic claim on profits if and when they occur. It is assumed that in a "market economy" all other participants receive a market-determined, risk-free payment for productive goods and services rendered. Hence, unlike shareholders, according to agency theory, those other participants do not bear the risk of whether the company turns a profit or sustains a loss. The proponents of MSV claim that its pursuit enables shareholders, as the economy's risk-bearers, to reallocate resources to their most efficient uses, with distributions of cash to shareholders in the form of dividends and buybacks funding this process. As a corollary, as the economy's sole risk-takers, it follows from MSV ideology that only shareholders have a legitimate claim to be directly engaged in the exercise of corporate decision-making by having representation on corporate boards of directors.

The argument that risk-takers should have claims on corporate profits (and bear the burden of corporate losses) and sit on corporate boards is a valid approach to the governance of the value-creating business enterprise. The problem, however, is that, as we have stressed in this book, public shareholders are not the only, or even the most important, risk-takers in the uncertain process of transforming investments in the firm's productive capabilities into the revenue-generating products that can enable the firm to reap profits. Indeed, with limited liability and access to the liquid stock market on which they can buy and sell shares, public shareholders take little risk at all. If a stock price falls or a company fails to pay a dividend, public shareholders can limit their losses instantaneously by selling their shares. And they can choose to diversify their shareholdings across a vast array of highly liquid stocks, which is a primary reason why such a large proportion of household savings is in the hands of institutional investors.

Workers and taxpayers are risk-takers who invest in the firm's productive capabilities, and from the perspective of innovation theory, the risks that workers and taxpayers take are far more fundamental to a value-creating economy than the risks that public shareholders take. When, according to the tenets of agency theory, senior executives make corporate allocation decisions "to disgorge the free cash flow," as leading agency theorist Michael Jensen put it,[7] they are advocating the extraction of value from those households as workers and taxpayers that helped to create that value. The modes of corporate resource allocation prescribed by agency theory and legitimized by MSV have resulted in the extreme imbalance

[7] Jensen (1986).

between value creation and value extraction that we have labeled predatory value extraction.

To recap our argument, households as workers take risks when they supply their skills and efforts to invest in improving the firm's productive capabilities, the purpose of which is to generate product revenues and profits in the future. They take the economic risk that, for technological, market, and competitive reasons, these investments in productive capabilities may in fact be unsuccessful in generating future revenues and profits. They take the political risk that even if future competitive products generate future revenues and profits, predatory value extractors will gain control over the allocation of corporate resources and will use that control to reap where they have not sown. Indeed, the history of the growing power of predatory value extractors that we have recounted in this book reveals that the political risk that workers as value creators face is very real. The overall result in the United States has been an extreme imbalance between value creation and value extraction, manifested by a concentration of income among the very richest U.S. households and the loss of middle-class employment opportunities.

As we have also argued, households as taxpayers take risks when, through government agencies, they pay a portion of their incomes to support investments in physical infrastructure and human knowledge that business enterprises utilize, and indeed require, to conduct their economic affairs. The return to households as taxpayers for making these productive capabilities available to business derives in large part from the taxes that businesses pay on the profits that they generate. Households as taxpayers take the economic risk that the firms that utilize these public resources will not generate the profits to pay the business taxes that reimburse households for their tax contributions. Households as taxpayers also take the political risk that business executives will convince legislators that, in order to make adequate profits, they need lower business taxes—as indeed happened (by no means for the first time) in the United States with the Republican tax-break act that passed Congress at the end of 2017. As expected, a main result of the Tax Cuts and Jobs Act of 2017 was a record-breaking level of stock buybacks in 2018—in excess of $800 billion by the companies in the S&P 500 Index.[8]

By the logic of ensuring the balance between risks and rewards, households as workers and households as taxpayers should have representatives on corporate boards of directors.[9] Households as savers—which is what most public

---

[8] Yardeni et al. (2019).

[9] In March 2018, U.S. Senator Tammy Baldwin (D-WI) introduced the *Reward Work Act* (S.2605), which would make open-market repurchases subject to manipulation charges by rescinding Rule 10b-18 and allot seats on corporate boards for workers' representatives (Baldwin, 2018). The Reward Work Act was reintroduced in March 2019 as S.915 (Baldwin, 2019). In August 2018, U.S. Senator Elizabeth Warren (D-MA) introduced the *Accountable Capitalism Act* (S.3348), aimed at companies with annual revenues of $1 billion or more, which complements the Reward Work Act by placing worker representatives on corporate boards and restraining the realized gains from stock-based

shareholders are—should also have board representation, but to a lesser extent than households as workers and as taxpayers. To repeat: Public shareholders have limited liability, and, given a liquid stock market—which is the reason why they are able and willing to buy shares in the first place—they can cut their losses by selling the shares at any instant that they so choose. In sharp contrast, in working long, hard, and smart for a company, workers have their livelihoods and careers at stake, and the only highly liquid markets for jobs are ones with low pay and insecure employment—and these are buyers' markets. Most households as taxpayers—especially those that derive their incomes mainly from wages and salaries—have no choice but to pay their taxes, no matter how business corporations abuse their access to the publicly funded resources that households as taxpayers provide and avoid paying business taxes, thus increasing the burden of households as taxpayers to fund government spending. In the United States, high-income taxpaying households have all manner of ways to avoid paying taxes (see the plank on fixing the tax system below). Bottom line: Households as workers and taxpayers need to be represented on corporate boards.

Why should households as savers have any representation at all on boards of directors? The answer is that, as demonstrated in Chapter 3, the most important positive function of the stock market is to separate managerial control from asset ownership by means of firms going public. To effect this separation, households as savers need to have an incentive to hold shares of companies. For that, they need liquidity and they need limited liability, both of which the stock market gives them. Given alternative ways of getting yields on their financial portfolios, households as savers also need a flow of income on their savings if they are going to allocate those savings to publicly traded stocks. Households as savers need a representative on the board, with insider knowledge of the company, to argue the case for the payment of dividends when the company can afford to pay them as well as to assent to the reduction or non-payment of dividends when the company needs to reinvest more or all of its cash flow in productive capabilities.

For these reasons, we argue for a prioritizing of corporate board representation that places households as workers first, households as taxpayers second, and households as savers third. It is also necessary to have board representation at publicly listed corporations for what can be called households as founders—entrepreneurs and financiers who invest time, effort, and money in the productive capabilities of a company prior to its initial public offering, at which point they can easily cash in their shares. Insofar as they continue to hold founder shares in the publicly listed company, households as founders should have

---

executive pay (Yglesias 2018a). In December 2018, five House Democrats introduced a version of the Accountable Capitalism Act in the U.S. House of Representatives (Yglesias 2018b).

board representation. At the same time, sustainable prosperity requires a system of board representation that excludes predatory value extractors from exercising strategic control—a far cry from the situation that now exists in the corporate-governance era of MSV.

In effect, we are calling for a robust stakeholder democracy rooted in the social conditions of innovative enterprise to replace the broken and corrupt regime of so-called "shareholder democracy" that has legitimized a system in which corporate board members represent shareholders exclusively. Once it is recognized that households as savers are not investors in the productive assets of companies, the rationale vanishes for a public shareholder's having a vote *that reflects an ownership stake.* Public shareholders would continue to have voting rights under a "stakeholder" corporate-governance regime, but their votes for board members would be only for that subset of the board seats that represent households as savers. Currently, besides voting on a decision to sell or merge the company, the only substantive role of shareholder voting is for board representation. Shareholder proposals at the annual meeting are limited to issues that concern the company that are NOT based on business judgement, such as whether the company is engaged in age discrimination or environmental pollution. Under a stakeholder scheme of corporate governance, the proxy statements would be sent to and the annual meeting would be open to all stakeholders.

Our argument for extending to workers and taxpayers the right to representation on corporate boards is radical. But then all extensions of democratic rights to previously disenfranchised groups of people represent major social change—take, for example, the extension of the political vote to women. And, given the damage that the current system of corporate governance is inflicting on the attainment of stable and equitable economic growth, radical change is urgently required. Shaped by the highly flawed ideology that public shareholding represents "ownership" of productive assets, the proxy-voting system as it now exists undermines sustainable prosperity.

In the Old Economy era, when shareholding was fragmented among households, one could live with the ideology that voting rights were based on ownership of the firm's assets because shareholding was too dispersed for that purported ownership right to be exercised. By the 1980s, however, shareholding was no longer fragmented, and the very definition of proxy voting changed. When shareholding was fragmented, individual shareholders who could not attend the annual meeting could give someone in attendance the proxy to vote their shares in a certain way. But now, as a result of the institutional changes that we described in Chapter 5, proxy voting means giving institutional investors the *obligation*—not just the right—to vote shares in their portfolios. This rule, adopted by the SEC in 1992, has put concentrated influence over voting power in the hands of two proxy-advisory firms, ISS and Glass Lewis. And the dropping of the non-engagement rule means that a hedge fund with a very small percentage of outstanding shares can use its influence with the proxy advisers, fund managers, corporate executives, and board members to secure management decisions that boost stock yields.

As part of the process of reforming the system of corporate board representation, the following three changes must be made. First, abolish the obligation that shareholders exercise voting rights on the shares that they hold. If those who have the right to vote do not want to vote, perhaps because they have not taken the time and effort to inform themselves how to vote. Then they should not have to vote. Second, eliminate the power of the managers of institutional funds to exercise the voting rights attached to savers' shares. This practice leaves the door wide open for hedge-fund managers, as value-extracting outsiders, to collaborate with institutional-fund managers, as value-extracting enablers, to gain access to or influence over corporate boards—with predatory value extraction as the result. Third, end the right of public shareholders to directly engage corporate executives. Direct engagement creates a system in which hedge-fund activists can use their wealth, visibility, hype, influence, and insider information to shape the thinking and actions of corporate management, bypassing the legitimate role of corporate boards of directors in performing these functions. Without these three reforms, predatory value extraction will remain the corporate-governance norm.

8.4 Reform the Corporate Tax System

Fundamental to MSV ideology is the myth that the United States is a "free market" economy. The United States has highly developed markets in product, labor, finance, and land. But these markets are the result, not the cause, of a highly productive economy.[10] The foundation of economic development is the "investment triad": household families, government agencies, and business enterprises. These families, agencies, and enterprises are *organizations (not markets) that invest in productive capabilities.* Household families invest in the present and future labor force; government agencies invest in physical infrastructure and the knowledge base; and business enterprises invest in collective and cumulative learning processes for the sake of generating innovative products. The investment strategies of these three types of organizations must be working in harmony to have a highly productive economy. This organizationally driven productivity permits markets in products, labor, finance, and land to flourish. There are lots of high-quality, low-cost products on the market. There are large numbers of well-paid employment opportunities available to the qualified labor force. There are vast quantities of savings looking for yields. And land increases in value in locations where the investment triad generates high levels of productivity.

---

[10] Lazonick (2003, 2017b).

Ultimately, given investments in productive capabilities by household families and by government agencies, we rely on business enterprises to generate the high-quality, low-cost products that are the essence of productivity. In the process, these business enterprises provide productive employment from which households obtain their incomes. Out of these incomes, households pay taxes to governments, which set up agencies to invest in the physical infrastructure and human knowledge that businesses need but in which even the largest business enterprises would be unable to undertake the necessary investment.

Big businesses and the households that grow wealthy from their involvement in these enterprises must pay their fair share of taxes to pay back the vast majority of households whose tax payments have supported government investments in infrastructure and knowledge. Yet MSV ideology proclaims that taxes on big business enterprises and the wealthiest households will undermine investment in the productive capabilities that can deliver more employment opportunities, higher incomes, and more rapid productivity growth. In the context of the Republican "tax-breaks-for-corporations-and-wealthy-households act" passed by the U.S. Congress in December 2017, both the advocates of MSV and the critics of MSV recognized that the main corporate use of the extra income from the lowering of corporate tax rates on domestic and repatriated profits would be increased distributions to shareholders in the form of cash dividends and stock buybacks.[11] This cynical attempt at "tax reform," carried out to capture the political financial contributions of the predatory value extractors, will make "the value-extracting economy" an even more apt description of what, in the twenty-first century, the U.S. economy has become.

8.5 Redeploy Corporate Profits and Productive Capabilities

In a world of rapid technological innovation and intense global competition, the value-creating economy depends on the continuous augmentation of the productive capabilities of the labor force. That means the constant upgrading of both the higher education and work experience of the national labor force. This upgrading of the labor force provides a necessary condition for producing innovative products, the productivity of which can be shared with workers in the form of higher wages and benefits. That is how a society's standard of living improves over time. The constant upgrading of the productive capabilities of the labor force and the return of a substantial portion of the productivity gains to these productive workers are fundamental to achieving stable and equitable economic growth—or what we call sustainable prosperity.

---

[11] Lazonick (2018a).

The learning that is the essence of the innovation process is collective and cumulative. Innovation cannot be done alone. People learn how to do their jobs better through interactions with others who are intent on the same organizational objectives. In the business enterprise, these collective interactions can result in the transformation of technologies and the accessing of markets that would not be possible if the large numbers of people involved in the complex hierarchical and functional division of labor were working in isolation from one another. Furthermore, innovation cannot be done all at once. What the learning collectivity learns today creates an indispensable foundation for what the learning collectivity can learn tomorrow. It is because of this cumulative character of the collective learning process that innovative companies seek to retain key employees over long periods of time. And in a complex division of labor producing complex products, the people who are "key" to the collective and cumulative learning process can be found deep down in the organizational hierarchy.

Just as companies need collective and cumulative learning to be innovative, employees need *collective and cumulative careers* (CCCs) to remain productive over working lives that now span four decades or more. Under the Old Economy business model, companies provided CCCs through the employment norm of a career-with-one-company (CWOC). But with the rise to dominance of the New Economy business model in the 1980s and 1990s, the CWOC norm disappeared. New Economy startups could not attract talent by holding out the promise of a career with one company. In a process that Lazonick has called "marketization," however, New Economy startups could induce talent to leave or eschew CWOC employment with Old Economy companies for the sake of stock options that could become very valuable if and when the company did an IPO on the NASDAQ exchange.[12]

This New Economy practice of using stock options to attract and retain a broad base of employees remained intact even after some startups became going concerns with employment in the tens of thousands. Over the course of the 1980s and 1990s, this marketization process corroded the CWOC norm at Old Economy companies, with IBM's deliberate downsizing of its labor force from 374,000 in 1990 to 220,000 in 1994 representing a pivotal case.[13] In the twenty-first century, the globalization of the labor force, particularly in high-tech fields, has completed the erosion of the CWOC norm in the United States, as key jobs are offshored to lower-wage areas of the world and as key employees are recruited, often on temporary non-immigrant visas, to fill these jobs in the United States.

---

[12] Lazonick (2015e).   [13] Lazonick (2009a: chs. 2–5).

This dramatic change in the dominant business model has created enormous challenges for members of the U.S. labor force to construct the CCCs that a middle-class existence requires. In a globalized economy with rapid technological change, the CWOC norm will not, cannot, and should not be restored. For the sake of sustainable prosperity, social institutions must be restructured to support CCCs across business enterprises, government agencies, and civil-society organizations. There are many different paths by which an individual can structure a CCC. Over the course of his or her career, an individual may develop skill through a series of jobs in different organizations, and the age of the Internet facilitates the individual pursuit of a CCC through participation in an interlinked network of business enterprises, government agencies, and civil-society organizations. In addition, a CCC may be followed across national borders, often with employment by one multinational organization or through a more individualized search for a globalized career path.[14]

In an economy in which the accumulation of knowledge provides an increasingly important foundation for sustaining high levels of productivity, the availability of CCCs has become more important than ever. In a world of rapidly changing technology and intense global competition, CCCs have become increasingly necessary for an individual to maintain a good standard of living over an expected forty to fifty years of his or her working life with sufficient savings from employment income to sustain him or her for another twenty to thirty years in retirement. Without a CCC, a person who was deemed to be highly productive in, say, his or her forties may become obsolete in his or her fifties or find that educated and experienced workers in lower-wage areas of the world have become well qualified to do his or her job.

Many of the most talented and ambitious young people embarking on careers may look—as indeed they have been doing since the late 1980s—for a quick hit on Wall Street or a NASDAQ IPO that can provide them with enough income for a lifetime without pursuing a CCC. These individual solutions just serve to concentrate income at the top, typically at the expense of stable and equitable economic growth. The problem is especially acute when the large corporations that used to be the bedrocks of CCCs support the dominance of the "financial economy" over the "productive economy" by distributing almost all, if not more, of their profits to shareholders in the form of stock buybacks and cash dividends.

How can the United States stifle predatory value extraction and put the nation back on a path to stable and equitable economic growth? Ban stock buybacks done as open-market repurchases. Structure executive remuneration to incentivize value creation, not value extraction. Place representatives of households as workers and taxpayers on corporate boards, while excluding the predatory

---

[14] Lazonick (2009a: ch. 5; 2015e).

value-extractors. Fix the broken tax system so that profitable corporations and rich households return value to the society to pay for the public resources that have helped make them profitable and rich. Finally, coordinate the investment triad to enable an ever-growing proportion of the population to pursue and prosper from collective and cumulative careers.

Bibliography

Ahuja, Maneet (2012), *The Alpha Masters*, John Wiley & Sons.

Alexander, Brian (2017), *Glass House: The 1% Economy and the Shattering of an All-American Town*, St. Martin's Press.

Allen, Franklin, and Douglas Gale (2001), *Comparing Financial Systems: A Survey*, MIT Press.

Anabtawi, Iman, and Lynn Stout (2008), "Fiduciary Duties for Activist Shareholders," *Stanford Law Review*, 60(5): 1255–308.

Ando, Ritsuko (2015), "Japan's Fanuc must do buybacks, capex plan no fix: Loeb," *Reuters*, February 21, at https://www.reuters.com/article/us-thirdpoint-fanuc/japans-fanuc-must-do-buybacks-capex-plan-no-fix-loeb-idUSKBN0LP04G20150221.

Appelbaum, Eileen, and Rosemary Batt (2014), *Private Equity at Work: When Wall Street Manages Main Street*, Russell Sage Foundation.

Apple Inc. (2014), "Apple reports first quarter results," press release, January 27, at https://www.apple.com/pr/library/2014/01/27Apple-Reports-First-Quarter-Results.html. bail-out-ends-as-u-s-sells-last-of-government-motors-.

Armstrong, Robert, and Stuart Kirk (2013), "HP and Autonomy: How to lose $8.8bn," *Financial Times*, May 8, at https://www.ft.com/content/7a52adb4-b70d-11e2-a249-00144feabdc0.

Bainbridge, Stephen M. (2005), "Shareholder Activism and Institutional Investors," *UCLA School of Law, Law-Econ Research Paper No. 05–20*, at https://papers.ssrn.com/sol3/papers.cfm?abstract_id=796227.

Bakija, Jon, Adam Cole, and Bradley T. Heim (2012), "Jobs and Income Growth of Top Earners and the Causes of Changing Income Inequality: Evidence from U.S. Tax Return Data," working paper, April, at https://web.williams.edu/Economics/wp/BakijaColeHeimJobsIncomeGrowthTopEarners.pdf.

Baldwin, Carliss Y. (1991), "How Capital Budgeting Deters Innovation—and What To Do About It," *Research Technology Management*, 34(6): 39–45.

Baldwin, Clare, and Soyoung Kim (2010), "GM IPO raises $20.1 billion," *Reuters*, November 16, at http://www.reuters.com/article/us-gm-ipo-idUSTRE6AB43H20101117.

Baldwin, Tammy (2015), Correspondence with SEC Chair Mary Jo White on April 23, 2015 at www.baldwin.senate.gov/imo/media/doc/Baldwin%20Letter%20to%20SEC%204%2023%2015.pdf; July 13, 2015 at www.documentcloud.org/documents/2272283-sec-response-to-baldwin-07132015.html#document/p1; November 16, 2015 at www.baldwin.senate.gov/imo/media/doc/111615%20Letter%20to%20SEC.pdf; and January 29, 2016 (copy in the possession of the authors).

Baldwin, Tammy (2018), "U.S. Senator Tammy Baldwin introduces legislation to rein in stock buybacks and give workers a seat at the table," press release, March 22, at https://www.baldwin.senate.gov/press-releases/reward-work-act.

Baldwin, Tammy (2019), "U.S. Senator Tammy Baldwin reintroduces legislation to rein in stock buybacks and give workers a voice on corporate boards," press release, March 27, at https://www.baldwin.senate.gov/press-releases/reward-work-act-2019.

Bassett, Ross Knox (2002), *To the Digital Age: Research Labs, Start-Up Companies, and the Rise of MOS Technology*, Johns Hopkins University Press.

Bebchuk, Lucian (2013), "The Myth that Insulating Boards Serves Long-Term Value," *Columbia Law Review*, 113(6): 1637–94.

Bebchuk, Lucian, and Jesse Fried (2004), *Pay Without Performance: The Unfulfilled Promise of Executive Compensation*, Harvard University Press.

Bebchuk, Lucian, and Scott Hirst (2018), "Index Funds and the Future of Corporate Governance: Theory, Evidence, and Policy," *Harvard Law School John M. Olin Center Discussion Paper No. 986*, at https://papers.ssrn.com/sol3/papers.cfm?abstract_id=3282794##

Bebchuk, Lucian, Alon Brav, and Wei Jiang (2015), "The Long-Term Effects of Hedge-Fund Activism," *Columbia Law Review*, 115(5): 1085–155.

Becht, Marco, Julian Franks, Jeremy Grant, and Hammes F. Wagner (2015), "The Returns to Hedge Fund Activism: An International Study," *ECGI Working Paper No. 402/2014*, in Finance, at http://ssrn.com/abstract=2376271.

Beech, Eric (2014), "U.S. government says it lost $11.2 billion on GM bailout," *Reuters*, April 30, at http://www.reuters.com/article/us-autos-gm-treasury-idUSBREA3T0MR-20140430.

Bell, Bob, Marie Carpenter, Henrik Glimstedt, and William Lazonick (2014), "Cisco's Evolving Business Model: Do Massive Stock Buybacks Affect Corporate Performance?," paper presented at the Edith Penrose Centenary Conference, SOAS University of London, November 15.

Benoit, David (2016), "Trump names Carl Icahn as adviser on regulatory overhaul," *Wall Street Journal*, December 21, at https://www.wsj.com/articles/trump-to-name-icahn-as-adviser-on-regulatory-overhaul-1482354552.

Benoit, David, and Joann S. Lublin (2014), "Third Point revives 'golden leash' pay plan in Dow Chemical fight," *Wall Street Journal*, November 16, at https://www.wsj.com/articles/third-point-revives-golden-leash-pay-plan-in-dow-chemical-fight-1416171616.

Berger, Suzanne (2014), "How Finance Gutted Manufacturing," *Boston Review*, April 1, at http://bostonreview.net/forum/suzanne-berger-how-finance-gutted-manufacturing.

Berle, Adolf A. (1954), *20th Century Capitalist Revolution*, Harcourt, Brace & World.

Berle, Adolf A., and Gardiner C. Means (1932), *Modern Corporation and Private Property*, MacMillan.

Bethel, Jennifer E., and Stuart L. Gillan (2002), "The Impact of the Institutional and Regulatory Environment on Shareholder Voting," *Financial Management*, 31(4): 29–54.

Bew, Robyn, and Richard Fields (2012), "Voting Decisions at US Mutual Funds: How Investors Really Use Proxy Advisers," at https://ssrn.com/abstract=2084231.

Biden, Joe (2016), "How short-termism saps the economy," *Wall Street Journal*, September 27, at http://www.wsj.com/articles/how-short-termism-saps-the-economy-1475018087.

Birch, S. (2009), *Full Participation: A Comparative Study of Compulsory Voting*, Manchester University Press.

Birstingl, Andrew (2016), "FactSet Buyback Quarterly," December 19, at https://insight.factset.com/hubfs/Buyback%20Quarterly/Buyback%20Quarterly%20Q3%202016_12.19.pdf.

BlackRock (2018), "BlackRock Investment Stewardship," Annual Report, 241.

Blair, Margaret (1995), *Ownership and Control: Rethinking Corporate Governance for the Twenty-First Century*, The Brookings Institution.

Blair, Margaret (2003a), "Shareholder Value, Corporate Governance, and Corporate Performance," in Peter K. Cornelius and Bruce Kogut (eds.), *Corporate Governance and Capital Flows in a Global Economy*, Oxford University Press: 53–82.

Blair, Margaret (2003b), "Locking In Capital: What Corporate Law Achieved for Business Organizers in the Nineteenth Century," *UCLA Law Review*, 51(2), 387–455.

Block, Fred (2009), "Where Do Innovations Come From? Transformations in the US Economy, 1970–2006," *Socio-Economic Review*, 7(3): 459–83.

Block, Fred, and Matthew Keller (eds.) (2010), *State of Innovation: The U.S. Government's Role in Technology Development*, Paradigm.

Board of Governors of the Federal Reserve System (2018), Federal Reserve Statistical Release Z.1, "Financial Accounts of the United States: Flow of Funds, Balance Sheets, and Integrated Macroeconomic Accounts," December 6, at https://www.federalreserve. gov/datadownload/Chart.aspx?rel=Z1&series=75cf7aa5c5495b9ba5194795df5ee426& lastobs=&from=01/01/1945&to=12/31/2017&filetype=spreadsheetml&label=include&lay out=seriesrow&pp=Download.

Bogle, John (2005), *The Battle for the Soul of Capitalism*, Yale University Press.

Boyarsky, Bill (2007), *Big Daddy: Jesse Unruh and the Art of Power Politics*, University of California Press.

Brennan, Jason, and Lisa Hill (2014), *Compulsory Voting: For and Against*, Cambridge University Press.

Briggs, Thomas W. (2007), "Corporate Governance and the New Hedge Fund Activism: An Empirical Analysis," *Journal of Corporation Law*, 32(4): 682–738.

Brooks, John (1973), *The Go-Go Years: The Drama and Crashing Finale of Wall Street's Bullish 60s*, Dutton.

Bruck, Connie (1989), *The Predator's Ball: The Inside Story of Drexel Burnham and the Rise of the Junk Bond Raiders*, Penguin Books.

Burton, Jonathan (2003), "Cash in the cubicle," *MarketWatch*, December 2, at http://www. marketwatch.com/story/employee-stock-purchase-plans-are-worth-every-dollar.

Business Week (1960), "Blue-ribbon venture capital," October 29.

Business Week (1979), "What makes Tappan such a hot target," October 22.

Calio, Joseph Evan, and Rafael Xavier Zahralddin (1994), "The Securities and Exchange Commission's 1992 Proxy Amendments: Questions of Accountability," *Pace Law Review* 14(2): 460–539.

Carlisle, Tobias E. (2014), "The Icahn Manifesto," *Journal for Applied Corporate Finance*, 26(4): 89–97.

Carosso, Vincent (1970), *Investment Banking in America*, Harvard University Press.

Carpenter, Marie, and William Lazonick (2017), "Innovation, Competition, and Financialization in the Communications Technology Industry," ISIGrowth Working Paper, at http://www.isigrowth.eu/2017/06/14/innovation-competition-and-financialization-in-the-communications-technology-industry-1996-2016.

Carpenter, Marie, William Lazonick, and Mary O'Sullivan (2003), "The Stock Market and Innovative Capability in the New Economy: The Optical Networking Industry," *Industrial and Corporate Change*, 12(5): 963–1034.

Cassidy, John (2002), *Dot.Con: The Greatest Story Ever Sold*, Harper.

Chandler, Jr., Alfred D. (1962), *Strategy and Structure: Chapters in the History of the American Industrial Enterprise*, MIT Press.

Chandler, Jr., Alfred D. (1977), *The Visible Hand: The Managerial Revolution in American Business*, Harvard University Press.

Chandler, Jr., Alfred D. (1990), *Scale and Scope: The Dynamics of Industrial Capitalism*, Harvard University Press

Chandler, Beverly (2016), "Event driven paper finds investors disenchanted," *AlphaQ*, June 6, at http://www.alphaq.world/2016/06/20/240734/event-driven-paper-finds-invest ors-disenchanted.

Chandler, Susan (1994), "Between TWA and a hard place," *Business Week*, November 21, at https://www.bloomberg.com/news/articles/1994-11-20/between-twa-and-a-hard-place.

Chang, Ha-Joon (2002), *Kicking Away the Ladder: Development Strategy in Historical Perspective*, Anthem Press.

Cheffins, Brian R. (2013), "The History of Corporate Governance," in Mike Wright, Donald S. Siegel, Kevin Keasey, and Igor Filatotchev (eds.), *The Oxford Handbook of Corporate Governance*, Oxford University Press: 46–64.

Christensen, Clayton (1997), *The Innovator's Dilemma: When New Technologies Cause Great Firms to Fail*, Harvard Business School Press.

Christensen, Clayton, Stephen P. Kaufman, and Willy C. Shih (2008), "Innovation Killers: How Financial Tools Destroy Your Capacity to Do New Things," *Harvard Business Review*, January: 98–105.

Christian Science Monitor (1983), "Coming to terms with takeover lingo," *Christian Science Monitor*, July 12, at http://www.csmonitor.com/1983/0712/071234.html.

Cioffi, John W. (2005), "Corporate Governance Reform, Regulatory Politics, and the Foundations of Finance Capitalism in the United States and Germany," CLPE Research Paper No. 6, at https://ssrn.com/abstract=830065.

Citizens for Tax Justice (2016), "Fortune 500 Companies Hold a Record $2.4 trillion Offshore," March 3, at http://ctj.org/pdf/pre0316.pdf.

Clark, John Bates (1900), "Disarming the Trusts," *Atlantic Monthly*, January: 47–53.

Coates, IV, John C. (2018), "The Future of Corporate Governance Part I: The Problem of Twelve," *Harvard Public Law Working Paper No. 19–07*, at https://ssrn.com/abstract=3247337.

Coffee, John C., and Darius Palia (2016), "The Wolf at the Door: The Impact of Hedge Fund Activism on Corporate Governance," *Annals of Corporate Governance*, 1 (1): 1–94.

Cook, David T. (1983), "Fairness to shareholders invoked; Tighter rules asked for the takeover game," *Christian Science Monitor*, July 12, at http://www.csmonitor.com/1983/0712/071232.html.

Corbett, Jenny, and Tim Jenkinson (1996), "The Financing of Industry, 1970–1989: An International Comparison," *Journal of the Japanese and International Economies*, 10(1): 71–96.

Craig, Susanne (2013), "The giant of shareholders, quietly stirring," *New York Times*, May 18, at http://www.nytimes.com/2013/05/19/business/blackrock-a-shareholding-giant-is-quietly-stirring.html.

Crystal, Graef (1978), *Executive Compensation: Money, Motivation, and Imagination*, American Management Association.

Crystal, Graef (1991), *In Search of Excess: The Overcompensation of American Executives*, W. W. Norton & Company.

Dayen, David (2015), "SEC admits it's not monitoring stock buybacks to prevent market manipulation," *The Intercept*, August 13, at https://theintercept.com/2015/08/13/sec-admits-monitoring-stock-buybacks-prevent-market-manipulation/.

Dayen, David (2016), "What Good are Hedge Funds?," *The American Prospect*, April 25, at http://prospect.org/article/what-good-are-hedge-funds.

Demsetz, Harold (1995), *The Economics of the Business Firm: Seven Critical Commentaries*, Cambridge University Press.

Denning, Steve (2014), "When pension funds become vampires," *Forbes*, December 10, at http://www.forbes.com/sites/stevedenning/2014/12/10/when-pension-funds-become-vampires/#704aac67510c.

Desai, Mihir (2012), "The Incentive Bubble," *Harvard Business Review*, March: 124–33.

Dodd–Frank Act (2011), Section 404, "Final Rule," at https://www.sec.gov/rules/final/2011/ia-3308.pdf.

Donaldson, Gordon (1961), *Corporate Debt Capacity: A Study of Corporate Debt Policy and the Determination of Corporate Debt Capacity*, Graduate School of Business Administration, Harvard University (republished by Beard Books, 2000).

Donlan, Thomas G. (2000), "Cisco's Bids: Its Growth by Acquisition Will Cause Problems," *Barron's*, 80(19): 31–4.

Drucker, Peter (1976), *The Unseen Revolution: How Pension Fund Socialism Came to America*, Harper & Row.

Eisenhower, Dwight (1961), "Military-Industrial Complex Speech," at http://coursesa.matrix.msu.edu/~hst306/documents/indust.html.

Eisinger, Jesse (2014a), "Repeated good fortune in timing of CEO's stock sale," *New York Times Dealbook*, February 19, at http://dealbook.nytimes.com/2014/02/19/repeated-good-fortune-in-timing-of-c-e-o-s-stock-sale/.

Eisinger, Jesse (2014b), "Failed Allergan deal strains Valeant's business model," *New York Times*, November 26, at https://dealbook.nytimes.com/2014/11/26/failed-allergan-deal-strains-valeants-business-model/.

Ferleger, Louis, and William Lazonick (1993), "The Managerial Revolution and the Developmental State: The Case of U.S. Agriculture," *Business and Economic History*, 22(2): 67–8.

Ferleger, Louis, and William Lazonick (1994), "Higher Education for an Innovative Economy: Land-Grant Colleges and the Managerial Revolution in America," *Business and Economic History*, 23(1): 116–28.

Ferleger, Louis, and William Lazonick (2002), "The Role of the US Government in the Emergence of the Commercial Airline Industry," unpublished note, University of Massachusetts, 2002 (available from William Lazonick on request).

Foley, Steven (2016), "The so-called death of event-driven investing," *Financial Times*, March 6, at https://www.ft.com/content/cc45d8ee-e135-11e5-9217-6ae3733a2cd1.

Foley, Steven, and Miles Johnson (2014), "'Event-driven' hedge funds leap into lead after rush to invest," *Financial Times*, May 8, at https://www.ft.com/content/d9a8b122-d61b-11e3-a239-00144feabdc0

Foley, Steven, and Daniel Thomas (2013), "Activist investor Loeb pressures Nokia for cash return," *Financial Times*, October 22, at https://www.ft.com/content/41da69a4-3b2e-11e3-87fa-00144feab7de.

Foroohar, Rana (2014), "Why Warren Buffett should vote 'no' on Coke," *Time*, April 24, at http://time.com/76556/warren-buffett-coke-buyback/.

Foroohar, Rana (2016), *Makers and Takers: The Rise of Finance and the Fall of American Business*, Penguin House.

Foroohar, Rana (2017), "Donald Trump's trickle-down delusion on tax," *Financial Times*, October 1, at https://www.ft.com/content/736ca456-a50f-11e7-b797-b61809486fe2.

Fortune (1970), *The Conglomerate Commotion*, Viking.

Fortune (2016), "Emerson: #128 for ranking by revenue in 2015," at https://fortune.com/fortune500/2016/emerson-electric/

Fried, Jesse M. (1988), "Reducing the Profitability of Corporate Insider Trading through Pretrading Disclosure," *Southern California Law Review*, 71(2): 303–92.

Fried, Jesse M. (2000), "Insider Signaling and Insider Trading with Repurchase Tender Offers," *University of Chicago Law Review*, 67(2): 421–77.

Fried, Jesse M. (2001), "Open Market Repurchases: Signaling or Managerial Opportunism," *Theoretical Inquiries in Law*, 2(2): 865–84.

Fried, Jesse (2005), "Informed Trading and False Signaling with Open Market Re-purchases," *California Law Review*, 93: 1323–86.

Fried, Jesse, and Charles C. Y. Wang (2017), "Short-Termism and Capital Flows," Harvard Business School Working Paper 17–062.

Fujikawa, Megumi, and Kosaku Narioka (2016), "7-Eleven CEO resigns as Loeb's hedge fund prevails in Japan boardroom fight," *Wall Street Journal*, April 7, at https://www.wsj.com/articles/7-eleven-chief-resigns-as-hedge-fund-prevails-in-japan-boardroom-fight-1460019140

Fuller, Joseph, and Michael Jensen (2002), "Just Say No to Wall Street: Putting a Stop to the Earnings Game," *Journal of Applied Corporate Finance*, 14(4): 41–6.

Gandel, Stephen (2015), "How DuPont went to war with activist investor Nelson Peltz," *Fortune*, May 11, at http://fortune.com/2015/05/11/how-dupont-went-to-war/.

Gaughan, Patrick A. (1999), *Mergers, Acquisitions and Corporate Restructuring*, John Wiley & Sons.

GE Report (2012), "The Hush-Hush Boys: GE Engineer Speaks About a Top Secret Program That Launched the Jet Age in America," at https://www.rdmag.com/news/2012/07/hush-hush-boys-ge-engineer-speaks-about-top-secret-program-launched-jet-age-america.

Gelter, Martin (2013), "The Pension System and the Rise of Shareholder Primacy." *Seton Hall Law Review*, 43(3): 909–70.

Gimein, Mark (2002), "You bought. They sold," *Fortune*, September 2, at https://money.cnn.com/magazines/fortune/fortune_archive/2002/09/02/327903/index.htm

Goldstein, Matthew, and Alexandra Stevenson (2017), "Icahn quits as special adviser to President Trump," *New York Times*, April 18, at https://www.nytimes.com/2017/08/18/business/dealbook/carl-icahn-trump-adviser.html.

Gompers, Paul, and Josh Lerner (2002), *The Venture Capital Cycle*, The MIT Press.

Gould, Carole (1989), "Shaking up executive compensation," *New York Times*, April 9, at http://www.nytimes.com/1989/04/09/business/personal-finance-shaking-up-executive-compensation.html.

Grant, Elaine (2006), "TWA—Death of a Legend," *St. Louis Magazine*, July 28, at https://www.stlmag.com/TWA-Death-Of-A-Legend/.

Hansmann, Henry, and Reinier Kraakman (2000), "The Essential Role of Organizational Law," *Yale Law Journal*, 110(3): 367–440.

Hayes, Robert H., and William J. Abernathy (1980), "Managing Our Way to Economic Decline," *Harvard Business Review*, July–August: 67–77.

Helmore, Edward (2018), "Experts voice concern that corporate tax cuts benefit the wealthy," *The Guardian*, September 1, at https://www.theguardian.com/business/2018/sep/01/trump-corporate-tax-cuts-benefit-wealthy

Higgins, Tim, Ian Katz, and Kasia Klimasinska (2013), "GM bailout ends as U.S. sells last of 'Government Motors'," *Bloomberg*, December 10, at https://www.bloomberg.com/news/articles/2013-12-09/gm-bailout-ends-as-u-s-sells-last-of-government-motors-.

Holland, Max (1989), *When The Machine Stopped*, Harvard Business School Press.

Hopkins, Matt, and William Lazonick (2014), "Who Invests in the High-Tech Knowledge Base?" Institute for New Economic Thinking Working Group on the Political Economy of Distribution Working Paper No. 14, at https://www.ineteconomics.org/research/research-papers/who-invests-in-the-high-tech-knowledge-base.

Hopkins, Matt, and William Lazonick (2016), "The Mismeasure of Mammon: The Uses and Abuses of Executive Pay Data," Institute for New Economic Thinking Working Paper No. 49, at https://www.ineteconomics.org/research/research-papers/the-mismeasure-of-mammon-uses-and-abuses-of-executive-pay-data.

Horwitz, Morton (1979), *The Transformation of American Law, 1780–1860*, Harvard University Press.

HP Press Release (2011), "HP to Acquire Leading Enterprise Information Management Software Company Autonomy Corporation plc," August 18, at http://www8.hp.com/ba/bs/hp-news/article_detail.html?compURI=tcm:110-1051736&pageTitle=HP-to-Acquire-Leading-Enterprise-Information-Management-Software-Company-Autonomy-Corporation-plc

Huawei Investment & Holding Co., Ltd. (2016), "2016 Annual Report," at http://www-file.huawei.com/-/media/CORPORATE/PDF/annual-report/AnnualReport2016_en.pdf?la=en-US.

Hudson, Richard L. (1982), "SEC eases way for repurchase of firms' stock," *Wall Street Journal*, November 10.

Icahn, Carl (2013), "Our Letter to Tim Cook," October 24, at http://carlicahn.com/our_letter_to_tim_cook/.

Icahn, Carl (2014a), "Open Letter to Apple Shareholders," January 24, at http://carlicahn.com/apple_shareholder_letter/.

Icahn, Carl (2014b), "Sale: Apple shares at half price," October 9, at http://carlicahn.com/sale-apple-shares-at-half-price/.

Icahn, Carl (2015a), "Carl Icahn issues letter to Twitter followers regarding Apple," February 11, at http://carlicahn.com/letter-to-twitter-followers-regarding-apple/.

Icahn, Carl (2015b), "Carl Icahn issues open letter to Tim Cook," May 18, at http://carlicahn.com/carl-icahn-issues-open-letter-to-tim-cook/.

Iliev, Peter, and Michelle Lowry (2015), "Are Mutual Funds Active Voters?," *Review of Financial Studies*, 28(2): 446–85.

Isa, Margaret (1996), "Where, oh where, have all the corporate raiders gone?," *New York Times*, June 30, at http://www.nytimes.com/1996/06/30/business/where-oh-where-have-all-the-corporate-raiders-gone.html.

Israel, Spencer (2017), "A brief timeline of the Bill Ackman–Valeant relationship," *Benzinga*, March 14, at https://www.benzinga.com/general/biotech/17/03/9166359/a-brief-timeline-of-the-bill-ackman-valeant-relationship.

Jacobson, Ken, and William Lazonick (2015), "SEC Rule 10b-18: A License to Loot," presentation to the annual conference of the Society for the Advancement of Socio-Economics, London School of Economics, July 3.

Jacobson, Ken, and William Lazonick (2019), "A License to Loot: How the US Securities and Exchange Commission Adopted SEC Rule 10b-18 and Sanctioned Systemic Stock-Market Manipulation," The Academic-Industry Research Network, forthcoming.

Jensen, Michael (1986), "Agency Costs of Free Cash Flow, Corporate Finance, and Take-overs," *American Economic Review*, 76(2): 323–9.

Jensen, Michael (1989), "Eclipse of the Public Corporation," *Harvard Business Review*, 67(5): 61–74.

Jensen, Michael (1993), "The Modern Industrial Revolution, Exit, and the Failure of Internal Control Systems," *Journal of Finance*, 48(3): 831–80.

Jensen, Michael, and Kevin Murphy (1990), "Performance Pay and Top Management Incentives," *Journal of Political Economy*, 98(2): 225–64.

Johnson, Chalmers (1982), *MITI and the Japanese Miracle: The Growth of Industrial Policy, 1925–1975*, Stanford University Press.

Johnson, Steven C., and Jennifer Ablan (2013), "Rise of shareholder activism gives bond investors headaches," *Reuters*, December 19, at http://www.reuters.com/article/us-investing-activism-bondholders-analys-idUSBRE9BI10420131219.

Jones, Chris, Jason Low, Mo Jia, and Tim Coulling (2017), "Media alert: Apple Watch has its best quarter and takes nearly 80% of total smartwatch revenue in Q4," *Canalys*, February 7, at https://www.canalys.com/newsroom/media-alert-apple-watch-has-its-best-quarter-and-takes-nearly-80-total-smartwatch-revenue-q.

Jones, T. L. (n.d.), "Frank Whittle's W2B Turbojet: United Kingdom versus United States Development," at http://www.enginehistory.org/GasTurbines/EarlyGT/W2B/W2B.shtml

Kahan, Marcel, and Edward Rock (2010), "Embattled CEOs," *Texas Law Review*, 88: 987–1051.

Kaplan, Steven N. (2017), "Are U.S. Companies Too Short-term Oriented? Some Thoughts," National Bureau of Economic Research Working Paper 23464, at https://www.nber.org/papers/w23464

Kashkari, Neel (2008), "Treasury Update on Implementation of Troubled Asset Relief Program," referenced at https://en.wikipedia.org/wiki/Troubled_Asset_Relief_Program.

Keeper, Big Al (2006), "The Gloster Meteor: Britain's First Operational Military Jet," at http://www.bbc.co.uk/dna/ptop/plain/A12746162.

Keizer, Gregg (2015), "Microsoft writes off $7.6B., admits failure of Nokia acquisition," *Computerworld*, July 8, at http://www.computerworld.com/article/2945371/smartphones/microsoft-writes-off-76b-admits-failure-of-nokia-acquisition.html.

Klein, William A., and John C. Coffee (2004) (9th edn.), *Business Organization and Finance: Legal and Economic Principles*, Thomson Reuters/Foundation Press.

Kroll, Luisa, and Kerry A. Dolan, eds. (2018), "The definitive ranking of the wealthiest Americans," *Forbes*, October 3, at https://www.forbes.com/forbes-400/#314e62ec7e2f

Lahart, Justin (2016), "Share buybacks: The bill is coming due," *Wall Street Journal*, February 28, at https://www.wsj.com/articles/share-buybacks-the-bill-is-coming-due-1456685173

Laide, John (2014), "Activists increasing success gaining board seats at U.S. companies," March 10, at https://www.sharkrepellent.net/pub/rs_20140310.html.

Lamkin, Paul (2016), "Apple Watch sales hit 12 million in 2015," *Wareable*, February 9, at https://www.wareable.com/smartwatches/apple-watch-sales-hit-12-million-in-2015-2279.

La Roche, Julia (2014), "Dan Loeb releases a mini-documentary slamming Dow Chemical's board for 'broken promises," *Business Insider*, November 14, at https://www.businessinsider.com.au/dan-loeb-video-on-dow-chemical-2014-11.

Lazonick, William (1986), "Strategy, Structure, and Management Development in the United States and Britain," in Kesaji Kobayashi and Hideaki Morikawa (eds.), *Development of Managerial Enterprise*, University of Tokyo Press: 101–46.

Lazonick, William (1990), *Competitive Advantage on the Shop Floor*, Harvard University Press.

Lazonick, William (1991), *Business Organization and the Myth of the Market Economy*, Cambridge University Press.

Lazonick, William (1992), "Controlling the Market for Corporate Control," *Industrial and Corporate Change*, 1(3): 445–8.

Lazonick, William (1994a), "Creating and Extracting Value: Corporate Investment Behaviour and American Economic Performance," in Michael Bernstein and David Adler (eds.), *Understanding American Economic Decline*, Cambridge University Press: 79–113.

Lazonick, William (1994b), "The Integration of Theory and History: Methodology and Ideology in Schumpeter's Economics," in Lars Magnusson (ed.), *Evolutionary Economics: The Neo-Schumpeterian Challenge*, Kluwer: 245–63.

Lazonick, William (1998), "Organizational Learning and International Competition," in Jonathan Michie and John Grieve Smith (eds.), *Globalization, Growth, and Governance*, Oxford University Press.

Lazonick, William (2002), "Innovative Enterprise and Historical Transformation," *Enterprise & Society*, 3(1): 35–54.

Lazonick, William (2003), "The Theory of the Market Economy and the Social Foundations of Innovative Enterprise," *Economic and Industrial Democracy* 24(1): 9–44.

Lazonick, William (2004), "Indigenous Innovation and Economic Development: Lessons from China's Leap into the Information Age," *Industry & Innovation*, 11(4): 273–98.

Lazonick, William (2005), "The Innovative Firm," in Jan Fagerberg, David Mowery, and Richard Nelson (eds.), *The Oxford Handbook of Innovation*, Oxford University Press.

Lazonick, William (2006), "Corporate Restructuring," in Stephen Ackroyd, Rosemary Batt, Paul Thompson, and Pamela S. Tolbert (eds.), *The Oxford Handbook of Work and Organization*, Oxford University Press.

Lazonick, William (2007a), "The U.S. Stock Market and the Governance of Innovative Enterprise," *Industrial and Corporate Change*, 16(6): 1021–2.

Lazonick, William (2007b), "Varieties of Capitalism and Innovative Enterprise," *Comparative Social Research*, 24, 2007: 21–69.

Lazonick, William (2008), "Everyone is paying the price for share buy-backs," *Financial Times*, September 25, at https://www.ft.com/content/e75440f6-8b0e-11dd-b634-0000779fd18c

Lazonick, William (2009a), *Sustainable Prosperity in the New Economy? Business Organization and High-Tech Employment in the United States*, Upjohn Institute Press.

Lazonick, William (2009b), "The New Economy Business Model and the Crisis of U.S. Capitalism," *Capitalism and Society*, 4(2): 1–67.

Lazonick, William (2009c), "The buyback boondoggle," *BusinessWeek*, August 13, at https://www.bloomberg.com/news/articles/2009-08-13/the-buyback-boondoggle.

Lazonick, William (2010), "Innovative Business Models and Varieties of Capitalism: Financialization of the U.S. Corporation," *Business History Review*, 84(4): 675–702.

Lazonick, William (2011a), "The global tax dodgers: Why President Obama and Congress lack job creation plans," *Huffington Post*, August 18, at http://www.huffingtonpost.com/william-lazonick/offshore-job-profits_b_930531.html.

Lazonick, William (2011b), "The Innovative Enterprise and the Developmental State: Toward an Economics of 'Organizational Success'," paper prepared for Institute for New Economic Thinking Annual 2011 Conference, at https://www.ineteconomics.org/research/research-papers/the-innovative-enterprise-and-the-developmental-state-toward-an-economics-of-organizational-success.

Lazonick, William (2012), "Alfred Chandler's Managerial Revolution," in William Lazonick and David Teece (eds.), *Management Innovation: Essays in the Spirit of Alfred D. Chandler, Jr.*, Oxford University Press.

Lazonick, William (2013), "The Financialization of the US Corporation: What Has Been Lost, and How It Can Be Regained," *Seattle University Law Review*, 36(2): 857–909.

Lazonick, William (2014a), "Innovative Enterprise and Shareholder Value," *Law and Financial Markets Review*, 8(1): 52–64.

Lazonick, William (2014b), "Numbers show Apple shareholders have already gotten plenty," *Harvard Business Review*, October 16, at https://hbr.org/2014/10/numbers-show-apple-shareholders-have-already-gotten-plenty.

Lazonick, William (2014c), "Taking Stock: How Executive Pay Results in an Inequitable and Unstable Economy," Franklin and Eleanor Roosevelt Institute White Paper, at http://www.theairnet.org/v3/backbone/uploads/2014/08/Lazonick_Executive_Pay_White_Paper_Roosevelt_Institute.pdf.

Lazonick, William (2014d), "Profits Without Prosperity: Stock Buybacks Manipulate the Market and Leave Most Americans Worse Off," *Harvard Business Review*, September: 46–55.

Lazonick, William (2014e), "What Apple should do with its massive piles of money," *Harvard Business Review*, October 20, at https://hbr.org/2014/10/what-apple-should-do-with-its-massive-piles-of-money.

Lazonick, William (2015a), "Clinton's proposals on stock buybacks don't go far enough," *Harvard Business Review*, August 11, at https://hbr.org/2015/08/clintons-proposals-on-stock-buybacks-dont-go-far-enough.

Lazonick, William (2015b), "Innovative Enterprise or Sweatshop Economics? In Search of Foundations of Economic Analysis," *Challenge*, 59(2), 65–114.

Lazonick, William (2015c), "The Theory of Innovative Enterprise: Foundation of Economic Analysis," Academic-Industry Research Working Paper #13–0201.

Lazonick, William (2015d), "Buybacks: From Basics to Politics," AIR Special Report, The Academic-Industry Research Network, August 19, at http://www.theairnet.org/v3/back bone/uploads/2015/08/Lazonick-Buybacks-Basics-to-Politics-20150819.pdf.

Lazonick, William (2015e), "Labor in the Twenty-First Century: The Top 0.1% and the Disappearing Middle-Class," in Christian E. Weller (ed.), *Inequality, Uncertainty, and Opportunity: The Varied and Growing Role of Finance in Labor Relations*, Cornell University Press, 143–92.

Lazonick, William (2016a), "The Value-Extracting CEO: How Executive Stock-Based Pay Undermines Investment in Productive Capabilities," Institute for New Economic Thinking, Working Paper No. 54, at https://www.ineteconomics.org/research/research-papers/the-value-extracting-ceo-how-executive-stock-based-pay-undermines-investment-in-productive-capabilities.

Lazonick, William (2016b), "How Stock Buybacks Make Americans Vulnerable to Globalization," paper presented at the Workshop on Mega-Regionalism: New Challenges for Trade and Innovation, East-West Center, University of Hawaii, Honolulu, January 20, at http://papers.ssrn.com/sol3/papers.cfm?abstract_id=2745387.

Lazonick, William (2017a), "Review of *Glass House: The 1% Economy and the Shattering of an All-American Town* by Brian Alexander," *Industrial and Labor Relations Review*, 70(5), 1285–87.

Lazonick, William (2017b), "Innovative Enterprise and Sustainable Prosperity," paper presented at the conference of the Institute for New Economic Thinking, Edinburgh, October 23, at https://www.ineteconomics.org/research/research-papers/innovative-enterprise-and-sustainable-prosperity.

Lazonick, William (2018a), "Congress can turn the Republican corporate tax cuts into middle-class jobs," *The Hill*, February 7, at https://thehill.com/opinion/finance/372760-congress-can-turn-the-republican-tax-cuts-into-new-middle-class-jobs

Lazonick, William (2018b), "Apple's 'Capital Return Program': Where are the Patient Capitalists?" Institute for New Economic Thinking Blog Post, November 13, at https://www.ineteconomics.org/perspectives/blog/apples-capital-return-program-where-are-the-patient-capitalists.

Lazonick, William (2018c), "The secret of Amazon's success," *New York Times*, November 19, at https://www.nytimes.com/2018/11/19/opinion/amazon-bezos-hq2.html.

Lazonick, William (2018d), "Comments on Gary Pisano, 'Toward a Prescriptive Theory of Dynamic Capabilities: Connecting Strategic Choice, Learning, and Competition'," *Industrial and Corporate Change*, 27(6): 1161–74.

Lazonick, William (2018e), "The Functions of the Stock Market and the Fallacies of Shareholder Value," in Ciaran Driver and Grahame Thompson (eds.), *What Next for Corporate Governance?* Oxford University Press: 117–51.

Lazonick, William (2019), "Innovative Enterprise and Sustainable Prosperity," AIR Working Paper #17-10/01, January, at http://www.theairnet.org/v3/backbone/uploads/2019/03/Lazonick-IESP-20190118.pdf

Lazonick, William, and Matt Hopkins (2015), "GM's stock buyback is bad for America and the company," *Harvard Business Review*, March 11, at https://hbr.org/2015/03/gms-stock-buyback-is-bad-for-america-and-the-company.

Lazonick, William, and Edward March (2011), "The Rise and Demise of Lucent Technologies," *Journal of Strategic Management Education*, 7(4): 1–66.

Lazonick, William, and William Mass (1995), "Indigenous Innovation and Industrialization: Foundations of Japanese Development and Advantage," MIT Japan Program Working Paper 95–03.

Lazonick, William, and Mariana Mazzucato (2013), "The Risk–Reward Nexus in the Innovation–Inequality Relationship: Who Takes the Risks? Who Gets the Rewards?," *Industrial and Corporate Change*, 22(4): 1093–128.

Lazonick, William, and Mary O'Sullivan (1997), "Finance and Industrial Development, Part I: The United States and the United Kingdom," *Financial History Review*, 4(1): 7–29.

Lazonick, William, and Mary O'Sullivan (2000a), "American Corporate Finance," in Candace Howes and Ajit Singh (ed.), *Competitiveness Matters*, Michigan University Press: 106–24.

Lazonick, William, and Mary O'Sullivan (2000b), "Maximizing Shareholder Value: A New Ideology for Corporate Governance," *Economy and Society*, 29(1): 13–35.

Lazonick, William, and Andrea Prencipe (2005), "Dynamic Capabilities and Sustained Innovation: Strategic Control and Financial Commitment at Rolls-Royce plc," *Industrial and Corporate Change*, 14(3): 1–42.

Lazonick, William, and Mustafa Erdem Sakinç (2010), "Do Financial Markets Support Innovation or Inequity in the Drug Development Process?," DIME Workshop, Innovation and Inequality, at http://fiid.org/wp-content/uploads/2012/11/Lazonick-and-Sakinc-FINAL-20100510.pdf.

Lazonick, William, and Öner Tulum (2011), "US Biopharmaceutical Finance and the Sustainability of the Biotech Business Model," *Research Policy*, 40(11): 1170–87.

Lazonick, William, Mariana Mazzucato, and Öner Tulum (2013), "Apple's Changing Business Model: What Should the World's Richest Company Do With All Those Profits?," *Accounting Forum*, 37(4): 249–67.

Lazonick, William, Philip Moss, Hal Salzman, and Öner Tulum (2014), "Skill Development and Sustainable Prosperity: Collective and Cumulative Careers versus Skill-Biased Technical Change," Institute for New Economic Thinking Working Group on the Political Economy of Distribution Working Paper No. 7, at https://ineteconomics.org/ideas-papers/research-papers/skill-development-and-sustainable-prosperity-cumulative-and-collective-careers-versus-skill-biased-technical-change.

Lazonick, William, Matt Hopkins, and Ken Jacobson (2016a), "What we learn about inequality from Carl Icahn's $2 billion Apple 'no brainer'," June 6, at https://www.ineteconomics.org/perspectives/blog/what-we-learn-about-inequality-from-carl-icahns-2-billion-apple-no-brainer.

Lazonick, William, Matt Hopkins, Ken Jacobson, Mustafa Erdem Sakinç, and Öner Tulum (2016b), "U.S. Pharma's Business Model: Why It Is Broken, and How It Can Be Fixed," in David Tyfield, Rebecca Lave, Samuel Randalls, and Charles Thorpe (eds.), *The Routledge Handbook of the Political Economy of Science*, Routledge: 83–100.

Lazonick, William, Matt Hopkins, Ken Jacobson, Mustafa Erdem Sakinç, and Öner Tulum (2017), "U.S. Pharma's Financialized Business Model," Institute for New Economic

Thinking Working Paper No. 60, at https://www.ineteconomics.org/research/research-papers/us-pharmas-financialized-business-model.

Lazonick, William, Phillip Moss, and Joshua Weitz (2019), *Fifty Years After: Black Employment in the United States Under the Equal Employment Opportunity Commission*, Institute for New Economic Thinking Report, forthcoming.

Lee, Hailey (2014), "Icahn: Will never be proxy fight with Apple," October 9, at http://www.cnbc.com/2014/10/09/icahn-we-would-like-to-see-a-massive-tender-offer-as-much-as-100-billion.html.

Lerner, Josh (2002), "Boom and Bust in the Venture Capital Industry and the Impact on Innovation," *Economic Review*, 87(4): 25–39.

Li, Yin (2017), Innovation Pathways in the Chinese Economy, PhD dissertation, Georgia Institute of Technology.

Linnane, Ciara (2017), "Share buybacks will continue to pose a threat to bondholders in 2017," *MarketWatch*, January 20, at http://www.marketwatch.com/story/share-buybacks-will-continue-posing-a-risk-to-bondholders-in-2017-2017-01-19.

Lippert, Inge, Tony Huzzard, Ulrich Jürgens, and William Lazonick (2014), *Corporate Governance, Employee Voice, and Work Organization: Sustaining High Road Jobs in the Automotive Supply Industry*, Oxford University Press.

Lipton, Martin (2013), "Bite the Apple; Poison the Apple; Paralyze the Company; Wreck the Economy," Harvard Law School Forum on Corporate Governance and Financial Regulation, February 26, at https://corpgov.law.harvard.edu/2013/02/26/bite-the-apple-poison-the-apple-paralyze-the-company-wreck-the-economy/.

List, Friedrich (1885), *The National System of Political Economy*, Longmans, Green, and Company (first published 1841).

Lloyd, William A. (1936), "County Agricultural Agent Work Under the Smith Lever Act, 1914 to 1924," at https://archive.org/stream/countyagricultur59lloy#page/n3/mode/2up.

Long, William, and David Ravenscraft (1993), "LBOs, Debt, and R&D Intensity," *Strategic Management Journal*, 14(1): 119–35.

Loomis, Carol (1966), "The Jones nobody keeps up with," *Fortune*, December 29, at http://fortune.com/2015/12/29/hedge-funds-fortune-1966/

Loomis, Carol (1970), "Hard times come to the hedge funds," *Fortune*, January, at http://archive.fortune.com/magazines/fortune/fortune_archive/1970/01/00/hedge_fund/pdf.html.

Loomis, Carol (2013), "The comeuppance of Carl Icahn (Fortune, 1986)," August 18, at http://fortune.com/2013/08/18/the-comeuppance-of-carl-icahn-fortune-1986/.

Loomis, Carol (2014), "BlackRock: The $4.3 trillion force," *Fortune*, July 7, at https://fortune.com/2014/07/07/blackrock-larry-fink/

Lorsch, Jay W., and Elizabeth MacIver (1989), *Pawns or Potentates: The Reality of Corporate Boards*, Harvard Business School Press.

Lu, Carmen X. W., (2016), "Unpacking Wolf Packs," *Yale Law Journal*, 125(3), at http://www.yalelawjournal.org/comment/unpacking-wolf-packs.

McCrank, John (2018), "Old rules, algorithmic traders add costs to U.S. share buybacks," *Reuters*, April 27, at https://www.reuters.com/article/us-usa-stocks-buybacks/old-rules-algorithmic-traders-add-costs-to-u-s-share-buybacks-idUSKBN1HY0GD.

McDonald, Duff (2017a), "Harvard Business School and the propagation of immoral profit strategies," *Newsweek*, April 6, at http://www.newsweek.com/2017/04/14/harvard-business-school-financial-crisis-economics-578378.html.

McDonald, Duff (2017b), *The Golden Passport*, HarperCollins Publishers.

McGee, Patrick (2018), "ThyssenKrupp splits after pressure from investors," *Financial Times*, September 27, at https://www.ft.com/content/6c7044fc-c267-11e8-95b1-d36dfef1b89a.

McGrath, Charles (2017), "80% of equity market cap held by institutions," *Pension & Investments*, April 25, at http://www.pionline.com/article/20170425/INTERACTIVE/170429926/80-of-equity-market-cap-held-by-institutions.

McKinsey & Co. (2018), "The Rise and Rise of Private Markets." *McKinsey Global Private Market Review*, February, at https://www.mckinsey.com/~/media/mckinsey/industries/private%20equity%20and%20principal%20investors/our%20insights/the%20rise%20and%20rise%20of%20private%20equity/the-rise-and-rise-of-private-markets-mckinsey-global-private-markets-review-2018.ashx

Machan, Dyan, and Riva Atlas (1994), "George Soros, meet A.W. Jones," *Forbes*, January 17.

Mackenzie, Michael, and Eric Platt (2016), "US corporate bonds: The weight of debt," *Financial Times*, December 4, at https://www.ft.com/content/41213b02-b87e-11e6-ba85-95d1533d9a62.

Malanga, Steven (2013), "The pension fund that ate California," *City Journal*, Winter, at https://www.city-journal.org/html/pension-fund-ate-california-13528.html.

Mani (2014), "Loeb unveils website in new era of Dow Chemical campaign," *Valuewalk*, November 14, at https://www.valuewalk.com/2014/11/value-dow-dan-loeb/.

Marriage, Madison (2013), "Activist investors fuel event-driven returns," *Financial Times*, July 13, at https://www.ft.com/content/faafbd08-ea1b-11e2-b2f4-00144feabdc0.

Martin, Roger L. (2011), *Fixing the Game: Bubbles, Crashes, and What Capitalism Can Learn from the NFL*, Harvard Business Review Press.

Matsusaka, John G., Oguzhan Ozbas, and Irene Yi (2018), "Opportunistic Proposals by Union Shareholders," USC CLASS Research Paper No. CLASS15-25; Marshall School of Business Working Paper No. 17–3, at https://ssrn.com/abstract=2666064 or http://dx.doi.org/10.2139/ssrn.2666064.

Mayer, Colin (1988), "New Issues in Corporate Finance," *European Economic Review*, 32 (5): 1167–83.

Means, Gardiner C. (1983), "Hessen's 'Reappraisal'," *Journal of Law & Economics*, 26(2): 297–300.

Melvin, Tim (2016), "Beware of firms that borrow cash for stock buybacks," *Real Money*, March 28, at http://realmoney.thestreet.com/articles/03/28/2016/beware-firms-borrow-cash-stock-buybacks.

Merrill Lynch Advisory Services (1994), *Mergerstat Review*, W. T. Grimm.

Merrill Lynch Advisory Services (2002), *Mergerstat Review*, W. T. Grimm.

Microsoft Press Release (2013), "Microsoft to Acquire Nokia's Devices & Services Business, License Nokia's Patents and Mapping Services," Microsoft press release, September 3, at https://news.microsoft.com/2013/09/03/microsoft-to-acquire-nokias-devices-services-business-license-nokias-patents-and-mapping-services/#pBTLPTPvpcDsUDvR.97

Modigliani, Franco, and Merton Miller (1958), "The Cost of Capital, Corporation Finance and the Theory of Investment," *American Economic Review*, 48(3): 261–97.

Monks, Robert (2013), "Robert Monks: It's Broke, Let's Fix it," *Listed Magazine*, at https://www.scribd.com/document/149758170/Anderson-in-Dialogue-With-Monks-the-Director-s-Chair-Listed-Jun-2013.

Monks, Robert (2015), "Careless Language or Cunning Propaganda," RFK Compass event, at http://www.ragm.com/careless-language/.

Morgenson, Gretchen (2016), "BlackRock wields its big stick like a wet noodle on C.E.O. pay," *New York Times*, April 15, at https://www.nytimes.com/2016/04/17/business/blackrock-wields-its-big-stick-like-a-wet-noodle-on-ceo-pay.html?_r=0.

Morrell, Alex (2016), "Steve Jobs sold most of his Apple stock when he was ousted from the company in 1985—today it would be worth $66 billion," *Business Insider*, April 1, at https://www.businessinsider.com/steve-jobs-original-apple-stock-would-be-worth-66-billion-today-2016-4?r=US&IR=T.

Morrill Act (1862), at https://www.ourdocuments.gov/doc.php?flash=true&doc=33&page=transcript.

Morrow, Adrian, and Greg Keenan (2015), "Ontario sells remaining GM shares acquired from bailout," *Globe and Mail,* February 4, at http://www.theglobeandmail.com/report-on-business/ontario-sells-gm-shares-for-11-billion/article22797007/.

Moudud, Jamee K. (2010), *Strategic Competition, Dynamics, and the Role of the State: A New Perspective,* Edward Elgar.

Mowery, David, and Nathan Rosenberg (1989), *Technology and the Pursuit of Economic Growth,* Cambridge University Press.

Mundy, Simon (2016), "Elliott targets Samsung again with call to split flagship," *Financial Times,* October 5, at https://www.ft.com/content/8a75ad02-8b0a-11e6-8cb7-e7ada1d123b1

National Institutes of Health (2019), "Office of the Budget, History," at https://officeofbudget.od.nih.gov/history.html.

National Research Council (1999), *Funding a Revolution: Government Support for Computing Research,* National Academy Press.

Navin, Thomas, and Marion Sears (1955), "The Rise of a Market for Industrial Securities, 1887–1902," *Business History Review,* 29(2): 105–38.

Noble, David (1979), *Design: Science, Technology, and the Rise of Corporate Capitalism,* Knopf Doubleday.

Nocera, Joe (2014), "Buffett punts on pay," *New York Times,* April 25, at https://www.nytimes.com/2014/04/26/opinion/nocera-buffett-punts-on-pay.html?_r=0.

Noked, Noam (2014), "'Greenmail' makes a comeback," Harvard Law School Forum on Corporate Governance and Financial Regulation, at https://corpgov.law.harvard.edu/2014/01/22/greenmail-makes-a-comeback/.

Online Investor (2015), "Emerson Electric Now #118 Largest Company, Surpassing Reynolds American," at https://www.theonlineinvestor.com/article/201504/emerson-electric-now-118-largest-company-surpassing-reynolds-american-EMR04132015-mbumped.htm/.

O'Reilly, Charles (2002), "Cisco Systems: The Acquisition of Technology is the Acquisition of People," Case No. HR10, Stanford Graduate School of Business.

Orol, Ronald (2014), "Teaming up with CalSTRS Helps Activist Funds Get Their Way," Harvard Roundtable on Shareholder Engagement—Consolidated Background Materials, June 16–17, at http://www.law.harvard.edu/programs/corp_gov/shareholder-engagement-roundtable-2015-materials/Harvard-Roundtable-on-Shareholder-Engagement-Consolidated-Background-Materials.pdf.

O'Sullivan, Mary (2000), *Contests for Corporate Control: Corporate Governance and Economic Performance in the United States and Germany,* Oxford University Press.

O'Sullivan, Mary (2007), "The Expansion of the Stock Market, 1885–1930: Historical Facts and Theoretical Fashions," *Enterprise and Society,* 8(3): 489–542.

O'Sullivan, Mary (2016), *Dividends of Development: Securities Markets in the History of U.S. Capitalism, 1865–1922,* Oxford University Press.

Ott, Julia (2011), *When Wall Street Met Main Street: The Quest for Investors' Democracy,* Harvard University Press.

Owusu, Tony (2015), "Alcatel-Lucent (ALU) stock declines after activist hedge fund builds 1.3% stake," *The Street,* June 29, at https://www.thestreet.com/story/13202033/1/alcatel-lucent-alu-stock-declines-after-activist-hedge-fund-builds-13-stake.html.

Parisian, Elizabeth, and Saqib Bhatti (2016), "All That Glitters Is Not Gold—An Analysis of US Public Pension Investments in Hedge Funds," Roosevelt Institute, at http://rooseveltinstitute.org/wp-content/uploads/2015/12/All-That-Glitters-Is-Not-Gold-Nov-2015.pdf.

Parrish, Michael E. (1970), *Securities Regulation and the New Deal.* Yale University Press.

Pearlstein, Steven (2018), "Beware 'the mother of all credit bubbles'," *Washington Post,* June 8, at https://www.washingtonpost.com/business/economy/beware-the-mother-of-all-credit-bubbles/2018/06/08/940f467c-69af-11e8-9e38-24e693b38637_story.html?utm_term=.30ca2ffa1586.

Penrose, Edith (1959), *The Theory of the Growth of the Firm,* John Wiley and Sons.

Penrose, Edith (1960), "The Growth of the Firm—A Case Study: The Hercules Powder Company," *Business History Review,* 34(1): 1–23.

Perino, Michael (2010), *The Hellhound of Wall Street: How Ferdinand Pecora's Investigation of the Great Crash Forever Changed American Finance.* Penguin Press.

Pichhadze, Aviv (2010), "Private Equity, Ownership, and Regulation," *Journal of Private Equity,* 14(1): 17–24.

Pichhadze, Aviv (2012), "Institutional Investors as Blockholders," in P. M. Vasudev and Susan Watson (eds.), *Corporate Governance after the Financial Crisis,* Oxford University Press, 145–60.

Pollack, Andrew, and Sabrina Tavernise (2015), "Valeant's drug price strategy enriches it, but infuriates patients and lawmakers," *New York Times,* October 4, at https://www.nytimes.com/2015/10/05/business/valeants-drug-price-strategy-enriches-it-but-infuriates-patients-and-lawmakers.html.

Potts, Mark (1985), "Phillips, Icahn settle," *Washington Post,* March 5, at https://www.washingtonpost.com/archive/business/1985/03/05/phillips-icahn-settle/7bc631ac-ab1d-4646-8a25-570333be3c33/?utm_term=.484230768c40.

Preqin (2016), "2016 Preqin Global Hedge Fund Report—Sample pages," at https://www.preqin.com/docs/samples/2016-Preqin-Global-Hedge-Fund-Report-Sample-Pages.pdf.

PricewaterhouseCoopers (2019), "Explore the data," at https://www.pwc.com/us/en/industries/technology/moneytree/explorer.html#/currentQ=Q3%202018&qRangeStart=Q3%202013&qRangeEnd=Q3%202018.

Quinn, James (2017), "Unilever Chief Paul Polman hits out at 'fast money' hedge funds as he prepares to meet government over takeover rules," *The Telegraph,* April 8, at http://www.telegraph.co.uk/business/2017/04/08/unilever-chief-paul-polman-hits-fast-money-hedge-funds-prepares/.

Quint, Michael (1989), "Texaco and Icahn end feud," *New York Times,* January 30, at http://www.nytimes.com/1989/01/30/business/texaco-and-icahn-end-feud.html.

Ramsay, John (2018), "Request for rulemaking petition to modernize Rule 10b-18 under the Securities Exchange Act of 1934 by allowing executions priced at the midpoint of the national best bid and offer to qualify for the safe harbor treatment provided by the Rule," U.S. Securities and Exchange Commission, March 27, at https://www.sec.gov/rules/petitions.shtml

Rappaport, Alfred, and Mark Sirower (1999), "Stock or Cash? The Trade-offs for Buyers and Sellers in Mergers and Acquisitions," *Harvard Business Review,* November–December: 147–58.

Ravenscraft, David, and Frederic Scherer (1987), *Mergers, Sell-offs, and Economic Efficiency,* Brookings Institution.

Rayburn, Frank, and Ollie Powers (1991), "A History of Pooling of Interests Accounting for Business Combinations in the United States," *Accounting Historians Journal,* 18(2): 155–92.

Reiff, Nathan (2017), "The Greatest Investors," May 4, at http://isites.nhu.edu.tw/yschao/doc/5141

Relational Investors and CalSTRS (2013), "Relational Investors LLC and CalSTRS Urge Timken's Board to Take Action to Separate the Company's Businesses to Unlock Shareholder Value," press release, February 19, at http://www.businesswire.com/news/home/20130219006721/en/Relational-Investors-LLC-CalSTRS-Urge-Timken%E2%80percent99s-Board.

Riordan, Michael, and Lillian Hoddeson (1997), *Crystal Fire: The Invention of the Transistor and the Birth of the Information Age*, W. W. Norton.

Ripley, William (1927), *Main Street and Wall Street*, Little Brown.

Robé, Jean-Philippe (2011), "The Legal Structure of the Firm," *Accounting, Economics, and Law*, 1(1): 5, at https://www.degruyter.com/view/j/ael.2011.1.1/ael.2011.1.1.1001/ael.2011.1.1.1001.xml

Rodrigues, Vivianne (2014), "Bondholders pay price of share buybacks," *Financial Times*, February 26, at https://www.ft.com/content/675b7f0a-9e53-11e3-95fe-00144feab7de.

Roe, Mark (1990), "Political and Legal Restraints on Ownership and Control of Public Companies," *Journal of Financial Economics* 27(1): 7–41.

Roe, Mark (1991), "Political Elements in the Creation of Mutual Fund Industry," *University of Pennsylvania Law Review*, 139(6): 1469–511.

Romano, Roberta (1993), "Public Pension Fund Activism in Corporate Governance Reconsidered," *Columbia Law Review*, 93(4): 793–853.

Rose, Paul (2007), "The Corporate Governance Industry," *Journal of Corporation Law*, 32 (4): 887–926.

Rosen, Jan M. (1991), "New regulations on stock options," *New York Times*, April 27, at http://www.nytimes.com/1991/04/27/business/your-money-new-regulations-on-stock-options.html.

Rosenberg, Hilary (1999), *A Traitor to His Class*, John Wiley & Sons.

Sakinç, Mustafa Erdem, and Öner Tulum (2012), "Innovation versus Financialization in the Biopharmaceutical Industry: The PLIPO Business Model," Ford Foundation Conference on Finance, Business Models, and Sustainable Prosperity, December 6, at http://fiid.org/wp-content/uploads/2012/11/Sakinc-Tulum-Biopharma-FINAL-20121205.pdf.

Scherer, Frederic, and David Ross (1990), "Industrial Market Structure and Economic Performance," University of Illinois at Urbana-Champaign's Academy for Entrepreneurial Leadership Historical Research Reference in Entrepreneurship, at https://papers.ssrn.com/sol3/papers.cfm?abstract_id=1496716.

Schumpeter, Joseph (1942), *Capitalism, Socialism and Democracy*, Harper.

Schumpeter, Joseph (1954), *History of Economic Analysis*, Oxford University Press.

Schwartz, Nelson D. (2014), "How Wall Street bent steel," *New York Times*, December 6, at https://www.nytimes.com/2014/12/07/business/timken-bows-to-investors-and-splits-in-two.html?_r=0.

Securities and Exchange Commission (SEC) (1969), "35th Annual Report," at https://www.sec.gov/about/annual_report/1969.pdf.

Securities and Exchange Commission (SEC) (1983), Advisory Committee on Tender Offers—Report on Recommendations.

Securities and Exchange Commission (SEC) (1992), Final Proxy Rule Amendments, Exchange Act Release No. 31,326, [1992 Transfer Binder] Fed. Sec. L. Rep. (CCH) 1185,051, at 83,353.

Securities and Exchange Commission (SEC) (2000), "Final Rule: Selective Disclosure and Insider Trading," at https://www.sec.gov/rules/final/33-7881.htm.

Securities and Exchange Commission (SEC) (2003), "Final Rule: Proxy Voting by Investment Advisers," 17 CFR Part 275, Release No. IA2106; File No. S73802, RIN 3235AI65, at https://www.sec.gov/rules/final/ia-2106.htm.

Securities and Exchange Commission (SEC) (2008), "General Electric Company—Form 10-K," at http://www.ge.com/pdf/investors/financial_reporting/ge_10K2009.pdf.

Securities and Exchange Commission (SEC) (2011), "General Motors Company—Form 10-K," at https://www.sec.gov/Archives/edgar/data/1467858/000146785812000014/gm201110k.htm.

Securities and Exchange Commission (SEC) (2016a), "Private Funds Statistics: Second Calendar Quarter 2016," at https://www.sec.gov/divisions/investment/private-funds-sta tistics.shtml.

Securities and Exchange Commission (SEC) (2016b), "Cisco Systems, Inc.—Form 10-K," at http://d18rn0p25nwr6d.cloudfront.net/CIK-0000858877/f8a35c54-4523-4e24-8255-2888181af3d7.pdf.

Securities and Exchange Commission (SEC) (2017), "Private Funds Statistics—Second Calendar Quarter 2016," at https://www.sec.gov/divisions/investment/private-funds-sta tistics/private-funds-statistics-2016-q2-accessible.pdf.

Seligman, Joel (1995), *The Transformation of Wall Street*, Northeastern University Press.

Serwer, Andrew, and Wilton Woods (1997), "Who's afraid of Carl Icahn?," *Fortune*, February 17, at http://archive.fortune.com/magazines/fortune/fortune_archive/1997/02/17/222196/index.htm.

Sharara, Norma M., and Anne E. Hoke-Witherspoon (1993), "The Evolution of the 1992 Shareholder Communication Proxy Rules and Their Impact on Corporate Governance," *The Business Lawyer*, 49(1): 327–58.

Sherr, Ian, and David Benoit (2013), "Icahn pushes Apple on buyback," *Wall Street Journal*, August 13, at https://www.wsj.com/articles/icahn-takes-large-bite-of-apple-1376420592?tesla=y.

Shin, Jang-Sup (2015), "The Reality of 'Actions' by Activist Hedge Funds and Public Policies on *Chaebols*," The KERI Insight, at http://fiid.org/wp-content/uploads/2015/07/Activist-fund-and-chaebol-policy-KERI-Insight-2015-7-1.pdf.

Singh, Shane P. (2015), "Compulsory Voting and the Turnout Decision Calculus," *Political Studies*, 63(3): 548–68.

Smiley, Gene, and Richard Keehn (1988), "Margin Purchases, Brokers' Loans and the Bull Market of the Twenties," *Business and Economic History*, 2(17): 129–42.

Smith, Michael P. (1996), "Shareholder Activism by Institutional Investors: Evidence from CalPERS," *Journal of Finance*, 51(1): 227–52.

Solomon, Steven Davidoff (2015), "Remaking Dow and DuPont for the activist shareholders," *New York Times*, December 15, at https://www.nytimes.com/2015/12/16/busi ness/dealbook/remaking-dow-and-dupont-for-the-activist-shareholders.html?_r=0.

Spector, Mike, and Joann S. Lublin (2015), "Bailout architect presses GM," *Wall Street Journal*, February 10, at https://www.wsj.com/articles/gm-shareholder-seeks-spot-on-board-1423577927.

Spence, Michael (1981), "The Learning Curve and Competition," *Bell Journal of Economics*, 12(1): 49–70.

Steinberg, Theodore (1991), *Nature Incorporated: Industrialization and the Waters of New England*, University of Massachusetts Press.

Sterling, Toby (2017), "Hedge fund goes to court, seeking to oust Akzo Nobel chairman," *Reuters*, May 9, at http://www.reuters.com/article/us-akzo-nobel-m-a-shareholder-idUSKBN1850E7.

Stevens, Mark (1993), *King Icahn: The Biography of a Renegade Capitalist*, Penguin Books.

Stevenson, Alexandra (2017), "Carl Icahn scrutinized for shaping policy that helped him profit," *New York Times*, May 9, at https://www.nytimes.com/2017/05/09/business/dealbook/carl-icahn-scrutinized-for-shaping-policy-that-helped-him-profit.html

Stewart, Robb M. (2017), "BHP Billiton CEO meets activist shareholder Elliott amid pressure," *Wall Street Journal*, May 17, at https://www.wsj.com/articles/bhp-billiton-ceo-to-meet-with-activist-shareholder-elliott-amid-pressure-1495014075.

Stout, Lynn A. (2004), "On The Nature of Corporations," *Deakin Law Review*, 9 (2): 775–89.

Strickland, Deon, Kenneth Wiles, and Marc Zenner (1996), "A Requiem for the USA—Is Small Shareholder Monitoring Effective?" *Journal of Financial Economics*, 40(2): 319–38.

Strine, Jr., Leo E. (2005), "The Delaware Way: How We Do Corporate Law and Some of the New Challenges We (and Europe) Face," *Delaware Journal of Corporate Law*, 30(3): 673–96.

Strine, Jr., Leo E. (2007), "Toward Common Sense and Common Ground?—Reflections on the Shared Interests of Managers and Labor in a More Rational System of Corporate Governance," Harvard Law and Economics, Discussion Paper No. 585.

Stulz, René M. (2007), "Hedge Funds: Past, Present, and Future," *Journal of Economic Perspectives*, 21(2): 175–94.

Syre, Steven (2012), "Internet-era boom icon's quiet bust," *Boston Globe*, October 26, at https://www.bostonglobe.com/business/2012/10/25/quiet-end-for-sycamore-networks-brief-star-internet-era/7GA6J0LQ1bz6NMrms4osoN/story.html.

Taggart, Robert (1988), "The Growth of the 'Junk' Bond Market and its Role in Financing Takeovers," in Alan J. Auerbach (ed.), *Mergers and Acquisitions*, University of Chicago Press.

Tax Foundation (2010), "Federal Capital Gains Tax Collections, 1954–2009," at https://taxfoundation.org/federal-capital-gains-tax-collections-1954-2009/.

Teece, David J. (2011), *Dynamic Capabilities and Strategic Management: Organizing for Innovation and Growth*, Oxford University Press (2nd edition).

Teece, David J. (2012), *Strategy, Innovation, and the Theory of the Firm*, Edward Elgar Publishing.

Tellis, Gerard J. (2013), "Microsoft and Nokia: A marriage made in hell," Forbes, September 4, at https://www.forbes.com/sites/forbesleadershipforum/2013/09/04/microsoft-and-nokia-a-marriage-made-in-hell/#7ee50cef5536.

Terrell, Ellen, (2016), "When a Quote is Not (Exactly) a Quote: General Motors," The Library of Congress Blogs, at https://blogs.loc.gov/inside_adams/2016/04/when-a-quote-is-not-exactly-a quote general-motors/.

Tilton, John E. (1971), *International Diffusion of Technology: The Case of Semiconductors*, Brookings Institution.

Tufano, Peter (1993), "Financing Acquisitions in the Late 1980s: Sources and Forms of Capital," in Margaret Blair (ed.), *The Deal Decade*, Brookings.

Tulum, Öner, and William Lazonick (2019), "Financialized Corporations in a National Innovation System. The US Pharmaceutical Industry," *International Journal of Political Economy*, 47(3–4): 281–316.

Uhlig, Mark (1987), "Jesse Unruh, a California political power, dies," *New York Times*, August 6, at http://www.nytimes.com/1987/08/06/obituaries/jesse-unruh-a-california-political-power-dies.html.

United States Census Bureau (1976), *Historical Statistics of the United States from the Colonial Times to the Present*, Government Printing Office.

United States Census Bureau (2016), "Statistics of U.S. Businesses," at https://www.census.gov/programs-surveys/susb/data/datasets.html.

U.S. Department of Agriculture (2016), "Table 8—Food expenditures by families and individuals as a share of disposable personal money income," at http://www.ers.usda.gov/data-products/food-expenditures.aspx.

U.S. Senate Committee on Banking and Currency (2009), *The Pecora Report: The 1934 Report on the Practices of Stock Exchanges from the Pecora Commission*.

Vaughn, David (2003), "Selected Definitions of 'Hedge Fund'," Comments for the U.S. Securities and Exchange Commission Roundtable on Hedge Funds, at https://www.sec.gov/spotlight/hedgefunds/hedge-vaughn.htm.

Vise, David A., and Steve Coll (1991), *Eagle on the Street*, Scribner's.

Wakabayashi, Daisuke (2014), "Apple repurchases $14 billion of its own shares in two weeks," *Wall Street Journal*, February 6, at https://www.wsj.com/articles/apple-re purchases-14b-of-own-shares-in-2-weeks-1391734918?tesla=y.

Walker, Owen (2016), *Barbarians in the Boardroom: Activist Investors and the Battle for Control of the World's Most Powerful Companies*, Pearson.

Wallman, Steven, Kathleen Wallman, and Geoffrey Aronow (1999), "Pooling-of-Interests Accounting and High Growth Economy Companies," at http://www.wallman.com/pdfs_etc/fasb.pdf.

Wall Street Journal (1982a), "Anchor Hocking buys Icahn's 6.2% holding; His profit is $2,995,321," August 23.

Wall Street Journal (1982b), "Owens-Illinois pays total of $38.4 million for Icahn-held stakes," September 13.

Wall Street Journal (1982c), "Icahn group acquires 6.9% Dan River stake; Might seek control," September 16.

Wapner, Scott (2016), "CNBC exclusive: CNBC transcript: Carl Icahn, Chairman of Icahn Enterprises, on CNBC's 'Power Lunch' today," April 28, at http://www.cnbc.com/2016/04/28/cnbc-exclusive-cnbc-transcript-carl-icahn-chairman-of-icahn-enterprises-on-cnbcs-power-lunch-today.html.

Warren, Tom (2016), "Microsoft wasted at least $8 billion on its failed Nokia experiment," *The Verge*, May 25, at https://www.theverge.com/2016/5/25/11766540/microsoft-nokia-acquisition-costs.

Weiss, Leonard W. (1979), "The Structure–Conduct–Performance Paradigm and Anti-trust," *University of Pennsylvania Law Review*, 127(4): 1104–40.

Whyte, William H. (1956), *The Organization Man*, Simon & Schuster.

Wikipedia (n.d.), "Troubled Asset Relief Program," at https://en.wikipedia.org/wiki/Troubled_Asset_Relief_Program#cite_note-ProPublica-TARP-list-46.

Williams, Harold M. (1981), "The Corporation as Continuing Enterprise," address delivered to the Securities Regulation Institute, San Diego, California, January 22, at www.sec.gov/news/speech/1981/012281williams.pdf.

Williams, Winston (1986), "Carl Icahn's wild ride at TWA," *New York Times*, June 22, at http://www.nytimes.com/1986/06/22/business/carl-icahn-s-wild-ride-at-twa.html?pagewanted=all.

Winter, Jaap W. (2011), "Shareholder Engagement and Stewardship: The Realities and Illusions of Institutional Share Ownership" at https://ssrn.com/abstract=1867564.

Woo-Cumings, Meredith (ed.) (1999), *The Developmental State*, Cornell University Press.

Woodyard, Chris (2013), "GM bailout played out over five years," *USA Today*, December 9, at https://www.usatoday.com/story/money/cars/2013/12/09/gm-bailout-timeline/3929953/.

World Wealth and Income Database (2017a), Database: United States, Top 0.1% income composition, at https://wid.world/.

World Wealth and Income Database (2017b), Database: United States, P99.9 income threshold, at http://topincomes.parisschoolofeconomics.eu/#Database.

Yardeni, Edward, Joe Abbott, and Mali Quintana (2019), Stock Market Indicators: S&P 500 Buybacks & Dividends, Yardeni Research, Inc., at https://www.yardeni.com/pub/buybackdiv.pdf

Yglesias, Matthew (2018a), "Elizabeth Warren has a plan to save capitalism," *Vox*, August 15, at https://www.vox.com/2018/8/15/17683022/elizabeth-warren-accountable-capitalism-corporations.

Yglesias, Matthew (2018b), "Top House Democrats join Elizabeth Warren's push to fundamentally change American capitalism," *Vox*, December 14, at https://www.vox.com/2018/12/14/18136142/pocan-lujan-warren-accountable-capitalism-act

Index

Note: Tables and figures are indicated by an italic '*t*' and '*f*', following the page number.

For the benefit of digital users, indexed terms that span two pages (e.g., 52–53) may, on occasion, appear on only one of those pages.